TALL BUILDINGS
of CHINA

TALL BUILDINGS
of CHINA

Edited by Georges Binder

Forewords by

A. Eugene Kohn and James von Klemperer, Kohn Pederson Fox Associates

Antony Wood, Council on Tall Buildings and Urban Habitat

Council on Tall Buildings and Urban Habitat

images
Publishing

Published in Australia in 2015 by
The Images Publishing Group Pty Ltd
ABN 89 059 734 431
6 Bastow Place, Mulgrave, Victoria 3170, Australia
Tel: +61 3 9561 5544 Fax: +61 3 9561 4860
books@imagespublishing.com
www.imagespublishing.com

Copyright © The Images Publishing Group Pty Ltd 2015
The Images Publishing Group Reference Number: 1068

National Library of Australia Cataloguing-in-Publication entry:

Title:	Tall buildings of China / edited by Georges Binder.
ISBN:	9781864704129 (hardback)
Notes:	Includes index.
Subjects:	Architecture, Modern
	Tall buildings—China.
	Tall buildings—Asia.
	Skyscrapers—China.
	Skyscrapers—Asia.
Dewey Number:	720.4830951

Coordinating editor: Gina Tsarouhas
Graphic designer: Ryan Marshall

Digital production and printing by Everbest Printing Co. Ltd.,
in Hong Kong, China on 140gsm GoldEast Matt Art paper

IMAGES has included on its website a page for special notices
in relation to this and our other publications. Please visit
www.imagespublishing.com.

Contents

APPENDIX

Foreword

A. Eugene Kohn and James von Klemperer

■ In today's 21st-century China, supertall towers are rising at an unprecedented rate to meet the needs of millions of people flooding into cities. The supertall building is no longer seen as a singular icon to punctuate a skyline, but, rather, has become an exemplary architectural solution to rapid urbanisation, whereby clusters of skyscrapers both reflect and enable the densification of China's urban habitats.

By 2025, 350 million people will be added to China's urban population – more people than the total population of the United States in 2014. What will that degree of urbanisation look like in the built environment? We predict approximately 40 billion square metres (431 billion square feet) of space will be built throughout five million buildings, and 50,000 of these buildings could be skyscrapers. It can be said with certainty that China's future is tall.

The benefits of population density are well known. Urbanisation is a powerful agent for economic change. China's urbanisation and the economies of scale will radically increase its economic growth. In China's intensified race for global recognition, new cities take shape where small villages once stood; rapid foreign investment in China's Special Economic Zones (SEZs) has funnelled billions of dollars into some of the country's fastest-growing cities, hastening economic growth and the need for vertical development. Today, there are more than 160 cities with more than a million inhabitants. This includes at least six megacities: Shanghai, Beijing, Guangzhou, Tianjin and Chengdu.

Until the early 16th century, Asia long represented the centre of gravity in the global economy, producing nearly two-thirds of global GDP. Following the industrial revolution, European and American cities urbanised to dominate the global economy for nearly three centuries. The present-day economic transformation in China has reversed that trend, and the global economic balance is shifting to Asia's emerging cities at an unprecedented pace.

China's robust economic growth highlights the widening gap between its cities and countryside. More than half of the Chinese population now lives in cities. The push for urbanisation, moving millions of people a year into its dense urban environments by offering subsidies for relocation and promising work, called for the construction of hundreds of new cities.

This revolutionary urban transformation extends beyond the supertall. Vertical development necessitates large-scale infrastructure systems. New roads, highways, power grids, bridges, tunnels, airports, public transport and high-speed rail are being engineered with the capacity to support the millions of inhabitants flooding into China's cities. However, the most innovative urban infrastructure now centres on the concept of the 'city in the sky.'

Vertical transportation planning links city subways, buses and roads to the ground levels of buildings, and improves the efficiency of the land. Building upwards also joins the most skilled workers in urban centres, boosting urban productivity. Financial institutions, international corporations and other private enterprises are moving to China's cities in search of high efficiency, both in terms of operations and connectivity. The modern supertall has become a global icon of economic progress; thus, building height directly equates to GDP, and the number of completed projects has come to represent prosperity.

Urban habitats, and dense city centres in particular, have the greatest potential to improve quality of life for large populations across the world while mitigating climate change. Strictly speaking, large cities are most efficient in per-capita greenhouse gas emissions. New York City has the highest total greenhouse gas emissions of cities, but the emissions per capita are significantly lower than other, sprawling urban environments. This is true of all efficient, well-planned cities. Increasing density has the potential to reduce energy consumption citywide. In order to encourage growth and reduce the impacts of climate change cities need to build vertically and improve energy efficiency. To borrow a phrase from Edward Glaeser, 'To save the planet, build more skyscrapers.'

When the Chinese border opened at the end of the 1950s the country looked to the United States and its high-rise architectural practice, and sought the expertise of leading architects from the West. Having retained Americans for their expertise to build China's first skyscrapers, the Chinese eventually began to adopt the Western process in selecting architects, establishing budgets, gaining approvals, value engineering, and construction. China's 20th-century skyline began to take shape.

Brian Lee, a veteran designer over at SOM, once said he didn't think there is a China style, that the work is international because so many foreign architects are working in the country and bringing different ideas into the country. He's really quite right. But the architecture there has evolved dramatically. Over time, architects and engineers have learned how to work within China's building code to create more sophisticated designs that conserve resources and achieve greater efficiency. New, higher quality building suppliers have become available in China. They are sought after by the growing number of professionals, manufacturers and fabricators who are familiar with building in China.

But change is afoot. A generation or two of aspirational Chinese men and women trained in the United States as architects and engineers are bringing their skills back home. China's rapacious appetite for American steel has diminished and American factories are losing ground to manufacturers in Asia and Europe. Long the world's largest buyer of industrial commodities, such as iron ore and copper, China tightened trade finance policies on redirecting imports and exports. The country's imports continue to fall, while data reflect strong exports. Domestic demand for steel has weakened, too, but production is at its highest since 2008. China will continue to refine, patent and export a typology invented by Americans over the coming decades.

To be sure, the make-up of China in 2025 will bear no resemblance to its landscape of today. We will see taller buildings continue to reshape its skylines, reflecting broader changes in the country's social and economic underpinnings. It promises to be a more sustainable China, too. At the very least, its building technologies will be energy efficient and conserve materials as design and construction techniques modernise.

The Chinese interpretation of the supertall will become the global standard, and the image of the Chinese city will be replicated in rapidly growing cities across the world. China's dynamic vertical urbanisation has given supertalls global acceptance, particularly in the United States and Europe. Whereas the first supertall buildings were 'imported' from the United States, today's China fabricates and ships entire sections of buildings internationally. Considering the pace and scale of this unprecedented event — it will be difficult to extrapolate the results of China's growth to other developing nations. But given the conventions of the 21st-century supertall, the desire for green, vertical cities promises to become universal.

Although the momentum and scale of urbanisation in China outpace every precedent known to humankind, this type of rapid growth is characteristic of developing countries. Economic development in other emerging economies like Turkey and Nigeria, where cities like İstanbul and Lagos have experienced exponential population growth over the last four decades, has also picked up. McKinsey predicts the GDP of the 143 largest African cities, largely clustered along the continent's west coast, nearly tripling to generate almost US$1.5 trillion by 2025. Both North Africa and sub-Saharan Africa are well on their way to urbanisation.

Urbanisation across the African continent is boosting productivity, demand, and investment, which creates jobs, increases spending, and improves the quality of life. Ultimately, economic growth in Africa will be contingent on its connections to the global economy. Thanks to investors in China, Africa will see its first supertall in the Ethiopian city of Addis Ababa. On a smaller scale, skyscrapers have popped up in Cape Town, Lagos, and Nairobi in the last couple of years, due to heavy foreign investment. While the enormous potential of the African economy and the rapid pace of urbanisation does seem to share similarities with China, the quantity and quality of the continent's infrastructure will dictate whether it will follow a similar, vertical path.

A. Eugene Kohn
Chairman
Kohn Pedersen Fox Associates

James von Klemperer
President and Design Principal
Kohn Pedersen Fox Associates

Foreword

Antony Wood

■ As recently as a decade ago, an entire book on the tall buildings of China would hardly have been feasible, let alone very long. But, today, China is the absolute epicentre of tall-building construction globally. Many of the iconic towers now rising in China have lent world recognition to cities that relatively few Chinese — let alone Westerners — were previously aware of. The changes wrought by urbanisation, and the scale and ambition of the nation's vertical iconography, are stunning.

All around the country, both the design and technologies of the typology are being advanced. Tall buildings that gather renewable energy, like the remarkable Pearl River Tower in Guangzhou. Buildings that link themselves together through skybridges, like the Linked Hybrid building in Beijing. Buildings that employ significant double-skin façades and other ventilation strategies, like the Kingtown International Center (KIC) in Nanjing. Or those that take on anthropomorphic or zoomorphic shapes in the quest to provide a different expression, like the Wangjing SOHO in Beijing. At the same time, this concentration of population in vertically extrapolating urban centres is providing opportunities for a more sustainable pattern of life, through consolidating infrastructure and allowing greater sharing of resources, without consuming essential natural, agricultural and recreational land.

China is replete with good high-rise examples. The three iconic buildings that make up Shanghai's supertall trio are already well known, but the design of each points to potentially different avenues for the typology. The Jin Mao Tower, completed in 1999, is a rebuke of the idea that skyscrapers automatically have a homogenising cultural effect on cityscapes. Here, in its distinctive stepped profile, we recognise allusions to the pagodas of traditional Chinese architecture. Yet the story doesn't end at the door. The Jin Mao has one of the most spectacular and surprising interior spaces in any tall building. A 30-storey circular atrium with balconies leading to hotel rooms would be spectacular enough; the fact that it begins on the 55th floor and continues to the 88th is staggering.

Directly across the street, the Shanghai World Financial Center's expressive focus is on its upper void-crowning skybridge, and it is a fantastic experience to walk that space internally, with its vertigo-inducing side glimpses to street level through glass flooring. However, like so many new high-rises in China, the mix of uses in the building — office, hotel, retail, leisure and observation deck — is no less adventurous, as was the design intent of relating to Chinese culture in a more abstract way, in contrast to the more literal approach of the Jin Mao.

Meanwhile, the third 'neighbour' in the trio, the Shanghai Tower, is remarkable not only for its 632-metre (2,073-foot) height (upon completion, this will make it the second-tallest building in the world), but for its extensive use of communal sky gardens and double-skin façades to moderate the psychological isolation that can come from spending all day in a tall building far above the ground. Its necessary outriggers, mechanical floors and elevator transfer lobbies are turned into signature design assets – soaring social spaces with 14-storey ceilings, large plantings and curving glass, turning over received notions about what it means to be 'grounded' or 'in the clouds'.

If there is any caveat to this fantastical depiction it is that these myriad positive examples reveal just how much mediocrity often surrounds them. The sheer speed and scale at which construction is being undertaken has also delivered numerous alienating, pedestrian-unfriendly, environmentally unsound cityscapes that contrast harshly with the wonderful, catalytic projects such as those found in this book. It is thus not surprising that tall buildings are not universally celebrated in China, and this book thus serves also as a crucible for cautionary reflection. There is an increasing recognition among leading practitioners that tall buildings must contribute something beyond sheer height and maximisation of land value in order to continue to be viable instruments of urban life.

There is, however, clearly a great potential for tall buildings to become an integrated part of the solution towards more sustainable cities, and our continued existence on this planet. As this book demonstrates, there is no greater laboratory than China in which to urgently test this potential.

Dr. Antony Wood RIBA PhD
Executive Director, Council on Tall Buildings and Urban Habitat (CTBUH)
Research Professor of Tall Buildings, Illinois Institute of Technology, Chicago
Visiting Professor of Tall Buildings, Tongji University, Shanghai

Introduction

Georges Binder

1

2

3

4

■ For many people in the Western hemisphere the first buildings that come to mind that epitomise tall buildings are generally the Chrysler Building and the Empire State Building, both located in New York City and both completed in the early 1930s. It's difficult to determine if these projects had an impact on what was going on in China[1] in terms of architecture and urbanism, but we note that the first major early series of tall buildings appeared in China soon after these American buildings, in the mid-1930s, though on a quite lower scale than that of the projects mentioned here. Considering the low-rise urban landscape of the time, the New York City projects' impact on the Chinese urban environment may have been more significant than what we might imagine today.

While Shanghai would witness the construction of the famous New York City skyscrapers in the early 1930s, by 1929 there was already a 77-metre-tall (253-foot) building in Shanghai, the **Peace Hotel** (originally known as the Cathay Hotel and now called the Fairmont Peace Hotel) comprising only 13 levels. The architect of the Peace Hotel was Hong Kong–based Palmer and Turner (a firm known today as P&T Group) who was the architect of a series of early tall buildings in China. The hotel then formed only a part of Sasoon House, which also contained offices and shopping arcades.[2]

In 1934 the Commercial Bank of China office building (designed by Davies, Brooke & Gran) comprised 20 storeys, but then in the same year Shanghai saw the 83.8-metre-tall (275-foot), 21-storey **Park Hotel** on Nanjing Road (designed by Hungarian architect László Hudec), making it the then-tallest building in Asia. The Park Hotel that now faces Shanghai's People's Square was originally erected as the Joint Savings Society Building, as explained by Edward Denison and Guang Yu Ren in *Building Shanghai*,[3] and from the detailed project description we learn that the building was considered an early vertical mixed-use building as it used to comprise a banking hall, bank offices, the Park Hotel, private apartments and an octagonal observation deck at the top. Soon after, a series of buildings, including the **Bank of China** (1939; designed by Luke Him Sau and Palmer and Turner[4]), helped define Shanghai's skyline along the Bund. It's this preserved waterfront skyline that can be observed from the new supertall business district that was created in the 1990s on the other side of the Huangpu River in what is known as Pudong (part of the 1992 Master Plan of Pudong New Area[5]), an area that today accommodates the tallest buildings in the city.

1 Peace Hotel (left), Shanghai, 13 storeys, 1929 • Architect: Palmer and Turner • Bank of China (right), Shanghai, 17 storeys, 1939 • Architect: Luke Him Sau / Palmer and Turner • Photography: courtesy P&T Group • While Shanghai has changed tremendously in the last 20 years, the Bund waterfront has not only been preserved but gradually renovated allowing the now-called Fairmont Peace Hotel and the Bank of China to reclaim their former glory. 2 Park Hotel, Shanghai, 21 storeys, 83.8 metres (275 feet), 1934 • Architect: László Hudec • Photography: old postcard, coll. G. Binder • Tallest building in Asia at the time of its completion, the Park Hotel was originally erected in 1934 as the Joint Savings Society Building and can be considered as an early vertical mixed-use building. 3 Hongkong & Shanghai Banking Corporation, 13 storeys, 1935 (now demolished) and Bank of China, 17 storeys, 1950, Hong Kong • Architect: Palmer and Turner • Photography: Coll. G. Binder • Tallest building in Hong Kong upon completion in 1935, the Hongkong & Shanghai Banking Corporation was the first fully air-conditioned building in the city[6] while the Bank of China Building remained the new city's tallest building from 1950 till 1963. 4 Mandarin Hotel (now Mandarin Oriental Hong Kong), Hong Kong, 26 storeys, 86.68 metres (284 feet), 1963 • Architect: Leigh & Orange • Photography: courtesy Hongkong Land Limited

Hong Kong

Meanwhile in Hong Kong, the tallest buildings are being built by some of the same names seen in Shanghai. The **Hongkong & Shanghai Banking Corporation** (1935; now demolished) and the **Bank of China** (1950) buildings, both designed by Palmer and Turner, would lead the way in the central district's skyline for almost two decades. While mainland China will see almost no tall buildings erected from the late 1930s till the early 1980s, Hong Kong continued to erect its now-famous skyline; 1963 is perhaps a pivotal year as it is the year of the opening of both the **Mandarin Hotel** (now known as the Mandarin Oriental Hong Kong) and the **Hongkong Hilton** – both hotels being 26 storeys high they probably became the tallest buildings in the city for a short period at 86.68 metres (284 feet) and 89.4 metres (293 feet), respectively. If the Mandarin designed by Leigh & Orange could perhaps be considered the link between the earlier Art Deco buildings and the later Hong Kong contemporary buildings as we know them now, the Hilton designed by Palmer and Turner probably brought to Hong Kong (and China in general) its first major International Style building on a large scale, with a local flavour considering its lace-like podium façade. Palmer and Turner again puts its mark on the Hong Kong skyline during the next two decades with other projects growing ever taller. When the **Connaught Centre** (now known as Jardine House) was completed in 1973 it became an instant city landmark – surmounted by a half-trunked pyramid-shaped rooftop and with its unexpected round windows. At 52 storeys and 178.5 metres (584 feet) high, the waterfront Connaught Centre project in central Hong Kong then became the tallest building in all of Asia, allowing the continent to be mentioned whenever tall buildings from around the world were being discussed or published. Interestingly, 1973 also saw the completion of the 56-storey Tour Maine-Montparnasse in Paris, then the tallest in Western Europe, as well as the completion of the 110-storey World Trade Center in New York City, which then became the world's newest tallest building.

In the next decade Palmer and Turner, by then known by the name still used today, P&T Group, placed its mark on **Exchange Square**, a 52-storey twin tower building completed in 1985 and complemented in 1988 by a third tower. Exchange Square featured an array of indoor and outdoor public areas, a welcome amenity in the Central district of Hong Kong. Apart from it prominence on the city skyline next to the Connaught Centre, Exchange Square became well known internationally in real estate circles in such a way as to bring the fame of the project far beyond Hong Kong, Chinese or even Asian boundaries. If we are to single out an architectural firm that made its mark for several decades in the area, such as Palmer and Turner (P&T Group), then we should also note that Jardine House (1948), the Mandarin Hotel (1963), Connaught Centre (1973) and Exchange Square (1985) have all been completed by the same developer, Hongkong Land, a development company that proved to be a major player in creating the current image of Hong Kong. This city is known worldwide for its contemporary tall buildings, many of which are located centrally and are connected by elevated pedestrian bridges that are protected from both vehicle traffic and inclement weather, and shops in the lower levels of many buildings create a contiguous but varied and lively urban fabric. In 1965, upon completion of the Prince's Building, Hongkong Land added the the first enclosed air-conditioned footbridge known as the **Chater Road pedestrian bridge** in Hong Kong to create a connection with the Mandarin Hotel that had been completed a couple of years earlier. This footbridge linked the hotel's retail area with the Prince's Building shopping arcade. From this single bridge the network of interconnected tall

5

6

7

8

5 Hongkong Hilton, Hong Kong, 26 storeys, 89.4 metres (293 feet), 1963 (now demolished) • Architect: Palmer and Turner • Photography: courtesy Hilton International; coll. G. Binder • While the Hongkong Hilton has been replaced in 1999 by the 63-storey Cheung Kong Center office tower, the Mandarin Oriental (see image 4, page 12) remains one of the best hotels in the city. **6** Connaught Centre (now Jardine House), Hong Kong, 52 storeys, 178.5 metres (584 feet), office, 1973 • Architect: Palmer and Turner • Photography: courtesy Hongkong Land Limited • Upon completion in 1973, the Connaught Centre became the tallest building in Asia. **7** Exchange Square (centre), Hong Kong, 52 storeys, 188 metres (617 feet), office, 1985 • Architect: P&T Group • Photography: courtesy P&T Group • On the left side of Exchange Square we can see the Connaught Centre, now Jardine House, completed in 1973 by the same architect. For about two decades the two projects developed by Hongkong Land have been 'the face' of Hong Kong in terms of architecture, real estate and city marketing. **8** Chater Road Bridge, 1965 • Rendering: courtesy Hongkong Land Limited • The developer of Prince's Building (1963), Hongkong Land added in 1965 the first enclosed air-conditioned footbridge in Hong Kong. The Chater Road pedestrian bridge linked the Mandarin Hotel's retail area with the Prince's Building shopping arcade.

buildings increased dramatically over time in the Central district. Those connections transformed Hong Kong's urban fabric as much as it probably started the trend for creating large-scale complexes in Asia comprising multiple buildings – although initially they were mostly single buildings joined together via pedestrian links. Multitower Exchange Square followed in the mid-1980s and soon after that **Pacific Place**, completed in phases from 1988 to 1991. It was developed by Swire Properties and designed by Wong & Ouyang, who had started to establish large-scale multitower mixed-use ensembles in the region. Pacific Place is a mixed-use project comprising originally four 40- to 61-storey towers, providing space for luxury hotels, residences and offices; the whole project being built above a vast three-level shopping mall.

Hong Kong enabled Asian skyscrapers to be part of the world's tall building scenery, with several major projects emerging from the mid 1970s till the mid 1980s, indeed it was the 178.8-metre-high (587-foot) **Hongkong and Shanghai Banking Corporation Headquarters Building** (now HSBC Building) completed in 1985 and designed by Foster Associates Hong Kong that brought Hong Kong's architecture – and not only tall building architecture – to the world stage, with unprecedented media coverage. The architecture of this building was at the time considered such an event that the well-respected American magazine *Progressive Architecture* made the building not only the cover project of its March 1986 issue, but that issue was entirely devoted to the bank building with a 43-page main feature article, which started with the following headline: 'P/A hails Foster Associates' Hongkong Bank for its beauty, stylistic and social implications, and technical virtuosity'.[7] At at the time of its completion, the Foster building with its series of stacked suspension structures was indeed a departure from a series of postmodern skyscrapers recently completed or still in progress in the United States.

Mainland China

In the meantime in mainland China, a few tall buildings were being built as well, sometimes with the expertise of Hong Kong–based architects or American ones. The Jinling Hotel in Nanjing was completed in 1982 and at 110.4 metres (362 feet) it became the then-tallest building in mainland China. The 37-storey project (designed by Palmer and Turner) now comes equipped with an additional 242-metre-tall (794-foot) mixed-use hotel/office tower known as Asia Pacific Tower that was completed in 2014 by P&T Group to form a coherent ensemble in the heart of the city. The year 1983 saw the opening of a hotel in Beijing that was created by a team of American architects and developers: C.B. Sung, a Chinese-born American businessman who teamed up with the Chinese Government[8] to create the 1,007-room Great Wall Hotel, now **The Great Wall Sheraton Hotel Beijing** designed by Becket International (a firm related to American architect Welton Becket Associates). The 22-storey building is articulated around a seven-storey atrium equipped with four glass-enclosed elevators; the top-floor panoramic restaurant may have been an early trendsetter for so many Chinese-designed tall buildings that followed in the next 15 years which were to include a protruding revolving restaurant on the top level or a similarly-designed rooftop level. Although not that tall, the Great Wall Hotel introduced a series of 'firsts'[9] to mainland China, such as the hotel's insulated reflective glass façade (which reflected the surrounding traditional Chinese architecture and landscape), the glass-enclosed scenic elevators and the fact that the project was one of the first two joint ventures undertaken in China since the promulgation of its open-door policy and the largest Sino-American joint venture at the time.

The first multitower mixed-use ensembles built at the same time in mainland China are probably another two projects that were also designed by American architects that would pave the way for the stunning and ever-taller skylines we now see in Beijing and Shanghai. The two projects – China World

9 Pacific Place, Hong Kong, 40 to 61 storeys, 1988–1991 • Architect: Wong & Ouyang (HK) Ltd • Photography: courtesy Wong & Ouyang (HK) Ltd • An aerial view of an early large-scale multitower mixed-use ensemble completed in phases. 10 Hongkong and Shanghai Banking Corporation headquarters building, Hong Kong, 43 storeys, 178.8 metres (587 feet), office, 1985 • Architect: Foster Associates Hong Kong • Photography: Doc. *Progressive Architecture* cover, March 1986 | coll. G. Binder • With its series of stacked suspension structures, the Hongkong and Shanghai Banking Corporation headquarters Building (now HSBC Building) completed in 1985 has replaced the former 1935 headquarters building. 11 The Great Wall Hotel (now The Great Wall Sheraton Hotel Beijing), Beijing, 22 storeys, 83 metres (272 feet), 1983 • Architect: Becket International • Photography: courtesy The Great Wall Hotel | coll. G. Binder • One of the early mainland China tall buildings. Its revolving rooftop restaurant would pave the way for a series of hotels featuring noticeable rooftop restaurants completed in the country leading up to the turn of the new millennium. 12 China World Trade Center, Beijing, 38 storeys, 155.25 metres (509 feet), 1990 • Architect: Robert Sobel/Emery Roth & Sons • Associate architect: Nikken Sekkei Ltd • Photography: courtesy Robert Sobel • In 1990 the China World Trade Center (CWTC) became mainland China's first large-scale multitower mixed-use ensemble when it officially opened slightly earlier than the Shanghai Centre in Shanghai.

Trade Center in Beijing and the Shanghai Centre in Shanghai — are large-scale multiuse ensembles accommodating retail and exhibition space, serviced apartments, hotels and offices and they imposed a model that is now being implemented all over China in one form or another.

In Beijing, the 38-storey **China World Trade Center (CWTC)** was completed in 1990 as a joint venture between the Chinese Government and Hong Kong–based Kuok Group of companies. The architect for China World Trade Center was New York–based Robert Sobel/Emery Roth & Sons whith Tokyo-based Nikken Sekkei as associate architect. The bronze curved façade of the 155.25-metre-high (509-foot) office tower, along with the concave façade of the Shangri-La hotel together with a couple of twin 34-storey residential towers complemented by a mall, exhibition spaces and additional low-rise office areas offering large floor plates, became an instant landmark on the Beijing skyline. The location of the project was to become a significant crossroad in the Chinese capital as it now accommodated a new series of major Beijing projects, such as CCTV headquarters (across the road on one side), designed by OMA and completed in 2012, and on the other side, the 250-metre-tall (820-foot) mixed-use Beijing Yintai Centre, designed by John Portman & Associates and completed in 2008. Also in 1990, shortly after the opening of China World Trade Center in Beijing, John Portman & Associates became the first architect to create in Shanghai a contemporary multitower high-rise project of international stature. The 164.8-metre-tall (541-foot) **Shanghai Centre** would form the first multiuse ensemble in the heart of the city, directly opposite the Shanghai Exhibition Centre. The three-tower project is comprised of retail shops, a 1,000-seat theatre, a 48-storey 700-room luxury hotel tower, two 24-storey apartments towers as well as exhibition space. The project has been built according to the 'city-within-a-city' concept that became the trademark of John Portman. It may have seemed a bit isolated at the time of completion as there was almost no commercial activity in the city the way it has been seen in the Western world for decades and the way it is now widely known in mainland China, but Shanghai Centre eventually proved to be well located and a catalyser of a series of projects that are now forming this lively part of Shanghai. Projects such as CITIC Square, designed by P&T Group and completed in 2000, or the 66-storey Plaza 66, designed by Kohn Pedersen Fox Associates and completed in phases in 2001 and 2006, and more recently, the 58-storey Jing An Kerry Centre, also designed by Kohn Pedersen Fox Associates and completed in 2013, are other types of mixed-used ensembles which create a now-contiguous urban fabric of contemporary projects along Nanjing Road.

In Shanghai, Kerry ParkSide, designed in 2011 by Kohn Pedersen Fox Associates, **CITIC Plaza** designed by Nikken Sekkei in 2010, or Jing An Kerry Centre, designed by Kohn Pedersen Fox Associates in 2013, to name a few, are among the first of another series of high-rise mixed-use ensembles that began to evolve around open-air courtyards and plazas and green squares; the early projects completed in the 1990s and 2000s in China had been more often designed inwardly — taking into consideration that these projects had to live more self-sufficiently given that there was not as much urban commercial life to connect to the way we know it today. Today, with dense city locations like Beijing and Shanghai, in particular, the use of open, high-rise mixed-use projects makes more sense, and these types of projects are more often expected in densely built city centres.

Apart from Hong Kong, and with the exception of the aforementioned projects) at the turn of the millennium very few tall buildings had been built in China to the standards people had been accustomed to in Europe, North America, Japan or Singapore (to name a few locations with tall buildings). In mainland China, many buildings became obsolete after only a few years and the first-time visitor to a city like Shanghai might have imagined, when seeing a tall building in the 1990s, that it has been erected 20 or 25 years earlier though it may have been built most probably less than 10 years earlier. Design considerations and poor maintenance could perhaps explain this. When it comes to design, we are here talking about the overall

Tall shopping malls

Most of the shopping malls around the world do not usually have more than two to three levels. In 1976, Chicago started to witness taller shopping malls, such as in the case of Water Tower Place, comprising a seven-storey shopping mall as part of the 74-storey mixed-use tower designed by Loebl Schlossman Dart & Hackl and C.F. Murphy Associates, the latter firm now known as JAHN. A few additional multilevel malls were erected in the 1980s in Chicago and in New York City, but otherwise few are found elsewhere in the world aside from in Asia in locations such as Singapore and Hong Kong, in particular. Indeed, Hong Kong includes some of the tallest shopping malls in the world. Some are part of mixed-use office/retail towers and as recent as 1993 we noted the 41- and 48-storey twin-towered Times Square designed by Wong & Ouyang, featuring a retail and entertainment mall up to level +14. Other projects are entirely devoted to accommodating retail, food and beverages and entertainment areas, such as in the case of the 24-storey The ONE designed by Tange Associates and LWK & Partners (2010); the 25-storey CUBUS designed by Woods Bagot (2010); or the 27-storey iSQUARE designed by Rocco Design (2009). In Europe, The ONE would be among the tallest buildings at 172.1 metres (565 feet) and to imagine that it accommodates retail and entertainment activities only may come as a surprise for many living in the Western part of the world.

iSQUARE, Hong Kong, 27 storeys, 139.55 metres (458 feet), shopping mall, 2009 • Architect: Rocco Design Architects Limited • Photography: ©Marcel Lam

13

14

13 Shanghai Centre, Shanghai, 48 storeys, 164.8 metres (541 feet), 1990 • Architect: John Portman & Associates • Associate architect: East China Architectural Design & Research Institute (ECADI) • Photography: Michael Portman • First major mixed-use ensemble and tallest building in Shanghai upon completion in 1990, Shanghai Centre comprises a 700-room central luxury hotel tower, two apartment towers, offices, a retail village, exhibition spaces as well as a 1,000-seat theatre. Originally known as The Portman Shangri-La and now as the Portman Ritz-Carlton, the hotel bears the name of its architect. 14 CITIC Plaza, Shanghai, 228 metres (748 feet), 49 storeys, 2010 • Architect: Nikken Sekkei Ltd • Architects of record: Shanghai Institute of Architectural Design & Research; Shanghai Mingkong International Design Co., Ltd • Photography: ©Nacasa & Partners Inc • The CITIC Plaza in Shanghai is one of those new tall buildings introducing to mainland China refined outdoor landscaped spaces integrated with high-rise architecture.

15

16

project design and not only the 'aesthetic' part of it. For instance, many of the early mainland Chinese mixed-use projects – such as the 28-storey China Mayors Plaza completed in 1996 in Guangzhou, or the 47-storey Golden Crown Tower completed in 2001 in Tianjin – both comprised offices in the upper part and a hotel in the lower part, but in contrast to what is now common in mainland China (and everywhere else), the lobby is often common for both uses; and in the case of China Mayors Plaza, office tenants and visitors, along with hotel guests, are sharing the same elevators – something that would not be acceptable for any new project conceived today.

While in several parts of the world the central business district (CBD) is not always seen to be the best part of the city, sometimes seen as a decaying location or as a place with not much to offer, the CBD has gained a totally different appeal in mainland China in recent years. Newly built and still-developing CBDs in cities like Beijing, Guangzhou or Shenzhen have probably helped to create a mark of quality and success in a descriptive name with regards to a location masterplanned by city officials. In some cases, like in Wuhan, where Wuhan CBD Investment & Development Co., Ltd., the developer of Wuhan Central Business District (a.k.a. Wuhan CBD) one of the largest projects in the city – which include the 88-storey Wuhan Tower (designed by ECADI) – has included 'CBD/Central Business District' in the project name so that the term 'CBD' becomes associated with a brand.

Supertall projects

At around the same time as the series of projects being built all over China (like Pacific Place in Hong Kong, China World Trade Center in Beijing and Shanghai Centre in Shanghai) that had paved the way for large-scale, multitower, mixed-use ensembles, a new trend for building supertall buildings in Asia and in China (in particular) was emerging – starting with the completion of the Bank of China Tower, designed by New York–based I.M. Pei & Partners. When the 367.4-metre-tall (1,205-foot) Bank of China Tower appeared on the Hong Kong skyline in 1990 the project became the first Asian building to be included among the world's 10 tallest buildings. When the **Bank of China Tower** made the cover story of *Architectural Record*, in January 1991, architecture critic Peter Blake wrote.[10] 'Given that Pei's tower is located just two blocks east of Norman Foster's highly publicised Hong Kong and Shanghai Bank Headquarters, comparisons between the two structures are inevitable. The Foster building – a super-high-tech visual extravaganza – is, in reality, a fairly conventional structure with a central atrium and a brilliant display of structural and mechanical innards on its north and south façades. Foster's building seems to use its dramatic structure as a form of decoration, whereas Pei's tower is a flawless integration of pure structure, function, form, and urban symbolism. Nothing could be added to it and nothing could be subtracted without doing damage to the whole.' Soon after the completion of the Bank of China Tower, the 373.9-metre-tall (1,227-foot) Central Plaza, also in Hong Kong, became in 1992 the second Asian building to appear in the top 10 list, but the first to be designed by an Asian-based architect, Ng Chun Man & Associates Architects & Engineers (now known as Dennis Lau & Ng Chun Architects & Engineers). Central Plaza became the new tallest building in Asia. The 1990s saw the emergence of Chinese-based architects involved in a series of supertall projects in several Chinese cities. Among the tallest early Chinese supertall projects we note the 390.2-metre-high (1,280-foot) **CITIC Plaza** in Guangzhou in 1997, designed by Dennis Lau & Ng Chun Man Architects & Engineers, and the 384-metre-tall (1,260-foot) **Shun Hing Square**, completed earlier in 1996 in Shenzhen and designed by K.Y. Cheung. Chinese-born Cheung had been educated in the United States and had won the competition for the Shun Hing Square with his firm K.Y. Cheung Design Associates (then based

15 Bank of China Tower, Hong Kong, 72 storeys, 367.4 metres (1,205 feet), 1990 • Architect: I.M. Pei & Partners • Associate architect: Wong/Kung & Lee • Doc. *Architectural Record* cover, January 1991 | coll. G. Binder • Photography: ©Terri Meyer Boake • In 1990 the Bank of China Tower became the first Asian supertall building to be included among the world's 10 tallest buildings. 16 CITIC Plaza, Guangzhou, 390.2 metres (1,280 feet), 80 storeys, 1997 • Architect: Dennis Lau & Ng Chun Man Architects & Engineers (HK) Ltd • Photography: Frankie Wong & Michael Tse Photography | courtesy Dennis Lau & Ng Chun Man Architects & Engineers (HK) Ltd • Strategically located along a major central axis leading to Guangzhou's CBD still in progress, CITIC Plaza still proudly stands guard almost two decades after its completion.

in Beverly Hills); after moving back to China he completed the project from his Hong Kong–based American Design Associates firm. Shenzhen's Shun Hing Square became the tallest building in China and the tallest outside the United States, still holding the title of the world's tallest building at the time. Returning to I.M. Pei's Bank of China Tower we can probably trace back to this 1990 building the trend regarding putting 'spires' atop contemporary tall buildings in the last 25 years. Until then, only American buildings completed prior to World War II (such as the Chrysler Building) were crowned by a thin spire. Following the completion of the Bank of China Tower, we have seen again a new series of tall buildings with spires in Hong Kong and in China but actually, all over the world, and this is still true today especially when it comes to a series of supertall buildings.

17

Like the early North American buildings, those early 1990s Chinese supertall buildings (i.e. Bank of China Tower, Hong Kong; Central Plaza, Hong Kong; CITIC Plaza, Guangzhou; Shun Hing Square, Shenzhen; The Center, Hong Hong) are all office buildings, even if some of them are part of mixed-use ensembles, but by 1999 such supertall towers became mixed-use programs, often with a luxury hotel in the upper levels. An example is the 88-storey **Jin Mao Tower** (designed by Skidmore, Owings & Merrill) completed in Shanghai in 1999; the tower became the tallest building in China at 420.5 metres (1,380 feet) until the completion in 2008 of the 494.3-m (1,622 feet) 101-storey **Shanghai World Financial Center** located across the street (and designed by Kohn Pedersen Fox Associates). These two buildings introduced on a grand scale mixed-use supertall towers to the Chinese skyline and have become very common in recent years. Next to these two buildings, the 632-metre (2,073-foot), 128-storey Shanghai Tower (designed by Gensler) will finalise, at least for some time, the race for the sky in Shanghai while the race for ever-taller buildings continues in Shenzhen with the 660-metre (2,165-foot), 115-storey Ping An Financial Centre designed by Kohn Pedersen Fox Associates currently under construction and scheduled to be completed in 2016. It should be followed by the 729-metre (2,392-foot) 137-storey mixed-use Suzhou Zhongnan Center scheduled for completion by the year 2020 and the tallest building in progress in China, so far.

18

Considering the high number of supertall buildings in progress in China there are of course many designed by Chinese firms, Shanghai-based East China Architectural Design & Research Institute (ECADI) being one of the leading mainland architects, acting both as design architect and as an associate architect depending of the project; however, one has to admit that the tallest ones in the country (or in a particular city) are often designed by American architects as eight of the 10 tallest buildings completed or under construction in China have been designed by American architects. The only two exceptions not being designed by an American architect are the Goldin Finance 117 tower in Tianjin, designed by Hong Kong-based P&T Group (the architect that historically put its mark for several decades in both Shanghai and Hong Kong), and the World Financial Center designed by Atkins, a firm with offices in China but based in the United Kingdom. And if we have a look at the individual cities, with the exception of a few locations, the tallest buildings completed or still in progress in most of the major cities, such as Beijing, Chengdu, Chongqing, Dalian, Guangzhou, Hong Kong, Nanjing, Shanghai, Shenzhen, Suzhou or Wuhan, have all been designed by an American architect. A famous American architect compared the role of the American architects on the tall building scenery with the one of car makers as he once asked the author of these lines 'Who does the best cars in the world' – suggesting that it would be difficult to challenge the renowned German or Italian contingency in that field – that is, that the American expertise gained over more than a century would probably only continue in this field, regardless of the experience gained by others.

19

17 Shun Hing Square, Shenzhen, 69 storeys, 384 metres (1,260 feet), mixed-use, 1996 • Architect: K.Y. Cheung Design Associates / American Design Associates • Associate architect: The Second Architectural Design Institute of Shenzhen • Photography: ©G. Binder • Part of a mixed-use ensemble, the 384-metre (1,260-foot) office tower became the first mainland China building to be included in the 'top 10' of the world's tallest buildings and the tallest outside the United States. **18** Jin Mao Tower, Shanghai, 88 storeys, 420.5 metres (1,380 feet), 1999 • Architect: Skidmore, Owings & Merrill • Associate architects: East China Architectural Design & Research Institute (ECADI); The Shanghai Institute of Architectural Design & Research (SIADR) • Photography: ©SOM • Tallest building in China for almost a decade, the 420.5-metre (1,380-foot) mixed-use Jin Mao Tower placed mainland China on the worldwide supertall building skyline. **19** Shanghai World Financial Center, Shanghai, 101 storeys, 494.3 metres (1,622 feet), 2008 • Architects: Kohn Pedersen Fox Associates (design); Mori Building Architects and Engineers (project) • Associate architect: Irie Miyake Architects • Architect of record: East China Architectural Design & Research Institute (ECADI) • Photography: ©G. Binder • Upon completion, both the Jin Mao Tower and the Shanghai World Financial Center became the tallest buildings in the country for a few years. These two buildings, featuring a luxury hotel in the upper levels, introduced on a grand scale mixed-use supertall towers to the Chinese skylines. Such projects are now becoming rather 'common' in most major Chinese cities.

Hotels

If the 88-storey Jin Mao Tower (designed in 1999 by Skidmore, Owings & Merrill) popularised throughout China the model for supertall mixed-used towers — comprising offices in the lower part and a hotel in the upper tier of the building, often articulated around an atrium — we should recognise that an early model of this form of mix equipped with an atrium is found in the 42-storey Tour Crédit Lyonnais[11] in Lyon, France, designed by Araldo Cossutta in 1977. In both these aforementioned cases hotels sit perched high in the air, their lobby and main amenities are conventionally located in the lower levels of the hotel part of the building. However, a new hospitality trend has emerged in China in recent years where this is no longer the case, it's now seen that both reception and lobby, as well as the main amenities, such as restaurants and bars, are located in the upper levels so everybody can experience and enjoy the most dramatic views over the city each property has to offer. This is seen in mixed-use towers, such as the St. Regis hotel which sits atop the 100-storey KK100 in Shenzhen (designed by TPF Farrells), or at the Ritz-Carlton hotel that's located atop the 108-storey International Commerce Centre in Hong Kong (designed by Kohn Pedersen Fox Associates), and in single-use hospitality towers, such as in the case of the Grand Hyatt Shenzhen and Grand Hyatt Shenyang (both designed by RTKL) and the Grand Hyatt Guangzhou (designed by Goettsch Partners).

As in the case of the Zhejiang Grand Hotel in Hangzhou, renovations of existing Chinese hotels created an opportunity to move the main reception lobby to an upper level as a way to reposition the hotel in its market, and at the same time it allowed it to regain space at ground level to be leased for retail in areas where retail may not have even been much present in the street at the time of the hotel's initial completion. This also reflects the rapid rate of change and the consequent impact to the urban environment throughout China.

Grand Hyatt Shenzhen, Shenzhen, 42 storeys, 193 metres (633 feet), 2009 • Architect: RTKL Associates, Inc. • Associate architect: CCDI • Photography: courtesy City Crossing

Grand Hyatt Shenzhen, main reception at sky-lobby level (33/F) • Photography: courtesy City Crossing

An ever-growing number of tall and supertall buildings

When we look at supertall buildings that are at 300+ metres (984+ feet), if by the year 2000 there were only 26 such buildings completed in the world (including at the time the two World Trade Center towers in New York City) and six in China alone, by 2010 there were already 15 such buildings in China out of a total of 50 worldwide at that time. Considering the completed buildings and the projects already under construction, we can anticipate that by the year 2020 there will be well over 200 supertall buildings completed worldwide and slightly more than 50 percent of them will be located in China alone. With the rhythm of new supertall projects we have encountered in China in recent years we can expect more supertall projects to be announced; we could thus confidently anticipate that the percentage of completed Chinese supertall projects by the year 2020 will be even higher that the above scheduled figure of 50 percent.

On a worldwide basis, if we consider all tall buildings of 150+ metres (492+ feet) completed or still under construction — far exceeding the figure of 4,000 — there are already more than 40 percent located in China alone, and this percentage is expected to increase in the coming years. If we consider only the projects of that height under construction, more than 50 percent of such projects are located in China.

Supertall and mixed-use projects and the process of change of use

Of all tall buildings above 300 metres (984 feet) completed and under construction, about 50 percent are mixed-use projects, more than three times the percentage of similar projects over 150 metres (492 feet). These figures show that many of the supertall buildings in China are not only 'tall' buildings, but they are often the focal point of a particular city or a particular district — not just because of their height (allowing the building to act as a gigantic totem) but also because in many cases, depending on the mix of the project, the building becomes 'the' location in the city to do shopping, to do business or to meet people in the numerous hotels located atop those towers, not forgetting that with the ever-increasing number of observation decks, these buildings become tourist attractions as well.

As everywhere else, the increasing number of mixed-use towers is not just to cater to society but it is a response to the real estate market. An increase in the supply of tall buildings has meant that demand for office space is too low to fill in this ever-growing number of supertall projects thus building space hasn't been filled in the way it once might have been in the past decades (mainly with office space), thus the mixed-use program spreads the investment risk over several different types of markets. Moreover, the fact that the built floor area of these buildings is thus generally increased because of the building height, it seems that finding different users to fill supertall towers is more probably a necessity.

We note that supertall buildings may have the advantage of being opened for business in phases, meaning that return on investment can already be provided while the building may still be under construction (this is not especially linked only to the Chinese market as we see this phenomenon in the West as well, an example is the 92-storey Trump International Hotel & Tower in Chicago). This was the case with the 108-storey International Commerce Centre (2010) in Hong Kong, which opened in three phases: the first lower two tiers were opened for the office tenants in two phases while the third tier scheduled to accommodate the Ritz-Carlton hotel was still being built in the upper part of the building. The hotel eventually opened in 2011.

Also in Hong Kong, at the Landmark, a twin-tower project completed in 1983, a hotel was implemented in 2005 in the lower levels by Kohn Pedersen Fox Associates in one of the towers originally designed by P&T Group. Hongkong Land was the developer of both the original building and its transformation. This is to say (and this is not particular to China nor Asia) that well-thought projects can evolve and see their mix of uses changed over time, including possibly their number of different uses increased or decreased depending of the real estate market conditions. The 1978 Windsor House is another interesting case of change of use in Causeway Bay in Hong Kong, an area favoured by shopping enthusiasts. While the

42-storey Windsor House office building originally provided retail space on two above-ground levels in addition to the basement, another 15 levels have recently been converted from office use to retail and entertainment uses, so today the 17 lower levels of the tower are now totally devoted to a mall; something that would have probably never been envisioned when the project was being studied about 40 years ago.

After New York City, Hong Kong – together with Singapore – probably has the highest number of rather tall demolished buildings in the world, and these include sometimes very recent projects. This differs to what happens in New York City where most such buildings have often been demolished 55 to 60 years after their initial completion, with the exception of the four buildings destroyed or demolished following the 9/11 attacks, which did not survive that long. In Hong Kong, the 31-storey Ritz-Carlton Hong Kong hotel, completed in1993, closed for business after only about 15 years and was demolished in 2009 in the Central area. Located very near the Ritz-Carlton, the 26-storey 1963 Hongkong Hilton hotel has also been demolished, this one earlier in the mid 1990s, although the hotel benefitted from an extensive renovation only a few years earlier. Next to the Ritz-Carlton, the 33-storey **Furama Hotel** (1973; later known as the Furama Inter-Continental and eventually Kempinski Furama), characterised by its noticeable protruding La Ronda rooftop revolving restaurant overlooking Victoria Harbour, was demolished in 2001. All three hotel projects have been replaced by office towers.

Apart from the pure hospitality business considerations, for decades, the heart of the Central area has been confirmed as the place of choice for grade A offices in Hong Kong. It makes sense then not only that developers opt to replace hotels with offices, but by maximising the plot ratio or floor area ratio (FAR) – the plot ratio/FAR can be summarised as the ratio obtained when dividing the above-ground built area by the site area – allowed by the planning authorities on a particular site, it may lead to erecting larger buildings on the same site or a larger building on the same site enlarged after buying neighbouring pieces of land.

Also in Hong Kong but more recently in the Causeway Bay area, the 38-storey Hysan Place (completed in 2012) has replaced the 40-storey Hennessy Centre that was originally completed in 1983 and demolished in 2008. In this case, considering the ever growing success of retail businesses in Causeway Bay, combined with the ever-growing success of multilevel malls in Hong Kong, the site owner (Hysan Development Company Limited) opted to replace an obsolete office tower with a mixed-use retail/ office tower, accommodating retail, entertainment areas and landscaped garden terraces that are spread over the first 15 levels of the tower and office areas in the upper levels. These are a few Hong Kong examples of demolished buildings that have been replaced by new ones accommodating often more spaces and either different or more uses. Depending on each case, the obsolete character of the above examples of demolished buildings is to be considered in regard to the features of the building compared to recent competition, in regard to the appropriateness of building use(s) and in regard to the size of the project considering the potential of a site in terms of total allowed above ground areas to be built.[12] In Hong Kong Central the plot ratio could be as high as 15 for office towers, which is a higher ratio than that normally allowed for hotels.[13]

What about mainland China? If we take into account the projects to date completed and still under construction in mainland China, considering that about 90 percent of all 150+ metres (492+ feet) tall buildings have been built since the turn of this millennium, property owners don't have many such opportunities as yet to decide whether it is worth demolishing a tall building for whatever reason. However, several buildings have seen their façades reclad as it appears the quality was not up to the expected standards when starting to build tall buildings 20 to 25 years ago. One of the particulars of mainland China's tall building scenery is, as we have just

Mixed-use projects

More often than in other countries single-use and mixed-use towers are being built in many cases as part of larger multitower, mixed-use ensemble. This mix of uses and the scale of these projects create a series of destination places within the city and focal points where people can gather together both inside and outside. The great variety of outdoor spaces around many large-scale multiuse projects in many newly built projects around China has increased in recent years along with the quality to ensure they meet a higher level of standard. One of the most recent mixed-use projects that exemplifies the current trend of large-scale, mixed-use ensembles being built at the moment in China is Eton Place Dalian (in Dalian) designed by NBBJ. Eton Place Dalian is organised around a large shopping mall and includes three 43-storey residential towers completed in 2010 and two 62- and 80-storey commercial towers still in progress. The roof of the podium has been designed as a landscaped garden and promenade level and while such amenity is often for the sole use of the projects' occupants, in the case of Eton Place Dalian access is free to everyone and becomes an extension of the street. Perhaps more than the height of some buildings, these large-scale ensembles define and structure the new appearance of so many Chinese cities being heavily redeveloped at the moment.

Eton Place Dalian, Dalian, 80 storeys, 383 metres (1,257 feet), 2010–2017 • Architect: NBBJ • Architect of record: China Northeast Architecture Design Research Institute • Rendering: ©Crystal CG

20

20 Furama Hotel, Hong Kong, 33 storeys, 109.8 metres (360 feet), 1973 (now demolished) • Architect: Eric Cumine Associates • Photography: coll. G. Binder • The 1973 109.8-metre-tall (360-foot) Furama Hotel, characterised by its noticeable protruding La Ronda rooftop revolving restaurant overlooking Victoria Harbour, has been later known as the Furama Inter-Continental and eventually Kempinski Furama when it was demolished in 2001. In order to maximise the allowable buildable areas of the plot, the 185-metre-tall (607-foot) AIA Central office tower completed in 2005 has now replaced the demolished hotel.

19

Bridges connecting buildings up in the air

As often advocated by Antony Wood,[14] executive director of the Chicago-based Council on Tall Buildings and Urban Habitat (CTBUH), there is an increasing number of towers in the world and particularly in China, and often, but not only, residential ones, that are connected by bridges in the upper levels. Sometimes they are connected at mid-levels or in the upper levels or are conceived as 'bridges' connecting independent towers, or as part of the architecture of the building that forms in some cases a giant majestic arch. Depending on the project, those 'bridges' (comprising often several levels) provide room for residences or large office areas or in many cases communal spaces or luxury amenities and even open-air terraces. In addition, as stressed by Antony Wood, these 'bridges' allow for the safe transfer from one tower to another in cases of emergency and allow for additional escape routes. Some of the residential projects with those upper bridges linking individual towers are Linked Hybrid in Beijing (2009; designed by Steven Holl Architects) and EPI Residences in Shenzhen (2013; designed by Wong & Ouyang). Among the commercial and mixed-use buildings with upper connected levels creating multilevel bridges and arches are Gate to the East in Suzhou (2016; designed by RMJM Hong Kong), the Window of Canton in Guangzhou (2018; designed by Atkins Consultants (Shenzhen) Co., Ltd) and Raffles City Chongqing in Chongqing (2019; designed by Safdie Architects).

Linked Hybrid, Beijing, 21 storeys, 66 metres (217 feet), 2009 • Architect : Steven Holl Architects • Photography: ©Shu He

21

22

seen, that most of its city skylines have been completed in a rather short period of time, whereas the Chicago and New York City skylines took decades to be built, and that means that for a city like Shanghai or Beijing we may expect to witness in the future a great number of buildings to become obsolete at the same time, since many of them would have been completed during the same timeframes. This is something we have never experienced anywhere else to that scale. A city like Dubai will probably have to face the same process in the future since most of its buildings have also been erected during a short period of time as well. How China will address this scheduled situation will be a major challenge for everyone involved.

Conclusion

Seen from far away, the number of tall buildings being erected year after year and their ever-increasing heights seem to be the major changes to Chinese city skylines. But perhaps for the people living there it could be that these would probably not be the only major changes to witness and perhaps not even the most important. One has to admit that the overall building quality has increased over time not only in terms of the buildings but what appear to be 'simple things', such as sidewalks; the landscaped finishes of many recent large-scale projects compare favourably with the world's best sidewalks (see image 21 at left). Until the turn of the new millennium, any visitor to mainland China – whether a tourist or a professional from the building industry – could see that buildings, although recently completed, often looked as thought they'd been completed a long time ago. Whether due to design, construction or maintenance reasons, this has indeed changed in recent years because of an increasing number of projects being designed by foreign-based or Hong Kong-based architects (and developers) who have brought their own high-rise expertise, and also because the level of expertise of mainland-based Chinese architects has also increased over the years. While although many Chinese tall buildings today follow the best international standards, one side effect of this change is that often buildings have lost the regional character many projects completed up to 10 years ago used to present: some of these characteristics were seen to be a circular rooftop or a conical roof or whatever particular character (see image 22, below left). Today, one may still single out a series of particular projects designed by Chinese architects, such as buildings in the form of a ring or in the form of an ancient coin, or unique projects like CCTV designed by the Netherland's-based OMA, but in the great mass of buildings being completed every year in China those uncommon projects (although quite noticeable on the skyline) are not as common as media coverage might lead to believe. So it poses the question, 'Will the ever-increasing quality of construction of tall buildings in China gradually eradicate the local character of its buildings?'

When referring to the 1988 Jin Mao Tower, Adrian Smith (then design architect at Skidmore, Owings & Merrill) said once: 'It was important to relate the Jin Mao Tower to the culture and indigenous character of China and its people. The ancient pagoda, one of the precursors of the manmade skyscraper, was the basis for the memory of the tower. It is not a copy of a pagoda, but rather an analogy to the profile, in much the same way as in the 1950s simple rectangular International style glass box forms were evocative of the towers of San Gimignano, Italy.'[15] Still in Shanghai, if we look at the 1990 Shanghai Centre (designed by John Portman & Associates), the project evokes in its own way another type of contextualism related to the historic and regional context. Considering the limited number of tall buildings in mainland China up to the beginning of this millennium, we note that many tall buildings erected in the 20th century, whether designed by mainland China–based architects or foreign-based ones, had often a regional and/or contextual historic character. In recent years, considering the very large number of buildings being built, we could almost dare to say that this historic/regional character has disappeared from most of the newer projects.

21 Wuhan Tiandi, Wuhan, Lots A5 to A12, 2011 • Architect: P&T Group • Photography: ©G. Binder • Nicely detailed landscaped sidewalks can be observed at Wuhan Tiandi. Wuhan Tiandi (developed in phases by Shui On Land) is one of these large-scale multitower mixed-use ensembles bringing to mainland China added quality of life. 22 Portion of the city centre skyline in Hangzhou • Photography: ©G. Binder • With a number of tall buildings designed by Western architects or Chinese architects following Western standards – and flavours – skylines with a regional flavour, such as the city centre one in Hangzhou, will perhaps disappear from the Chinese scenery with newly designed buildings coming in.

While impressive supertall projects have advertised Chinese tall buildings throughout the world, when visiting China one will probably observe that tall building mixed-used ensembles comprising several towers (and not always the tallest ones in their respective location) are probably the high-rise projects that have most transformed the Chinese urban centres, by creating destination places where everybody converge for shopping, entertainment, business or general living. While the early major large-scale projects completed in 1990s and the early 2000s were often functioning like isolated islands because of the lack of contemporary neighboring projects to relate to, we noticed in recent years a series of projects articulated around open-air courtyards and plazas, where newly built tall building projects become part of a network of complementing projects constituting the new urban fabric.

Regarding supertall buildings, by the year 2020 China alone will have over 50 percent of the over 200 buildings 300+ metres (984 feet) completed in the world. Those 'uncommon' buildings are starting to be as 'common' for Chinese people as when in the 1960s Americans witnessed the completion of the 60-storey One Chase Manhattan Plaza and the 59-storey Pan Am Building (now MetLife Building) in New York or the 60-storey One First National Plaza (now Chase Tower) in Chicago or when the Europeans witnessed the completion of the 26-storey Thyssenhaus (now Dreischeibenhaus) in Dusseldorf or the now-demolished 30-storey Centre International Rogier in Brussels. Three different continents, thee different scales – but the skyscraper seems to remain a strong actor to enter eras of change.

In the introduction of an earlier book done by the same team, *Tall Buildings of Asia & Australia*[16] released in 2001, the author pondered the following: 'How long will it be before an Asian-based architect designs and builds a major skyscraper in another part of the world?' We can now answer this: a little bit more than a decade, as 2012 saw the completion of the 175.6-metre (576-foot) **Absolute World** residential twin towers in Mississauga, Canada, a project that won the *Best Tall Building Americas Award 2012*, awarded by the Council on Tall Buildings and Urban Habitat (CTBUH). The irony is that not only was it the first major tall building designed by an Asian-based architect and completed outside Asia, but it was also the first completed tall building ever designed by young architect Ma Yansong of Beijing-based MAD Architects, the architect who recently unveiled the design proposal for the Lucas Museum in Chicago. In parallel, we are also witnessing a series of major Chinese real estate investments outside Asia, such as in the case of the 1931 Waldorf Astoria in New York City.[17] If the ownership of the famous 47-storey American hotel can be transferred to the Anbang Insurance Group Co. of China in a US$1.95 billion deal, and if a mainland Chinese architect can design a 56- and 50-storey twin-towered project in Canada, China may perhaps surprise us – even outside its own boundaries – in unexpected ways in the field of tall buildings in the next 20 years. There are probably very few of us who could have imagined just a couple of decades ago what has been achieved in this field in China in the past 20 years alone.

Georges Binder
Managing Director, Buildings & Data SA
Fellow of the Council on Tall Buildings and Urban Habitat (CTBUH)
and CTBUH Country Representative for Belgium

Floor numbering systems

For decades, people travelling to the United States or staying in international luxury hotels have discovered that most of the American high-rise buildings and international hotels do not have a '+13' level, meaning that any floor number above level +13 was not labelled sequentially or accounted for because there was a 'missing' level in the overall floor count. This is a minor discrepancy compared to what is happening in many Chinese tall buildings and particularly in Hong Kong where most of its building floor numbering does not include the floor numbers +4, +14, +24, +34, +44, +54 and so on, since these are considered unlucky numbers. The same goes for the number of a particular tower in a multitower complex: should you need to visit a friend on a so-called level +67 in Tower 5 in Hong Kong, as an example, in a housing ensemble composed of several towers, that does not in fact mean that there is a minimum of five towers, since there are almost no towers named Tower 4 in multitower projects located in a city such as Hong Kong. Your friend is probably living in the fourth tower of the residence and the apartment is probably located on the actual level +60 since there are no levels ending with '4'. The same may also apply to level +13 as it happens in North America, but this is less common in China. Returning to the 'missing' levels ending with '4', it means that in a project such as the well-known International Commerce Centre (ICC) located in Kowloon, the top level is not the 118th floor as advertised to all people visiting the Ritz-Carlton hotel perched atop the tower, but the actual level +108. At the turn of the millennium several 88-storey towers have been completed. Opened in the same period as the 88-storey Petronas Twin Towers in Kuala Lumpur, the Jin Mao Tower has also – officially – 88 storeys as '8' is a lucky number in Asia. However, it should be noted that in the case of the Jin Mao Tower, the building has an additional four penthouse levels, meaning that developers like Donald Trump in New York City would have included them in the overall count to have a taller-looking building, but in this particular case the goal was just to preserve the 'facial' 88-storey count. With the new millennium, most of the supertall buildings having grown taller and taller, we are almost no longer witnessing '88-storey' buildings; most of these supertall towers are in fact taller.

23

Notes

1 Except when noted otherwise, the term 'China' includes Hong Kong and Macau, while 'mainland China' does not include Hong Kong or Macau.
2 Tess Johnston and Deke Erh, *A Last Look: Western architecture in old Shanghai*, Old China Hand Press, Hong Kong, China, 1993.
3 Edward Denison and Guang Yu Ren, *Building Shanghai: The Story of China's Gateway*, Wiley-Academy, Chichester, West Sussex, United Kingdom, 2006.
4 Edward Denison and Guang Yu Ren, *Luke Him Sau Architect: China's Missing Modern*, John Wiley & Sons Ltd, Chichester, West Sussex, United Kingdom, 2014.
5 Liu Wujun and Huang Xiang, *Shanghai Urban Planning*, Thomson, Singapore, 2007.
6 P&T Group: *130 Years Architecture in Asia*, PACE Publishing Limited, Hong Kong, 1998.
7 Peter Blake, *Progressive Architecture*, March 1986.
8 *TIME* magazine, 26 December, 1983.
9 *The Great Wall Hotel Bulletin*, Vol. 1, Winter 1984.
10 Peter Blake, *Architectural Record*, January 1991.

11 *Architectural Record*, March 1978.
12 Kin Chee Wong in Thomas N.T. Poon and Edwin H.W. Chan (eds), *Real Estate Development in Hong Kong*, PACE Publishing Limited, Hong Kong, China, 2002.
13 Building (Planning) Regulations, The Government of the Hong Kong Special Administrative Region of the People's Republic of China, www.legislation.gov.hk; accessed February 2015.
14 Antony Wood, 'Rethinking Evacuation: Rethinking Cities', *CTBUH Journal*, 2011, Issue III.
15 Adrian Smith (ed.), *The Architecture of Adrian Smith, SOM: Toward a Sustainable Future*, Images Publishing, Melbourne, Australia, 2007.
16 Georges Binder (ed.), *Tall Buildings of Asia & Australia*, Images Publishing, Melbourne, Australia, 2001.
17 *Wall Street Journal*, www.wsj.com, 6 October, 2014.

23 Absolute World Towers, Mississauga, Canada, 50 and 56 storeys, 2012 • Design architect: MAD Architects • Associate architect: Burka Architects • Photography: ©Terri Meyer Boake • The Absolute World Towers are the first major completed tall buildings outside Asia designed by a mainland China–based architect.

Projects

I

Anchored by the sublime hillside of the Peak, OPUS HONG KONG draws its inspiration from the breathtaking scenery surrounding the site. A collaborative project with an American design architect, extensive site analysis was carried out to obtain a complete picture of the terrain, while massing studies were employed to develop an understanding of the future structure's proportions in relation to the landscape of the Peak and the surrounding neighbourhood.

The building consists of 12 residential units. There are two garden duplexes on the lower levels, and 10 super-flats above, one per floor with an area of more than 500 square metres (5,300+ square feet) each.

The design responds to the site context by opening up panoramic views of Victoria Harbour through floor-to-ceiling **curved glass walls** surrounded by continuous balconies. These act as solar shades and enable 'pavilion' living when the glass walls are opened for natural ventilation. The building 'turns' as it rises, giving each apartment a unique floor plan and its own spectacular outlook over the city below and the hills around.

Two solid towers of 'boxes' create a continuous visual language, continuing from the quarry-like planter boxes around the site retaining structure. This integrates the building with the site and provides shading and privacy for individual units.

Structural columns are pushed to the exterior of the building, maximising the interior layout flexibility. These finely tuned glass-enclosed columns twist up and around the building like reeds swaying in the breeze.

The design was realised through a series of different scale-model studies, with the help of computer technology and real-size mockups, allowing teams to review the material composition and technical 'build-ability'. A close collaboration between the design team, executive architects and the construction team enabled consistency of design down to the last detail and allowed the project to be realised with the best workmanship.

1 Panoramic view from apartment
2 View from Stubbs Road
3 Duplex garden
4 Reflecting pool
5 Evening view from swimming pool
6 Floor plan (6/F)
7 Northeast elevation

Photography: courtesy Ronald Lu & Partners

OPUS HONG KONG

Location Hong Kong	**Main contractor** Gammon Construction Limited
Completion 2012	**Uses** Residential
Client Swire Properties Limited	**Number of buildings** I
Architect Gehry Partners, LLP	**Height** 56 m (184 ft)
Associate architect Ronald Lu & Partners	**Above-ground storeys** 13
Structural engineer Arup	**Basements** NIL
MEP engineer Arup	**Site area** 3,000 m² (32,292 ft²)
Vertical transportation consultant Arup	**Total gross area** 6,339 m² (68,232 ft²)
Façade engineer Emmer Pfenninger Partner AG	**Total number of elevators** 3
Landscape architect Urbis Limited	**Number of car parking spaces** 24
Lighting consultant L'Observatorie International	**Principal structure materials** Concrete, steel
Other consultants Gehry Technologies • Shen Milsom & Wilke (acoustic) • Oriental Landscape Limited (tree specialist) • Business Environment Council (BEAM)	

56 m | 184 ft

Source: Ronald Lu & Partners; OPUS HONG KONG sales brochure, coll. G. Binder

2

3

4

5

6

7

I

The Linked Hybrid complex aims to counter the current privatised urban developments in China by creating a 21st-century porous urban space, inviting and open to the public from every side. A filmic urban experience of space – around, over and through multifaceted spatial layers, as well as the many passages through the project – make Linked Hybrid an 'open city within a city'.

The ground level offers public passages that are 'micro-urbanisms' of small-scale shops, which also activate the urban space surrounding a large central reflecting pond that freezes over in winter to become an ice-skating rink. On the intermediate level of the lower buildings, public roof gardens offer tranquil green spaces, and at the top of the eight residential towers private roof gardens are connected to the penthouses. Elevators displace like a 'jump cut'

to another series of passages on higher levels. From the 12th to the 18th floors a multifunctional series of sky-bridges with a swimming pool, a fitness room, a café and gallery connects the residential towers and the hotel tower.

Programmatically this loop aspires to be **semi-lattice-like** rather than simplistically linear. Focused on the experience of passage of the body through space, the towers are organised to take movement, timing and sequence into consideration. The new 'Z' dimension of the towers' urban sectors aspire to individuation in urban living while shaping public space.

The Chinese Buddhist architecture inspires a polychromatic dimension. The undersides of the bridges and cantilevered portions are coloured membranes that glow with projected nightlight and the window jambs are based on the 'Book of Changes' with colours found in ancient temples.

Geothermal wells (655 at 100 metres [328 feet] deep) provide Linked Hybrid with cooling in summer and heating in winter, and make Linked Hybrid one of the largest green residential projects.

Five landscaped mounds to the north reuse the earth excavated from the new construction. The 'Mound of Childhood' is integrated with a kindergarten and has an entrance portal through it; the 'Mound of Adolescence' holds a basketball court, inline skating and skateboarding areas; the 'Mound of Middle Age' includes a public coffee-/ teahouse, a tai chi platform and two tennis courts; the 'Mound of Old Age' features a wine-tasting bar; and the 'Mound of Infinity' is carved into a meditation space with circular openings referring to infinite galaxies.

1 Detail view at ground level
2 View of polychromatic undersides of sky-bridges
3 View across public roof gardens
4 Central pond area
5 Elevation diagram
6 Section diagram
7 Typical program floor plan
Following pages:
8 Overall view in context

Credits: 1,4 ©Iwan Baan; 2,3,8 ©Shu He; 5,6,7 courtesy Steven Holl

Linked Hybrid

Location Beijing
Completion 2009
Client Modern Green Development Co., Ltd. Beijing
Architect Steven Holl Architects
Associate architect Beijing Capital Engineering Architecture Design Co. LTD
Structural engineers Guy Nordenson and Associates • China Academy of Building Research
MEP engineers Transsolar • Beijing Capital Engineering Architecture Design Co. LTD • Cosentini Associates
Landscape architects Steven Holl Architects • EDAW Beijing • Beijing Top-Sense Landscape Design Limited Co.
Lighting consultant L'Observatoire International
Other consultants Interior design: Steven Holl Architects; China National Decoration Co., LTD • curtain wall: Front Inc.; Xi'an Aircraft Industry Decoration Engineering Co. Ltd; Shenyang Yuanda Aluminum Industry Engineering Co., Ltd; Beijing Jianghe Curtain Wall Co., Ltd

Main contractor Beijing Construction Engineering Group
Uses Residential (644 apartments), hotel, commercial, entertainment, recreational, educational (kindergarten, Montessori school)
Number of buildings 9
Height 66 m (217 ft)
Above-ground storeys 21
Gross above-ground building area 162,932 m² (175,378 ft²)
Gross basement area 58,495 m² (629,640 ft²)
Total gross area 220,000 m² (2,368,060 ft²)
Gross floor area 221,462 m² (2,383,797 ft²)
Principal structure materials Exoskeletal concrete frame with insulation & sanded aluminium skin

Source: Steven Holl Architects

2

3

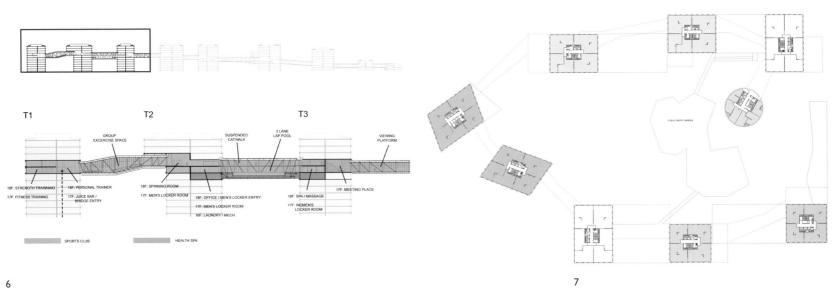

4

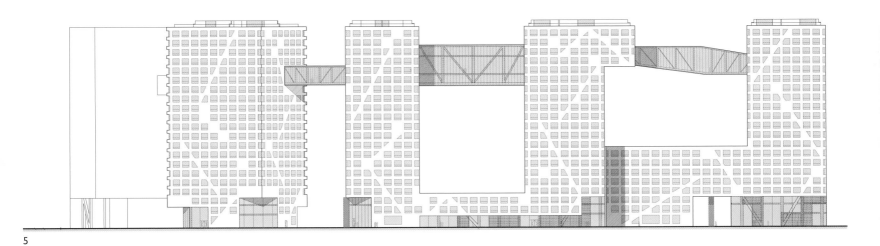

5

T1

T2

T3

GROUP
EXCERCISE SPACE

SUSPENDED
CATWALK

3 LANE
LAP POOL

VIEWING
PLATFORM

18F: STRENGTH TRAINNING

18F: PERSONAL TRAINER

18F: SPINNING ROOM

18F: OFFICE / MEN'S LOCKER ENTRY

18F: SPA / MASSAGE

17F: MEETING PLACE

17F: FITNESS TRAINING

17F: JUICE BAR /
BRIDGE ENTRY

17F: MEN'S LOCKER ROOM

17F: MEN'S LOCKER ROOM

17F: WOMEN'S
LOCKER ROOM

16F: LAUNDRY / MECH.

SPORTS CLUB

HEALTH SPA

PUBLIC ROOF GARDEN

6

7

■ The China Diamond Exchange Center is a 49,750-square-metre (535,504-square-foot) office building in Shanghai's Pudong district, the city's modern financial and commercial hub. The 15-storey-high building provides space for members of the China Diamond Exchange, as well as other related and speculative tenants.

The building is conceived as two rectangular office slabs connected by a sky-lit atrium, with a large cable-supported net wall (216 x 754 metres [66 x 230 feet]) at each end. One tower is fully dedicated to the Diamond Exchange members, with the adjacent tower serving other tenants. The relatively narrow, 20-metre-wide (feet) floor plate of each tower is unique, working in combination with the atrium to bring daylight to all offices.

The open elevator tower defines the focal point of the building, with three cabs traversing the atrium to sky bridges on each level that connect the two office blocks. The elevator activity is not only visible from the lobby but also from outside, through the full-height glass walls.

The major tenants' core business inspired the design, with **diamond-shaped elements** featured throughout, including the atrium's glass skylight, the structural geometry of the entry canopy, and the main lobby floor. Details provide punches of red, a colour that signifies prosperity and happiness in Chinese culture.

1   Diamond-patterned skylight of atrium
2   View of black horizontal grillwork of the office façades
3   View from building atrium through cable net wall
4   Ground floor plan
5   Typical floor plan

Photography: © 1st-image

China Diamond Exchange Center

Location Shanghai
Completion 2009
Client Shanghai Lujiazui Development Co., Ltd
Architect Goettsch Partners
Associate architect Shanghai Zhongfu Architectural Design Institute
Structural engineer Shanghai Tong-qing Technologic Development Co., Ltd
MEP engineer Shanghai Zhongfu Architectural Design Institute
Vertical transportation consultant ThyssenKrupp Elevator
Façade engineer Goettsch Partners (façade designer)
Landscape architect ADI Limited
Lighting consultant Shanghai New Century Co., Ltd
Main contractor Shanghai No. 2 Construction Co., Ltd
Uses Office
Number of buildings 1

Height 76.65 m (251 ft)
Above-ground storeys 15
Basements 2
Mechanical levels 17/F
Site area 6,430 m² (69,212 ft²)
Gross above-ground building area 39,870 m² (429,157 ft²)
Gross basement area 9,880 m² (106,347 ft²)
Total gross area 49,750 m² (535,504 ft²)
Floor area ratio (FAR)/Plot ratio 6.13
Gross typical floor area 2,480 m² (26,694 ft²)
Total number of elevators 6
Speed of fastest elevators 2.5 m (8 ft)/s
Number of car parking spaces 228
Principal structure materials Steel, concrete

700 m
600 m
500 m
400 m
300 m
200 m
100 m

77 m | 251 ft

Source: Goettsch Partners

2

3

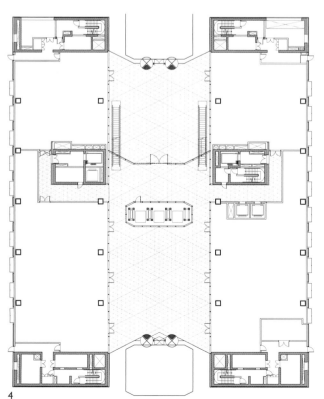

4

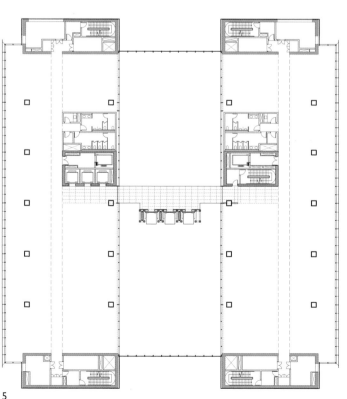

5

■ Due to its location on the 4th Ring Road the Zhongguancun Cultural Center is of particular significance within the development of the former 'Haidian book city' to a modern cultural forum. It was the overall approach to reflect the requirement of multimedia communication in the appearance of the building and to design it to be extremely efficient at the same time.

The large public areas of the cultural centre are accessed via a mall in a north–south direction, which offers a generous gallery space on the first six floors. The hall of the internal building part opens to the eastern road. This V-shaped space evokes a unique atmosphere, which is still increased by light and sound installations. The roof level is designed as a business centre with restaurants, bars, discotheques and terraces. At a height of 80 metres (262 feet) visitors can enjoy the panoramic views over Beijing.

Circumferential glass strips enclose the building in a seemingly flowing movement. In response to the inner courtyards the façade possesses curvilinear setbacks, which follow the trapezoidal plan and present great plasticity. At the same time the deliberate modelling of the glass strips characterises the entrances. Sharp-edged cornice profiles generate a vertical structure on the glass façade. The atria and the double layer façade serve as buffer zones. They take up sun protection facilities and ventilation aggregates, as well as special media strips with newsworthy information. Images can be projected onto the façades with the support of mirrors, making the building appear at nighttime as a symbol of modern media technology.

1 Looking up to glass atrium
2 Perspective
3 Overview
4 Close-up of circumferential glass strips
5 View of the internal void
6 Floor plan (1/F)
7 Floor plan (2/F)
8 Floor plan (4/F)

Credits: 1,2,3,4,5 ©Christian Gahl, Berlin; 6,7,8 ©gmp

Zhongguancun Cultural Center

Location Beijing
Completion 2006
Client China Zhongguancun Culture Development Co., Ltd
Architect gmp (von Gerkan, Marg and Partners | Architects)
Associate architect Sunlight Architects & Engineers Co., Ltd
Structural engineer Schlaich Bergermann und Partner
MEP engineer Sunlight Architects & Engineers Co., Ltd

Façade engineer Schlaich Bergermann und Partner
Uses Commercial, entertainment
Number of buildings 1
Height 80 m (262 ft)
Above-ground storeys 17
Gross above-ground building area 85,000 m² (914,932 ft²)
Principal structure materials Reinforced concrete

700 m

600 m

500 m

400 m

300 m

200 m

100 m

80 m | 262 ft

Source: gmp (von Gerkan, Marg and Partners | Architects)

3

2

4

5

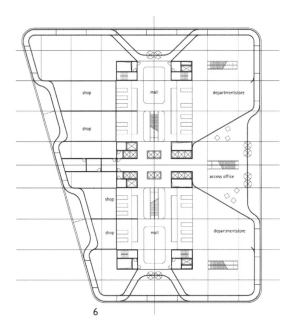

6

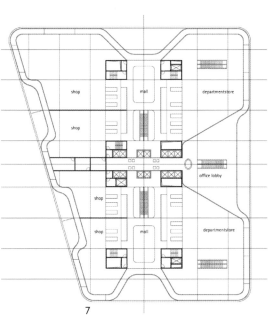

7

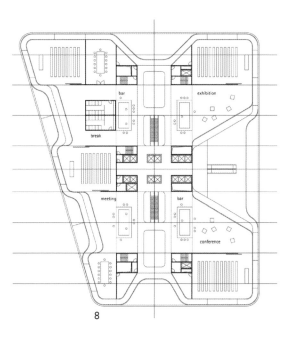

8

1

The concept for the 'Bamboo Towers' (Lot 14-01) strives for urban openness, physical and spiritual connectivity, simplicity in the organisation of functions, clarity in the use of materials and systems and the efficient use of space and resources.

The 'Bamboo Towers' will redefine the concept of the 'office environment'. Offering a place for human interaction in a campus setting, the open space is as important as the buildings themselves. The goal is to achieve harmony and dilute the boundaries between public and private space.

The plan configuration is bold and simple. The 'Bamboo Towers', anchored at opposite ends of the site, take their name from the strong vertical character of their façades – inspired by the image of **bamboo forests**, their branches overlay, forming abstracted patterns that appear to be in motion, illustrating the subtle yet constant presence of the wind.

The axial promenade bisects the complex in two, and becomes the *plano nobile* (noble level) that unifies and connects all the urban activity on the site. This is neither a civic nor a transitional space – it is intended to be a lively urban environment that promotes human engagement and ecological consciousness. Each user has a distinct point of entry at the ground plane. The tower's main access is oriented towards the promenade, within the space formed by the canopies and the screen walls, departing from the traditional concept of the arcade and giving the buildings a 'face' with a strong character.

The orthogonal geometry of the towers is in contrast to the 'organic' nature of their skins. The façade concept dilutes the boundaries at the edges of the buildings, giving the sense of continuity, while visually softening the edge of the rectangular shapes.

The landscape concept uses the strong architectural lines of the surrounding building grid – a carpet of pavers covers the entire site. The orientation of the striated granite provides a consistency and framework for other elements onsite. The framework of pavers is emphasised through the holistic integration of stripes of vegetation, water and light. The vegetation is arranged in layers to create a visual buffer, while the water plaza creates an area of calmness and reflectivity. The complex truly becomes a unique urban space that is elevated above all others.

1　Bird's-eye view
2　View from street level
3　Overall ground floor plan
4　Model rendering concept overview

Renderings: courtesy JAHN

Qiantan Enterprise World Phase II

Location Shanghai
Completion 2017
Client Shanghai Qiantan International Business District Investment (Group) Co., Ltd
Architect JAHN
Architect of record Shanghai Institute of Architectural Design & Research (SIADR)
Structural engineer SIADR
MEP engineer SIADR
Vertical transportation consultant SIADR
Façade engineers PFT • SIADR
Landscape architect Rainer Schmidt Landschaftsarchitekten (RSLA) • SIADR
Lighting consultants JAHN • SIADR
Uses Office, retail
Number of buildings 6
Height 99.2 m (325 ft)
Above-ground storeys 21
Basements 3

Mechanical levels B1/F, roof
Refuge levels 12/F
Site area 17,224 m² (185,397 ft²)
Gross above-ground building area Tower C: 36,682 m² (394,842 ft²) • Tower D: 36,682 m² (394,842 ft²) • Bldg A: 3,435 m² (36,974 ft²) • Bldg B: 1,440 m² (15,500 ft²) • Bldg E: 1,400 m² (15,500 ft²) • Bldg F: 3,435 m² (36,974 ft²)
Gross basement area 46,525 m² (500,791 ft²)
Total gross area 82,665 m² (889,798 ft²)
Floor area ratio (FAR)/Plot ratio 4.80
Gross typical floor area 1,800 m² (19,375 ft²)
Basic planning module 1.5 m (4.9 ft)
Total number of elevators 16
Speed of fastest elevators 6 m (20 ft)/s
Number of car parking spaces 750
Principal structure materials Steel and concrete composite

700 m
600 m
500 m
400 m
300 m
200 m

99 m | 325 ft

Source: JAHN

2

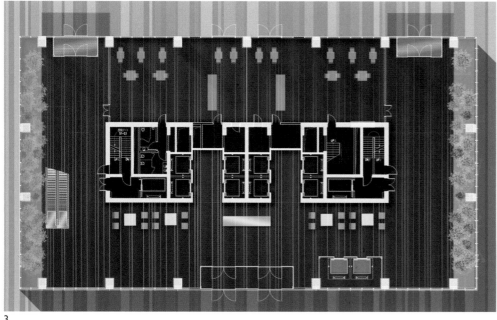

3

4

■ Also known as the Sheraton Moon Hotel, this resort is located next to Nan Tai Lake in Huzhou, a city situated west of Shanghai and north of Hangzhou, overlooking Suzhou and Wuxi across the lake. Since ancient times, Huzhou has been known as 'the house of silk' and 'the land of plenty' and is the only ancient city of culture in the surrounding area named after the lake. The favourable cultural and geographical environments bring both traditional and modern atmospheres to the hotel, distinguished by its unique design, which integrates the building into the waterscape of Nan Tai Lake, subsequently creating a poetic, yet artificial, echo of the natural landscape.

The hotel takes full advantage of its waterfront by directly integrating architecture and nature. The circular building corresponds with its reflection in the water, creating a surreal picture and connection between real and phantom. Beneath the sunlight and the reflection of the lake, the curved shape of the building is crystal clear. When night falls, both its interior and exterior lighting light up the entire building brightly. Soft light wraps around the hotel and the water, resembling the **bright moon** rising above the lake, blending classic and modern through the reflection.

The clear ring-shape posed a great challenge to the structural design: eventually, a reinforced concrete-core tube featuring high capacity, light-weight and excellent earthquake resistance was implemented, while simultaneously reducing environmental pollution during construction. The mesh curved surface structure makes the building more solid and it is this solidity that is further enhanced by the bridge-like bracing-steel structure that connects with the double-cone structure at the top floor. The hotel façade is covered with layers of fine-textured white aluminium rings and glass, bringing about illusion and drama of the building scale.

The annular shape of the hotel allows for all rooms to accommodate good views while increasing the natural light in all directions. The arc-like public space at the top has great open views and can act as a 'site in the air' for large-scale activities. The experience of being there is extraordinary as it feels like floating on the lake, putting emphasis on the harmony between humanity and nature.

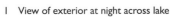

1 View of exterior at night across lake
2 View of exterior from lake
3 Site plan
4 Typical floor plan

Photography: ©Xia Zhi

Sheraton Huzhou Hot Spring Resort

Location Huzhou
Completion 2013
Client Feizhou Group
Architect MAD Architects
Associate architect Shanghai Xian Dai Architecture Design (Group) Co., Ltd
Structural engineer China Majesty Steel Structural Design Co., Ltd
MEP engineer China Majesty Steel Structural Design Co., Ltd
Façade engineers Zhejiang Zhongnan Curtain Wall Co., Ltd • Shanghai Timalco Curtain Wall Engineering Co., Ltd
Landscape architect EDSA – Landscape Design
Main contractor Shanghai Xian Dai Architecture Design (Group) Co., Ltd
Uses Hotel
Number of buildings 1

Height 102 m (335 ft)
Above-ground storeys 22
Basements 2
Site area 36,231 m² (389,987 ft²)
Gross above-ground building area 30,799 m² (331,517 ft²)
Total number of elevators 7
Speed of fastest elevators 3.5 m (11.5 ft)/s
Elevator brand Schindler
Number of car parking spaces 50
Hotel brand Sheraton
Principal structure materials Concrete, steel
Other materials Aluminium, glass

102 m | 335 ft

Source: MAD Architects

2

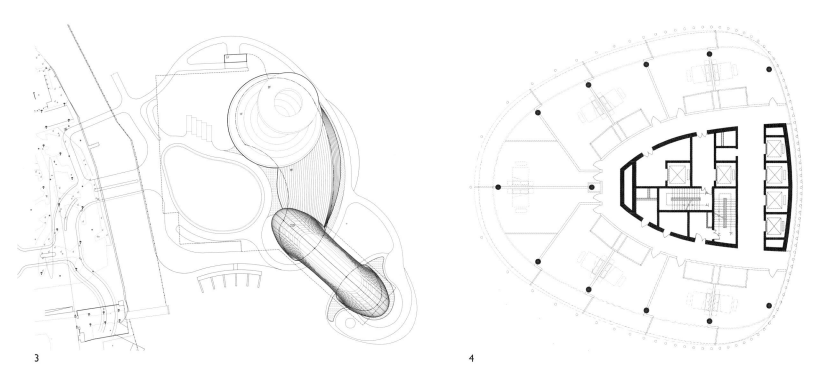

3

4

beijing

■ The two structures are to be understood as **abstract stone sculptures** from which vertical towers (hotel and office use) are developed out of a horizontal base (commercial use). The two buildings create a striking entity within the heterogeneous urban fabric by means of the towers' distinctive projection into the urban area around Jianguo Road.

Setback floors, as well as large-scale recesses at the entrances to the towers, act to organise the building. Shaded colonnades form the structure's base zone. The façade's natural materials — granulated granite of a light, warm color — reflect the sunlight and draw attention to the building ensemble.

The deep reveals and the sculptural effects of the architectural bodies thereby allow a staged image of light and shade to emerge that emphasises the overall form's effect in the urban environment.

1 Aerial view in context
2 Overall view from street level
3 Tower floor plan
4 Ground floor plan
Credits: 1,2 ©Christian Gahl, Berlin; 3,4: ©gmp

Wanda Plaza

Location Beijing
Completion 2007
Client Wanda Plaza Property Co., Ltd
Architect gmp (von Gerkan, Marg and Partners | Architects)
Associate architect China Beijing Institute of Architectural Design & Research
Structural engineer Jianghe Group (façade)
MEP engineer HL-Technik (Munich)
Façade engineer Jianghe Group

Project management gmp
Uses Office, hotel, commercial
Number of buildings 2
Height 104 m (341 ft)
Above-ground storeys 23
Site area 40,200 m² (432,709 ft²)
Gross above-ground building area 130,000 m² (1,399,308 ft²)
Principal structure materials Reinforced concrete

104 m | 341 ft

Source: gmp (von Gerkan, Marg and Partners | Architects)

2

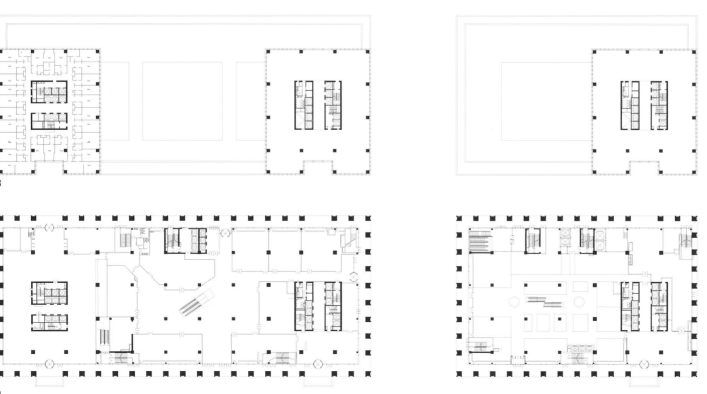

3

4

1

beijing

The project addresses the park as a 'quiet zone', while the project's eastern face looks out to the main street's 'loud zone'. The northern civic edge relates to the master plan corridor where most retail and commercial functions are planned. The southeast corner of this site is linked to a future train station. The office and residential towers anchor each side of the site, and natural movement is caught between them. The 100-metre-tall (328-foot) office tower stands on the intersection corner as a landmark, while the apartment tower is on the southwest corner, oriented towards the park and southern light. Daylight pours through skylights between the towers towards the ground, highlighting the entrances in the north, south and west sides of the site.

■ Anchoring the overall development, this project engages the natural forces of the site and celebrates its potential. It takes the adjacent park, main streets and the subway station as the three major forces that drive the design, which could be interpreted as water flowing between rocks.

The two towers are the **'rocks'** and can be accessed from the major streets; the retail podium, slightly twisted and deformed, is like water with a canyon-like atrium. Circulation paths inside the mall are planned like running water flowing down a stream. The floor plates create terraces and stepped landscapes for people to sit outside and enjoy.

1 Façade detail
2 Overview of development
3 Office tower
4 View from adjacent park
5 Internal atrium of shopping centre
6 Ground level of development

Photography: courtesy Aedas

North Star

Location Beijing	**Number of buildings** 3 (1 office building, 1 residential building, 1 shopping centre)
Completion 2010	**Height** 107 m (351 ft)
Client Beijing North Star Company Ltd	**Above-ground storeys** offices (2 towers): each 25 storeys • retail podium: 7 storeys
Architect Andrew Bromberg of Aedas	**Total gross area** 161,780 m² (1,741,385 ft²)
Local design institute China Electronics Engineering Design Institute	**Principal structure materials** Concrete, steel
Uses Mixed-use: office • residential • retail	**Other materials** Glass

2

3

4

5

6

Chaoyang Park Plaza pushes the boundary of the urbanisation process in modern cosmopolitan life by creating a dialogue between artificial scenery and natural landscapes. This project is located in Beijing's central business district, and comprises commercial, office and residential buildings. The site is on the southern edge of Chaoyang Park, one of the city's largest public parks.

By transforming features of Chinese classical **landscape painting**, such as lakes, springs, forests, creeks, valleys and stones into modern 'city landscapes', the urban space creates a balance between high urban density and natural landscape. The forms of the buildings echo what is found in natural landscapes, and re-introduces nature to the urban realm.

Like the tall mountain cliffs and river landscapes of China, a pair of asymmetrical towers creates a dramatic skyline in front of the park. Ridges and valleys define the shape of the exterior glass façade, as if the natural forces of erosion wore down the tower into a few thin lines; flowing down the façade, the lines

emphasise the smoothness of the towers and its verticality. The internal ventilation and filtration system of the ridges draws a natural breeze indoors, which not only improves the interior space but also creates an energy efficient system. The use of natural lighting, intelligent building and an air purification system make this project stand out; the ideal of 'nature' is not only embodied in the innovation of green technology, but also in the planning concept – transforming the traditional model of building in a modern city. (The project was awarded the LEED Gold certificate by the United States' Green Building Council.) Landscape elements are also injected into the interiors of the towers to augment the feeling of nature within an urban framework: the two towers are connected by a tall courtyard lobby with a ceiling height of up to 17 metres (56 feet); the site and sounds of flowing water make the entire lobby feel like a natural scene from a mountain valley. At the top of the towers, multilevel terraces shaped by the curving forms of the towers form public gardens, where people can gaze out over the entire city and look down at the valley scene created by the lower buildings on the site.

Located south of the towers, four office buildings are shaped like river stones that have been eroded over a long period – smooth, round, and each with its own features, they are delicately arranged to allow each other space while also forming an organic whole. Adjacent to the office buildings are two multilevel residential buildings in the southwest area of the compound. These buildings continue the 'mid-air courtyard' concept, and provide all who live here with the freedom of wandering through a mountain forest.

1 Office exterior as the mountain
2 Rendering of bird's-eye view
3 View from the street
4 Entrance lobby to high-rise
5 Lobby interior
6 Section diagram
7 Section diagram
8 Diagram of façade ventilation detail

Renderings: courtesy MAD Architects

Chaoyang Park Plaza

Location Beijing
Completion 2016
Client Junhao Real Estate Beijing Jingfa Properties Co., Limited
Architect MAD Architects
Structural engineer China Construction Design International (Shenzhen) Group Co., Ltd
Façade engineer RFR
Landscape architect Greentown Akin
Lighting consultant GD Lighting Design Co., Ltd

Uses Commercial, office, residential
Number of buildings 8
Height 120 m (394 ft)
Above-ground storeys 29
Basements 4
Site area 30,763 m² (331,130 ft²)
Gross above-ground building area 128,177 m² (1,379,686 ft²)
Gross basement area 94,832 m² (1,020,763 ft²)

120 m 394 ft

Source: MAD Architects

2

3

4

5

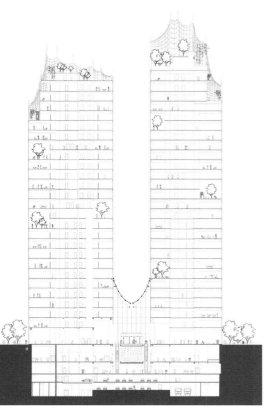

6

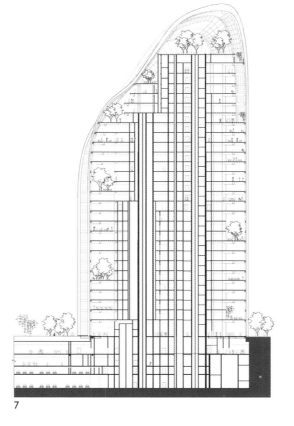

7

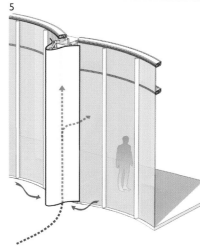

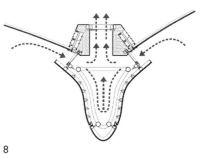

8

1

The large public space framed in the centre of the block is formed into three valleys inspired by a poem of the city's greatest poet, Du Fu (713–770), who wrote, 'From the northeast storm-tossed to the southwest, time has left stranded in Three Valleys.' The three plaza levels feature water gardens based on concepts of time – the Fountain of the Chinese Calendar Year, Fountain of Twelve Months, and Fountain of Thirty Days. These three ponds function as skylights to the six-storey shopping precinct below.

Establishing human scale in this metropolitan rectangle is achieved through the concept of 'micro-urbanism,' with double-fronted shops open to the street, as well as the shopping centre. Three large openings are sculpted into the mass of the towers as the sites of the Pavilion of History (designed by Steven Holl Architects), the Light Pavilion (by Lebbeus Woods) and the Local Art Pavilion (by Chinese sculptor Han Meilin).

■ In the centre of Chengdu, China, at the intersection of the first Ring Road and Ren Ming Nam Road, the Raffles City Chengdu project forms large public plazas with a hybrid of different functions. Creating a metropolitan public space instead of object-icon skyscrapers, this project takes its shape from its distribution of **natural light**. The required minimum sunlight exposures to the surrounding urban fabric prescribe precise geometric angles that slice the exoskeletal concrete frame of the structure. The building structure is white concrete organised in 1.8-metre-high (6-foot) openings with earthquake diagonals as required while the 'sliced' sections are glass.

The offices, retail and basement areas of the development are heated and cooled with geothermal technology, provided by 468, 90-metre-deep (295-foot) wells. The large ponds in the plaza harvest recycled rainwater, while the natural grasses and lily pads create a natural cooling effect. This, along with water thermal storage, daylight control, CO_2 monitoring, efficient interior lighting, and a high-performance building envelope, equipment and glazing, all result in an overall energy savings of 20 percent, with largest savings on space heating (68 percent) and space cooling (29 percent). Moreover, the use of regional materials is among the other methods employed to reach the LEED Gold rating.

1 Close-up of the sculpted opening in the Light Pavilion's façade
2 Aerial overview
3 View across a water garden
4 Plaza
5 Site plan
6 Site plan

Credits: 1,2 Shu He; 3 ©Iwan Baan; 4,5,6 ©Steven Holl Architects

Raffles City Chengdu

Location Chengdu
Completion 2012
Client CapitaLand Development
Architect Steven Holl Architects (design)
Associate architect China Academy of Building Research
Structural engineer China Academy of Building Research
MEP engineer Ove Arup & Partners
Other consultants Ove Arup & Partners (fire) • Davis Langdon & Seah (DLS) (quantity surveyor) • MVA Hong Kong Ltd (traffic)

Uses Office, serviced apartments, retail, hotel, commercial
Number of buildings 5
Height 123 m (404 ft)
Site area 17,500 m² (57,415 ft²)
Gross above-ground building area 195,000 m² (2,098,963 ft²)
Gross basement area 115,000 m² (1,237,850 ft²)
Gross floor area 310,000 m² (3,336,812 ft²)
Principal structure materials Exoskeletal concrete frame

123 m 404 ft

Source: Steven Holl Architects

2

3

4

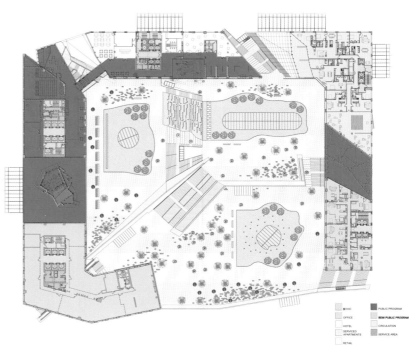

5

6

1

■ The Nanfung Commercial, Hospitality and Exhibition Complex is located outside Guangzhou on the Pazhou island, and is dedicated to exhibition related activities. The project contains four distinct programmatic uses, which split between two different sites, namely '1301' and '1401'. The complex is located opposite the government-funded exhibition centre (currently ranking the second largest in the world), which presents considerable design challenges; this complexity becomes even more strained by the realisation that the sites of the project are separated 160 metres (524 feet) from each other by another building. The introduction of four primary uses to the complex is to diversify its offering and create a mixed-use vibrancy, with an aim to raise competitiveness and establish a stronger likelihood of success.

The building '1301', also known as Guangzhou Commercial Showcase Complex, houses a retail exhibition area and an office showroom building; while '1401', the Guangzhou Nanfung International Convention and Exhibition Centre/Langham Place, is a traditional, multifloor exhibition centre and a 500-room five-star hotel.

The project design balanced the importance of 'frontage' for the visibility of the complex with basic functional constraints, including pedestrian flow, traffic flow, vehicular drop-offs and appropriate areas for loading/unloading zones.

This was formalised into a simple functional diagram that allows very efficient area layouts to be achieved.

The primary formal drivers for the design, however, are its contextual responses to the surrounding area as well as the **physical separation** of the two project sites. Contextually, the project, which initially seems large, is actually fragmented in comparison to its surrounding dominant neighbours. Consequently, urban design restrictions placed strong emphasis on the podiums: a simple and consistent presence was required on the major street wall to the north. The major entrances for the two sites are on the west side for '1301' and the east side for '1401'. These podium faces allowed for the exploration of more articulation and playfulness.

1 Exterior view of 1401
2 Night view of 1301
3 Exterior view of 1301
4 Floor plan of level 1 of 1401

Photography: courtesy Aedas

Nanfung Commercial, Hospitality and Exhibition Complex

Location Guangzhou

Completion 2013

Client Nan Fung Group

Architect Andrew Bromberg of Aedas

Local design institute Guangzhou Design Institute

Structural engineer Ove Arup & Partners Hong Kong Ltd

MEP engineer J. Roger Preston Limited

Façade engineer Ove Arup & Partners Hong Kong Ltd

Landscape architect Key Master Consultant Co.Ltd, and Earthasia Ltd (1401)

Lighting consultant Isometrix

Other consultants J. Roger Preston Limited (fire engineer) • Davis Langdon & Seah (quantity surveyor) • Graphia International (1401 signage)

Uses Office: 1301, tower • retail exhibition centre: 1301, podium • hotel: 1401, tower • exhibition centre: 1401, podium

Number of buildings 2 (1 office & retail exhibition centre; 1 hotel & exhibition centre)

Height 1301: 100 m (328 ft) • 1401: 126 m (413 ft)

Above-ground storeys 1301: 18 • 1401: 23

Site area Overall: 32,836 m² (353,443 ft²)

Total gross area Overall: 159,000 m² (1,711,461 ft²) • 1301: 74,000 m² (796,529 ft²) • 1401: 85,000 m² (914,932 ft²)

Hotel brand Langham Place

Principal structure materials Concrete, steel

Source: Aedas

126 m 413 ft

2

3

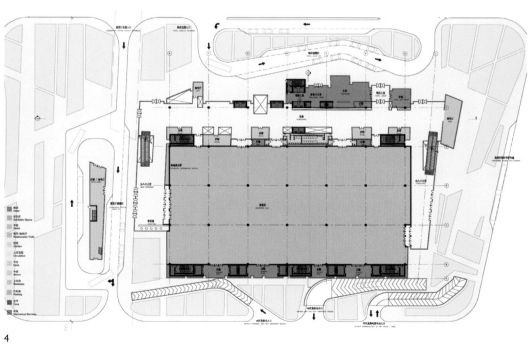

4

700 m | 2296 ft

600 m | 1968 ft

500 m | 1640 ft

400 m | 1312 ft

300 m | 984 ft

200 m | 656 ft

100 m | 328 ft

dalian

■ Located along Zhongshan Road in Dalian, a major boulevard connecting the famous Dalian port on the east with Asia's largest municipal square, Xinghai Square, on the west, the AVIC International Square covers four city blocks on a 5-hectare (12-acre) site. The 352,000 square-metre (3,788,896 square-foot) **mixed-use** program comprises four residential towers, each on two blocks, a high-rise office and apartment tower on the third block, and a mid-rise apartment building and a mid-rise office building on the fourth block. The project aims to establish a new hub of pedestrian activity for the Zhongshan financial district: the building's lower floors will provide shopfronts and a civic-scaled plaza will address a government building across the boulevard.

1 Entrance to office building, Lot A
2 Aerial view at dusk
3 Typical residential towers (C1–C4) floor plan (7/F–31/F)
4 Overall site plan

Credits: 1,2,4 ©AVIC Legend Co., Ltd;
3 ©Robert A.M. Stern Architects

AVIC International Square

129 m | 423 ft

Location Dalian

Completion 2015

Client AVIC Legend Co., Ltd • Dalian Hanghua Real Estate Development Co., Ltd

Architect Robert A.M. Stern Architects

Associate architect Hwa Yang Design Institute

Structural engineer Capol International (Shenzhen, China)

MEP engineer Architecture Design Institute Ltd

Cost consultant Dong Hui Cost Estimate

Landscape architect The Olin Studio (Philadelphia, Pennsylvania)

Lighting consultant Ying Liang Lighting Technology Ltd

Other consultants Kai Shun Teng

Main contractor China Architecture Number 8 Construction Unit

Uses Residential, retail, office

Number of buildings 4

Height 4 residential towers C1–C4 (phase 1): 129 m (423 ft) • 4 residential towers D1–D4 (future phase): 146 m (479 ft) • AVIC Center A office tower (future phase): 176.4 m (579 ft)

Above-ground storeys 4 residential towers C1–C4 (phase 1): 37 • 4 residential towers D1–D4 (future phase): 46 • AVIC Center A office tower (future phase): 40

Basements 2 (residential towers)

Source: Robert A.M. Stern Architects

Site area 46,800 m² (503,751 ft²) [phase 1]

Gross above-ground building area 70,319 m² (756,907 ft²) [phase 1]

Gross basement area 23,126 m² (248,926 ft²)

Total gross area Lot C Residential Buildings #1 & #2 (total 17,902 m² [192,695 ft²]): Ground–6/F: 535 m² (5,759 ft²) • 7/F–31/F: 487 m² (5,242 ft²) • 32/F–34/F: 445 m² (4,790 ft²) • 35/F–36/F: 400 m² (4,305 ft²) • 37/F: 382 m² (4,112 ft²) • Lot C Residential Buildings #3 & #4 (total 16,074 m² [173,019 ft²]): Ground–6/F: 486 m² (5,231 ft²) • 7/F–33/F: 446 m² (4,801 ft²) • 34/F–36/F: 382 m² (4,112 ft²) • 37/F: 352 m² (3,789 ft²)

Floor area ratio (FAR)/Plot ratio 6.32

Total number of elevators 8

Speed of fastest elevators 2.5 m (8 ft)/s

Elevator brand RI LI

Car parking area 23,126 m² (248,926 ft²)

Residence (and service) brand AVIC International Square

Principal structure materials Reinforced concrete shear wall

Other materials (Exterior building materials) base: yellow granite (honed finish) • wall & window sill: yellow granite (antique finish) • window frame: painted aluminium • (interior building materials): Jerusalem gold limestone • St. Laurent marble • antique mirrored walls • antique bronze grilles

2

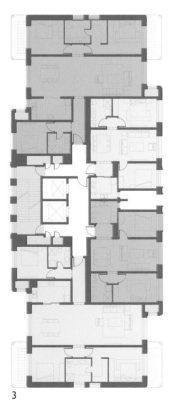

3

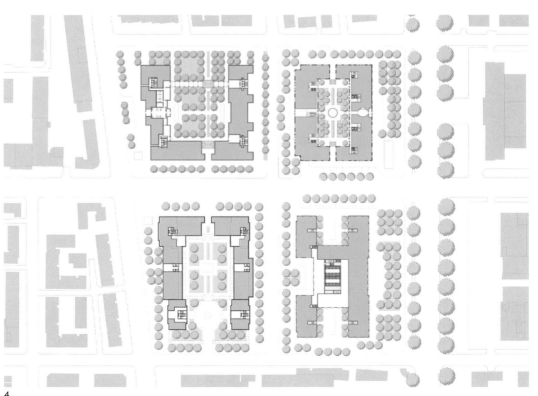

4

The mixed-use LHT Tower is flanked by Theatre Lane, a historic pedestrian alley that is the only such precinct in the core business district. While the new development does help to extend the width of this lane, its main intention is to energise the street by engaging the pedestrians.

Challenging the standard tower-and-podium development approach, while maximising the commercial value of podium retails, the LHT design features a dynamic folding façade on the long side of the building. It wraps the podium and the tower

in a formal continuum. On the other side, a ribbed wall together with the roof feature projects beyond to form the extension of the adjoining wall. The program is sandwiched between these two dialectical gestures, delineating the two different urban characters on either sides of the site. The escalator zones at the retail floors are strategically placed next to the external wall, forming an animated façade that responds to the busy pedestrian traffic along Theatre Lane. The folding curtain wall gives an impression of a **stage curtain**, opening to reveal the building and especially of the retail spaces within, making a subtle reference to the iconic Queen's Theatre, which occupied the site previously.

This is a building that takes cues from its urban context, both past and present, while rising above it to embody something new. The carefully modulated glazing systems of the two primary façades respond to the urban energy at street level and extend the public realm upwards, a creative intervention that enhances the dynamics of movement, encounters and interaction so vital to city life.

1 View of transparent façade
2 View overall and of folding curtain
3 View from street level, with pedestrianised Theatre Lane to the right
4 Interior view
5 Connection bridge at 2/F, looking over the main lobby for the office floors
6 Typical floor plan
7 Floor plan (3/F)
8 Floor plan (1/F)

Credits: 1,2,3,4,6,7,8 ©Rocco Design Architects Limited; 5 ©Marcel Lam

LHT Tower

Location Hong Kong
Completion 2011
Client The Luk Hoi Tong Co., Ltd
Architect Rocco Design Architects Limited
Structural engineer Greg Wong & Associates Ltd
MEP engineer J. Roger Preston Group
Façade engineer Arup
Project management consultants The Luk Hoi Tong Co., Ltd • C.K. Lau & Associates Ltd
Landscape architect Axxa Group Ltd
Lighting consultant Lightsource International (Asia) Ltd
Other consultants Greg Wong Associates Ltd. (geotechnical engineering) • J. Roger Preston Ltd. (building services) • Davis Langdon & Seah HK Ltd (quantity surveyor) • Allied Environmental Consultants Ltd (environmental) • Dcmstudios Ltd (interior design) • Duttonbray Design Ltd (graphic & signage)
Main contractor Gammon Construction Ltd
Uses Retail [B/F, G/F, 1/F, 2/F, 5/F] • F&B [3/F] • office [7/F–31/F]
Number of buildings 1

Height 130.55 m (430 ft)
Above-ground storeys 28
Basements 1
Mechanical levels 6/F, 22/F
Refuge levels R/F
Site area 1,059 m² (11,399 ft²)
Gross above-ground building area 15,642 m² (168,369 ft²)
Gross basement area 906 m² (9,752 ft²)
Total gross area 16,548 m² (178,121 ft²)
Floor area ratio (FAR)/Plot ratio 15.6 (approx.)
Gross typical floor area 575–614 m² (6,189–6,609 ft²)
Total number of elevators 8
Speed of fastest elevators 3.5 m (11.5 ft)/s
Elevator brand Schindler
Principal structure materials Reinforced concrete column & beam structure
Other materials Unitised curtain wall system (tower portion) • stick curtain wall system (podium portion)

131 m | 430 ft

Source: Rocco Design Architects Limited

3

4

5

2

6

7

8

700 m
600 m
500 m
400 m
300 m
200 m
136 m 446 ft
100 m

1

■ Wuhan Tiandi, located on the Yangtze riverfront with an unrivalled view of scenic Jiangtan Park, is a mixed-use city-core development comprising residential, office, hotel, retail, dining and entertainment facilities. Its goal is to conform to the long-term planning and development strategy for Wuhan's internationalisation.

Located in the commercial district of Wuhan Tiandi as the first Grade A office building, Corporate Center No. 5 (Lot A5) consists of a 30-storey office tower, a two-storey detached retail podium and a three-storey basement car park. The office tower has been carefully planned with the best views facing both southeast *and* southwest to capture

the panoramic views of Lots A11 and A12 residential developments, consisting of a pair of 41-storey-high twin towers, as well as other low-rise buildings ranging from five to eight storeys, surrounding a spacious central courtyard landscape. The basement contains a two-level car park and an exclusive clubhouse with swimming pool, gym, basketball court, etc. The buildings are sited in the most privileged location along the Changjiang River with the long frontage facing the exclusive views. The two lots are merged into a single plot without building the original road between the lots, allowing the twin high-rise towers to form a gateway along the central axis of the site. With its privileged location next to the river, the luxurious residential development fully benefits from the internal courtyard landscape. As there are no other buildings at similar heights, the duplexes on

the top floors enjoy the exclusive **panoramic views** of the river without other buildings impeding. The towers are clad in beige stone/tile in an elegant art deco style. The rooftop feature is designed like a glowing lantern to be seen at night, making the towers a river landmark.

In between the Corporate Center No. 5 and the twin residential towers A11/A12, stand a series of residential Lots A6 to A10, also designed and developed by the same teams, P&T Group and Wuhan Shui On Tiandi Property Development Co., Ltd.

1   Aerial view
2   Overall view in context
3   Overall view residential towers A11/A12
4   Situation plan (Lot A)
5   Residential towers A11/A12 typical floor plan
6   Office tower ground floor plan

Photography: courtesy P&T Group

Wuhan Tiandi – Lots A5 to A12

Location Wuhan

Completion 2011

Client Wuhan Shui On Tiandi Property Development Co., Ltd

Architect P&T Group

Structural engineer P&T Group

MEP engineer P&T Group

Cost consultant Langdon & Seah

Landscape architect WAA International Limited

Lighting consultant Brandston Partnership Inc.

Other consultants ADO Design & Public Art Consultants (HK) Ltd (signage) • Ove Arup & Partners (LEED) • Simon Wong Design Co., Ltd. (clubhouse)

Main contractor Residential towers: Shanghai Construction Group Co., Ltd • office tower: China Construction Third Engineering Bureau

Uses Office, residential, clubhouse

Height Residential towers A11/A12: 136 m (446 ft) • office tower: 130 m (426 ft)

Above-ground storeys Residential towers A11/A12: 41 • office tower: 30

Basements Residential towers (A11/A12): 2 • office tower: 3

Mechanical levels 16/F (office tower)

Refuge levels 16/F (office tower)

Site area Residential towers A11/A12: 15,422 m² (166,001 ft²) • office tower: 11,394 m² (122,644 ft²)

Gross above-ground building area Residential towers A11/A12: 51,677 m² (556,246 ft²) • office tower: 57,054 m² (614,124 ft²)

Gross basement area Residential towers A11/A12: 17,768m² (191,253 ft²) • office tower: 23,853 m² (256,751 ft²) • clubhouse 3,330m² (35,843 ft²)

Total gross area Residential towers A11/A12: 72,775 m² (783,343 ft²) • office tower: 80,907 m² (870,875 ft²)

Floor area ratio (FAR)/Plot ratio Residential towers A11/A12: 3.68 • office tower: 5.18

Gross typical floor area Residential towers A11/A12: 18,350 m² (197,517 ft²) • office tower: 54,000 m² (581,251 ft²)

Total number of elevators Residential towers A11/A12: 6 (per tower) • office tower: 16

Speed of fastest elevators Residential towers A11/A12: 3.5 m (11.5 ft)/s • office tower: 4 m (13 ft)/s

Elevator brand Residential towers A11/A12: KONE • office tower: ThyssenKrupp

Number of car/bike parking spaces Residential towers A11/A12: 232/95 • office tower: 459/300

Principal structure materials Reinforced concrete structure

Other materials Residential towers A11/A12: stone cladding, external wall tiling, external texture paint • office tower: glass curtain wall, external stone cladding

Source: P&T Group

2

3

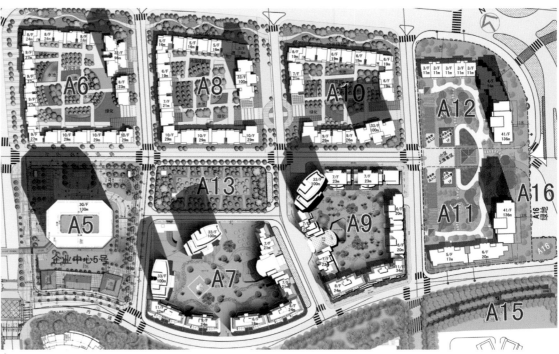

4

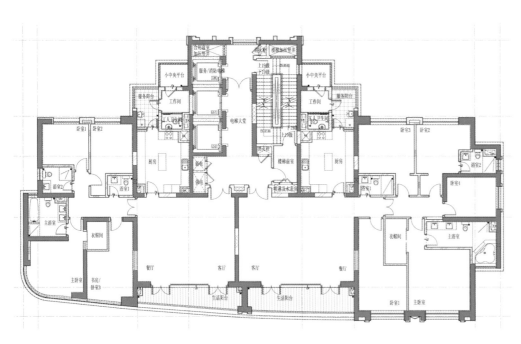

5

6

A7
足住

700 m

600 m

500 m

400 m

300 m

200 m

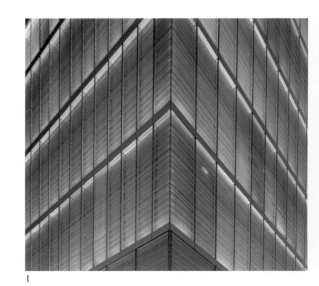

1

Located in the heart of busy Tsim Sha Tsui in Hong Kong, iSQUARE's tower is a **vertically stacking landscape** of retail and entertainment venues. The site formerly held a Hyatt Hotel that was demolished to make way for this 53,000-square-metre (570,487-square-foot) emporium whose mix of programs – shops, restaurants and cinema – are perfectly suited to contemporary Kowloon's frenetic, crowded character. Like all great cities, Hong Kong is constantly in a state of flux. The transformation of this site is a necessary response to the ever-increasing retail value of this location, but iSQUARE's unprecedented verticality poses challenges for the architecture in its pursuit of a new movement and spatial strategy.

Hong Kongers famously love to shop and eat, and iSQUARE gives them myriad options for indulging in both within its relatively narrow floor plate. This busy corner site with its proximity to both Kowloon Park and the harbour called for a very particular architectural form defined at street level by a setback that opens up a public plaza fronted by prime retail options; at higher floors the building splits into two towers and its interior reveals itself.

1 Close-up of façade curtain wall
2 Aerial view of podium corner (foreground) with projected restaurant terraces (at rear)
3 View of illuminated glazed cinema areas
4 Interior retail void
5 Floor plan (M2/F)
6 Floor plan (3/F)
7 Ground floor plan

Photography: ©Marcel Lam;

Illustrations: ©Rocco Design Architects Limited

iSQUARE

Location Hong Kong
Completion 2009
Client Associated International Hotel Ltd
Architect Rocco Design Architects Limited
Structural engineer Meinhardt (C&S) Ltd
MEP engineer Meinhardt (M&E) Ltd
Vertical transportation consultant Otis Elevator Co. (HK) Ltd
Façade engineer Meinhardt Facade Technology (HK) Ltd
Project management consultant Debenham Tie Leung Property Management Ltd
Cost consultants Davis Langdon • Seah Hong Kong Ltd
Lighting consultant Light and View Design Ltd
Other consultants Meinhardt (civil/geotechnical engineering/building services/acoustic)
 • Gammon Construction Ltd (ground investigation works, demolition) • MVA Hong Kong Ltd (traffic) • Benoy Ltd (interior design) • Tysan Foundation Ltd (foundation) • Shen Milsom & Wilke Ltd (audiovisual)

Main contractor Gammon Construction Ltd
Uses Retail complex with cinema, shops & restaurants
Number of buildings 1
Height 139.55 m (458 ft)
Above-ground storeys 27
Site area 4,043.8 m² (43,527 ft²)
Total gross area 53,047.8 m² (571,002 ft²)
Gross typical floor area 37,706 m² (405,864 ft²)
Total number of elevators 12
Number of car parking spaces 10
Principal structure materials Concrete

Source: Rocco Design Architects Limited

2

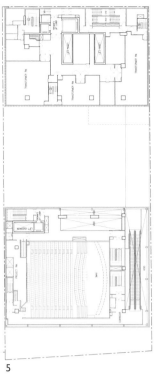

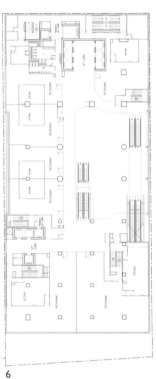

5

6

3

4

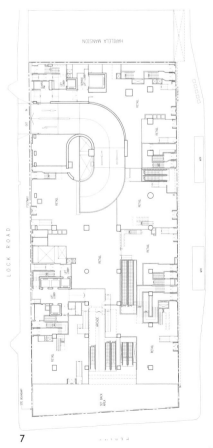

7

■ The Larvotto development provided an acute challenge for the design of a premium residential product. The site is located in the Ap Lei Chau area of Hong Kong Island, which has a sensitive green backdrop of Yuk Kwai Shan, and has long suffered from a low-grade reputation, that is, the noise pollution from the adjacent boatyard. The completed development of nine residential towers has proven to be an outstanding success, rapidly improving perceptions of the location and also creating a new benchmark for high-end residential development in Hong Kong.

Working with the natural geography of the site, the nine towers gently curve in a **linear arrangement** along the harbourfront that overlooks the typhoon shelter towards the Ocean Park theme park. All nine towers enjoy waterfront views. An innovative approach is adopted to the façades against noise pollution from the boatyards: by providing the main frontage with non-openable curtain

wall glazing (more commonly used in commercial offices), while also giving the majority of apartments dual aspects through the main living spaces and with balconies overlooking the green hills behind. The towers are positioned above a five-storey podium deck that houses the clubhouse and parking, with vehicular and pedestrian access taking residents immediately up to the first level offering raised views across the boatyards.

The apartments increase in both size and quality from the northern towers to the prime southern towers, ranging from 56-square-metre (600-square-foot) studios to 232-square-metre (2,500-square-foot) apartments and 362-square-metre (3,900-square-foot) duplexes at the upper levels. The two southern towers are also angled towards the

south to take in spectacular views towards the Outlying Islands and the South China Sea. Additional ideas for the design of these two towers include a clubhouse at a dramatic scale and a unique transfer plate design.

While quality of accommodation was paramount, the impact on the surrounding environment was also a key factor, and all the towers are clad in low-reflective glass to minimise glare perceived from the typhoon shelter. Open sky gardens are punctured through the mid-storeys of all three clusters of towers to maintain views through the development and provide a sense of lightness to the architectural design.

1 View from indoor swimming pool onto outdoor terrace
2 Overview
3 Main frontage curtain wall
4 Clubhouse interior
5 Clubhouse lounge
6 Key plan
7 Residential apartment floor plan (Tower 3, Flat A)

Photography: courtesy Ronald Lu & Partners

Larvotto

Location Hong Kong
Completion 2011
Clients Sun Hung Kai Properties Ltd • Kerry Properties Ltd • Paliburg Holdings Ltd
Architect Ronald Lu & Partners
Structural engineer Siu Yin Wai & Associates Ltd
MEP engineer Meinhardt (M&E) Ltd
Project management consultant Sun Hung Kai Properties Ltd
Cost consultant Rider Levett Bucknall
Landscape architect Sun Hung Kai Architects and Engineers Ltd
Lighting consultant Guava Hong Kong Limited
Other consultants BTR Workshop Limited (interior design, clubhouse) • Greg Wong & Associates Ltd (geotechnical) • Wilbur Smith Associates/ TMA Planning & Design Limited (traffic) • Environ Hong Kong Limited (environmental)
Main contractor Chun Fai Construction Co. Ltd
Uses Residential • clubhouse (3/F, 5/F, P/F) • shop (G/F)
Number of buildings 9 [no designation of tower 4]
Height 140.6 m (461 ft)

Above-ground storeys Towers 1 & 2: 35 • tower 3: 35 • tower 5: 35 • towers 6 & 7: 35 • tower 8: 35 • towers 9 & 10: 35 [No 13/F, 14/F, 24/F & 34/F for all towers]
Refuge levels Towers 1 & 2: sky garden [19/F] • tower 3: part of roof • tower 5: part of roof • towers 6 & 7: sky garden [20/F, 21/F] • tower 8: part of roof • towers 9 & 10: sky garden [20/F, 21/F]
Site area 16,770 m² (180,511 ft²)
Gross above-ground building area 83,850 m² (902,554 ft²) [domestic] • 1,000 m² (10,764 ft²) [nondomestic]
Gross typical floor area 84,850 m² (913,318 ft²)
Total number of elevators 3 (each tower) • 3 (shuttle lift lobby) • 4 (clubhouse)
Elevator brand Chevalier
Number of car parking spaces Residential: 400 • residential visitors: 45 • nondomestic visitors: 5
Number of motorbike spaces 40
Principal structure materials Reinforced concrete

Source: Ronald Lu & Partners

700 m
600 m
500 m
400 m
300 m
200 m

141 m 461 ft

100 m

2

3

4

5

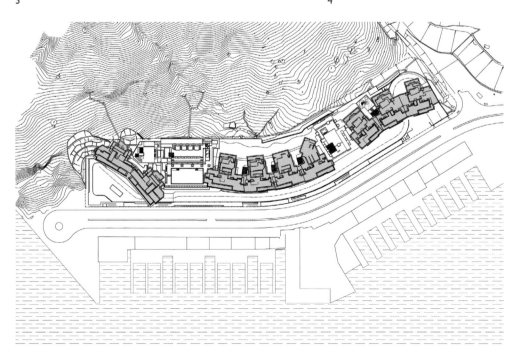

6

7

Divided into two L-shaped phases around a central garden space that is used by all residents, the project boasts five super-high-rise towers at the north end of the site, and a meandering arrangement of townhouse-villas stretching southward. The towers are over 40 storeys, with the two towers of the eastern block holding larger, innovatively stacked apartments sized from 250 to 500 square metres (2,691 to 5,382 square feet) with prime views. The three western block towers have apartments with floorplates between 170 and 260 square metres (1,830 and 2,799 square feet). Duplex units at the lower, mid- and rooftop levels maximise the site's urban views and offer design variety. The upper duplexes enjoy private rooftop pools, while the lower duplexes have private cantilevered terraces overlooking the common garden.

■ The brief was to create a **luxury development** comprising 370 apartments and 25 townhouse-villas, with a wide design variety for these innovative, high-density residences. The project is located in one of Guangzhou's fastest-growing areas, near the north bank of the Pearl River and just two blocks from the city's Civic Axis. The design required an innovative response to maximise residence quality and green views, both within the site and overlooking Zhujiang Park, while maintaining space and privacy for residents of the development.

Across the garden, the seven townhouse volumes each have two wings, accommodating two stacked townhouses per wing. Each villa has five aboveground floors with private access to basement parking and a private ground-level front yard. The upper villas have additional terraces, while the lower villas have backyards. The landscaped central garden space incorporates a rainwater collection system and is vehicle-free, with cars directed to the basement level, which includes light wells and vertical green walls to complement the access routes.

1 Façade facing Pearl River
2 Overview from Zhujiang Park
3 Typical floor plan
4 Semi-duplex floor plan (lower floor)
5 Semi-duplex floor plan (middle floor)
6 Semi-duplex floor plan (upper floor)

Photography: courtesy Ronald Lu & Partners

Virtue Court at Zhu Jiang Xin Cheng

Location Guangzhou
Completion 2014
Client Guangzhou Pearl River Industrial Development Co.
Architect Ronald Lu & Partners
Structural engineer Guangzhou Pearl River Foreign Investment Archi Design Institute (FIADI)
MEP engineer FIADI
Landscape architect AECOM
Uses Residential
Number of buildings 5 super high-rise, 13 low-rise
Height 149.9 m (492 ft)

Above-ground storeys 43
Basements 3
Refuge levels Sky garden [18/F]
Site area 22,196 m² (238,916 ft²)
Total gross area 88,503 m² (952,638 ft²)
Floor area ratio (FAR)/Plot ratio 4.0
Number of car parking spaces 657
Number of bike parking spaces 1,770
Principal structure materials Composite of steel & concrete

150 m | 492 ft

Source: Ronald Lu & Partners

2

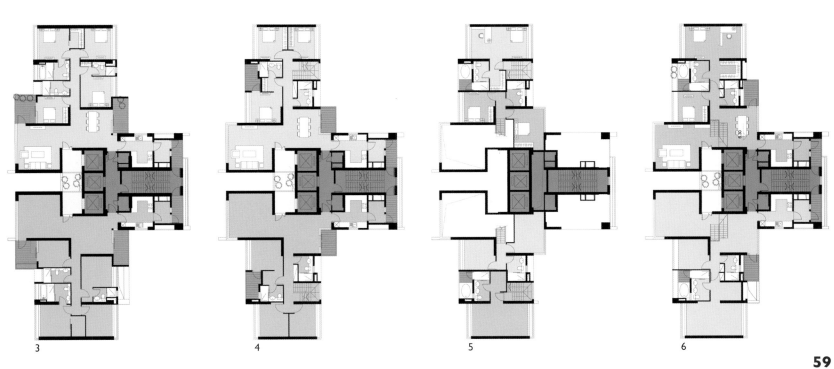

3   4   5   6

1

The overall master-planning concept is to create a 'butterfly-shaped' arrangement, which could capture the best sea view potential and – as part of a number of sustainable strategies – make use of the best natural light and natural ventilation. The changes of levels between the residential towers create a more **dynamic skyline** and interesting roofscape.

The residential clubhouse is situated at the front of the site facing the sea, and is integrated with a large artificial beach, providing various recreational facilities. These features and design enhance the unique character of the coastal site. The commercial district, about 6,700 square metres (72,118 square feet) in area, is located at the centre road of the site. There are also two levels of underground car parking.

■ This luxury residential project is located in the Meilisha District, in the northwest coastal area of Haidian Island, north of the city of Haikou, in Hainan.

The site is a combination of three plots of reclaimed lands (Plots 14, 15 and 16). Phase I of this development mainly comprises 17 high-rise towers, one large clubhouse building, a kindergarten, and some commercial facilities. The building heights of the towers vary from 90 metres (295 feet) to 155 metres (508 feet).

In terms of elevation design, a modern wavy language has been adopted for the elevation fronting the sea to echo the seaside nature, while the elevation facing the internal gardens and the city has a more artistic rectangular treatment.

1 Master layout plan (Plots 14–16)
2 Sea-facing perspective
3 Ground floor plan (T3)
4 Typical floor plan (T3)
5 Aerial view perspective (Plots 10–16)

Renderings: courtesy P&T Group

Meilisha Residential Development

155 m | 508 ft

Location Haikou
Completion 2017
Client New World China Land
Architect P&T Group
Associate Architect Hainan Province Institute of Architectural Design
Structural engineer China Architecture Design and Research Group
MEP engineer China Architecture Design and Research Group
Vertical transportation consultant China Architecture Design and Research Group
Uses Residential, commercial, educational
Number of buildings Residential towers: 17 • clubhouse: 1 • commercial buildings 2
Height Residential towers: 90.15 m (296 ft) [T16]; 109.05 m (358 ft) [T15]; 118.50 m (389 ft) [T13,T17]; 134.25 m (440 ft) [T12,T18]; 138.95 m (456 ft) [T6,T7]; 142.10 m (466 ft) [T1,T10]; 148.70 m (488 ft) [T5,T8,T11,T19]; 155 m (508 ft) [T2,T3,T9]

Above-ground storeys (Residential towers) T16: 26 • T15: 32 • T13,T17: 35 • T12,T18: 40 • T6,T7: 42 • T1,T10: 43 • T5,T8,T11,T19: 45 • T2,T3,T9: 47
Basements Plot 16: 1 • Plots 14 & 15: 2
Site area Plots 14, 15 & 16: 181,829 m² (1,957,191 ft²)
Gross above-ground building area 547,174 m² (5,889,732 ft²)
Gross basement area 229,750 m² (2,473,008 ft²)
Total gross area 776,924 m² (8,362,740 ft²)
Floor area ratio (FAR)/Plot ratio Plot 1401: 3.2; Plot 1501: 3.5; Plot 1601: 2.8; Plot 1602: 0.4
Gross typical floor area T3: 1,000 m² (10,764 ft²) • T2: 1,040 m² (11,194 ft²)
Total number of elevators 77
Number of car parking spaces 4,624
Principal structure materials Concrete
Other materials Metal, glass, tiles

Source: P&T Group

2

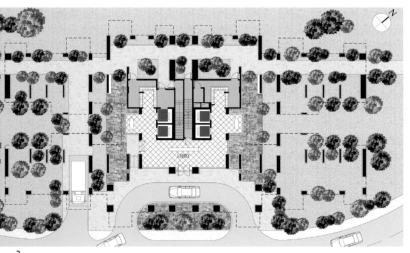

3

4

5

I

■ This residential project is located in the Tianjin New Technology Industrial Park, south of Haitai East-West Street and west of Haitai South-North Street. It is also close to the CBD and the polo club of the Tianjin Goldin Metropolitan project.

The site is a combination of three plots of land, separated by the Haitai Chuangxin 6th Road and the green belt that passes through the entire development. The residential project comprises 31 medium-rise to high-rise towers, and 42 villas. The height of each tower varies from around 55 metres (180 feet) to 160 metres (525 feet), while the villas are each about 16 metres (52 feet) high. In addition to the various residential facilities provided on the ground floor, and the club house/supporting commercial facilities, a golf park is also situated at the south side of the site. The proximity to the polo club and park also bring attractive views and greenery to the living quarters, as well as recreation facilities for the residents. There are also two levels of underground car parking, providing ample car parking space.

The overall master planning concept is to create a generally south-facing setting, stepping up from south to north with low-rise villas at the front, medium-rise towers in the middle, and high-rise towers at the back to capture the best views and sunlight potential for all building elements. Medium- and high-rise towers also vary in height from east to west to create a variation of skyline and interesting roofscape. A **contemporary classical** language has been adopted for the elevation design, to project an image of luxury and prestige on the buildings' external appearances.

1 Typical floor plan
2 Aerial view perspective
3 Tower section
4 Tower front view perspective
5 Tower rear view perspective

Renderings: courtesy P&T Group

Fortune Heights

Location Tianjin
Completion 2014
Client Goldin Properties Holdings Ltd
Architect P&T Group
Associate architect Academy of Architectural Design & Research, Tianjin University
Structural & MEP engineer P&T Group
Façade engineer Shenzhen Jinyuwan Decoration Engineering Co. Ltd
Uses Residential
Number of buildings 31 towers & 42 villas
Above-ground storeys Villas: 3 • M1, M2, M4, M5: 12; M3, M6, M7-14: 15 • T1, T5, T6: 20; T7: 24; T13, T16: 30; T2, T4, T9, T10: 31; T8: 33; T3: 35; T12, T15, T17: 36; T11, T14: 41
Height Villas: 16.40 m (53.80 ft) • M1, M2, M4, M5: 54.60 m (179 ft); M3, M6-M14: 65.40 m (214 ft) • T1, T5, T6: 84.65 m (277 ft); T7: 99.05 m (325 ft); T13, T16: 120.65 m (396 ft); T2, T4, T9, T10: 124.25 m (407 ft); T8: 131.45 m (431 ft); T3: 138.65 m (454 ft); T12, T15, T17: 142.25 m (466 ft); T11, T14: 160.25 m (525.75 ft)
Basements 2

Refuge levels 24/F [T11 & T14]
Site area 332,628 m² (3,580,378 ft²)
Gross above-ground building area 502,285 m² (5,406,550 ft²)
Gross basement area 260,455 m² (2,803,514 ft²)
Total gross area 762,740 m² (8,210,065 ft²)
Floor area ratio (FAR)/Plot ratio 1.51
Gross typical floor area 760 m² (8,180 ft²) each for T11 & T14
Total number of elevators 3 elevators each for T11 & T14
Number of car parking spaces 2,350
Number of bike parking spaces 1,078
Residence & service brands Goldin Properties
Principal structure materials Concrete
Other materials Stone cladding

Source: P&T Group

700 m

600 m

500 m

400 m

300 m

200 m

160 m 525 ft

100 m

2

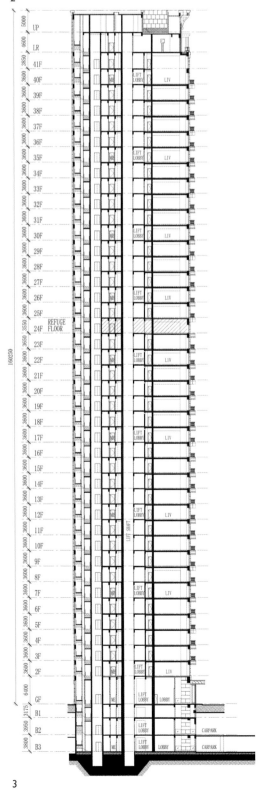

3

4

5

1

Poly Real Estate Headquarters overlooks the Pearl River in Pazhou, a commercial district in the city of Guangzhou. The office and retail complex comprises two office towers and two mixed-use pavilions housing retail and exhibition facilities. The four structures are set in a landscaped court of plazas water features and park areas. Underneath the plaza there is an exhibition hall and a trade centre. Teak-screened arcades on each side of the landscaped area link the towers and pavilions and serve as gateways to the complex.

The offices have 15-metre-wide (49-foot) floorplates, which are slender enough to admit daylight to the full depth of the workspace. The north façades, which are oriented to the river, are faced in glass vertical fins. Reinforced **concrete X-bracing,** part of the structural spine on the south façades, shades the offices and maximises the amount of column-free space inside.

Offset vertical elevator and service cores are encased in translucent and opalescent glass, making visible the activity within and allowing views from the elevator cabs and lobbies of the surrounding district. A three-storey horizontal opening perforates each tower at its midpoint, forming large central employee terraces that also reduce the building's wind load.

1   Office building interior
2   Overall view
3   Ground floor plan
4   View of lobby

Photography: SOM | ©Tim Griffith;
illustration: courtesy SOM

Poly Real Estate Headquarters

Location Guangzhou	**Number of buildings** 4
Completion 2007	**Height** 160.6 m (527 ft)
Client China Poly Real Estate Company Limited	**Above-ground storeys** 34
Architect Skidmore, Owings & Merrill LLP (SOM)	**Basements** 2
Architect of record Guangzhou Design Institute	**Site area** 57,565 m² (619,625 ft²)
Structural engineer SOM	**Gross above-ground building area** 168,000 m² (1,808,337 ft²)
MEP engineer Flack + Kurtz, Inc.	**Total gross area** 180,000 m² (1,937,504 ft²)
Vertical transportation consultant Edgett Williams Consulting Group, Inc.	**Speed of fastest elevators** 6 m (20 ft)/s
Landscape architect SWA Group	**No of car parking spaces** 850
Uses Office, retail	**Principal structure materials** Composite

161 m | 527 ft

Source: Skidmore, Owings & Merrill LLP (SOM)

2

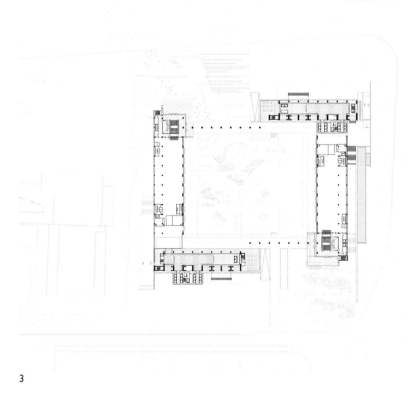

3

4

1

■ This project is a compact entertainment complex within an urban site. It comprises a gaming hall, a hotel with more than 500 guestrooms and suites, a number of private gaming rooms and casino facilities. The functions are vertically stacked on top of each other, forming an interlocking, and yet shifting, tower. A three-storey-high glass wall with wavy aluminium 'curtain' behind wraps the gaming hall, shielding the hall from public view (as required by law). At the same time, the light and the ambiance are allowed to filter through, especially at night, adding to the nightlife of the city.

The VIP games rooms and amenities are enclosed by a double façade with shifting **dot matrix patterns** on both the inner and outer surfaces, creating a swirling pattern and various lighting effects. Individual VIP rooms are expressed as glass boxes projecting from the building in difference sizes and scales.

The hotel portion is planned on top with a U-shaped plan to maximise the view to the sea and surroundings; it's deliberately jogging out from the lower tower and articulated with various colours and textures.

In effect, the building envelope is transformed into a billboard with distinctive glamour in a grand urban scale. The overall composition of the building form uniquely creates an architectural and luminous landmark among the numerous casinos in Macau.

1 Wavy aluminium skin and glass wall surrounding the podium
2 View of exterior at night
3 View of metal and glass building envelope
4 Double-skinned curtain wall façade
5 Floor plan (3/F)
6 Floor plan (14/F & 16/F)
7 Hotel guestrooms floor plan

Photography: ©Marcel Lam;
Illustrations: ©Rocco Design Architects Limited

StarWorld Hotel

Location Macau	**Number of buildings** 1
Completion 2006	**Height** 161.75 m (531 ft)
Client Galaxy Entertainment Group Ltd	**Above-ground storeys** 36
Architect Rocco Design Architects Limited	**Basements** 2.5
Associate architect CC Atelier De Arquitectura, lda (Macau)	**Refuge levels** 8/F, 18/F
Structural engineer Meinhardt (C&S) Ltd	**Site area** 6,864 m² (73,883 ft²)
MEP engineer Meinhardt (C&S) Ltd	**Gross above-ground building area** 100,000 m² (1,076,391 ft²) [approx.]
Vertical transportation consultant Meinhardt (C&S) Ltd	**Gross basement area** 6,200 m² (66,736 ft²)
Façade engineer Meinhardt (C&S) Ltd	**Total gross area** 100,000 m² (1,076,391 ft²)
Cost consultant Levett & Bailey Quantity Surveyors Ltd	**Floor area ratio (FAR)/Plot ratio** 14.5
Landscape architect Team 73 HK Ltd	**Gross typical floor area** 2,040 m² (21,958 ft²)
Lighting consultant Lightsource International (Asia) Ltd	**Basic planning module** 9 m x 4.2 m (30 ft x 14 ft)
Other consultants Shen Milson & Wilke Ltd. (acoustic) • LRF Designers Ltd (interior design) • Constructive Consultant Co., Ltd. (kitchen/catering) • The Design Partners Ltd (signage) • SKM Sinclair Knight Merz CCD, Australia (security)	**Total number of elevators** Total 22 [VIP guest lift: 5 • hotel guest lift: 4 • casino amenity lift: 2 • casino/hotel services lift: 6 • other: 5]
Main contractor San Meng Fai Engineering & Construction Company Ltd. (Macau)	**Speed of fastest elevators** 5 m (16 ft)/s
	Elevator brand Otis Elevator Company
Uses Parking, loading/unloading, garbage collection & hotel back-of-house [B2/F–G/F] • reception, hotel check-in, concierge, ticketing, cloakroom & lobby lounge [G/F] • mass gaming area [1/F & 3/F] • fine Chinese dining [2/F] • Japanese restaurant & club [5/F] • food & beverages outlets [6/F] • Grand Ballroom, function rooms & business centre [8/F] • VIP gaming areas [9/F–12/F, 15/F] • coffee shop & multipurpose room [16/F] • fitness club, outdoor swimming pool, beauty salon, business centre & meeting rooms [17/F] • guestroom floors [18/F–38/F] • sky suite [39/F]	**Number of car parking spaces** 270 (with double parking)
	Number of motorbike spaces 85
	Principal structure materials Reinforced concrete
	Other materials Glass curtain wall & aluminium cladding

Source: Rocco Design Architects Limited

2

3

4

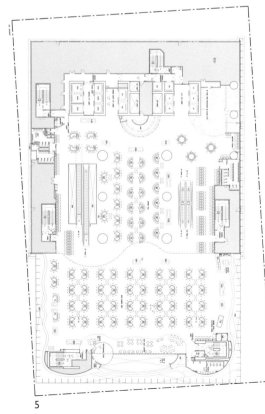

5

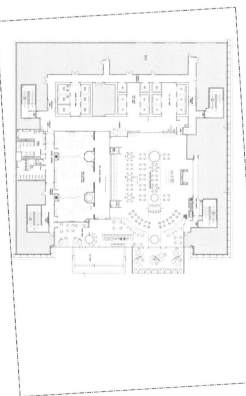

6

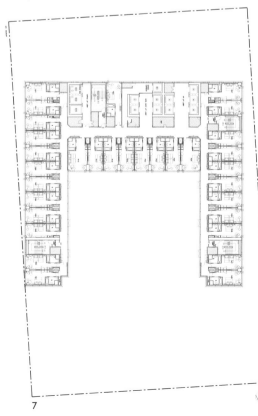

7

1

■ The Serenade is located on Tai Hang road, Causeway Bay. It is situated in one of the most prestigious commercial and shopping districts on Hong Kong island. The towers are arranged to provide panoramic views of Victoria Harbour. The **asymmetrical design** of the façades gives a unique identity to the buildings that stands apart from the surrounding community. The development consists of two residential towers that sit on a podium with two levels of clubhouse. The two towers contain 270 residential units; the three types of residential units (simplex, duplex and penthouse + roof) are designed to suit the occupants' different needs. The clubhouse contains many recreational facilities catering to children, such as a gymnasium, indoor/outdoor children play areas, kids' library and games room, and for the adults an oxygen spa suite, aerobics/yoga/piano room, gymnasium, table tennis room, music room, steam room, sauna and an infinity swimming pool.

1 Infinity swimming pool
2 Exterior view
3 Main lobby
4 Penthouse roof plan (tower 1)
5 Penthouse roof plan (tower 2)
6 Towers 1 & 2 upper duplex floor plan
7 Tower 1 simplex floor plan (69/F)
8 Towers 1 & 2 lower duplex floor plan
9 Tower 1 simplex floor plan (68/F)
10 Residential units floor plans (8/F–32/F)
11 Clubhouse floor plan (7/F)
12 Clubhouse floor plan (6/F)

Photography & illustrations: ©Wong Tung & Partners Ltd

The Serenade

165 m | 541 ft

Location Hong Kong	**Above-ground storeys** 52
Completion 2010	**Basements** 2
Client Hongkong Land (HK Glory Properties Ltd)	**Mechanical levels** Ground level, roof
Architect Wong Tung & Partners Ltd	**Refuge levels** 29/F
Structural engineer Siu Yin Wai & Associates Ltd	**Site area** 5,722.78 m² (61,599 ft²)
MEP engineer WSP HK Ltd	**Gross above-ground building area** Total: 16,332 m² (175,796 ft²) [usable floor area for residential towers] • T1: 8,165 m² (87,887 ft²) • T2: 8,167 m² (87,909 ft²)
Façade engineer Arup	**Total gross area** 29,096 m² (313,187 ft²)
Cost consultant Davis Langdon & Seah HK Ltd (quantity surveyor)	**Floor area ratio (FAR)/Plot ratio** 4.999
Landscape architect ADI Ltd	**Total number of elevators** 6 (3 for each tower)
Other consultants Siu Yin Wai & Associates Ltd (geotechnical) • Simon Wong Design Co. Ltd (interior design) • MVA Asia Ltd (traffic)	**Elevator brand** Jardine Schindler
Main contractor Gammon Construction Ltd	**Number of car parking spaces** 277
Uses Residential • clubhouse [6/F, 7/F] • basements [B1/F, B2/F, 1/F–3/F, 5/F]	**Number of motorbike spaces** 28
Number of buildings 2	**Principal structure materials** Reinforced concrete
Height 165.092 m (541 ft)	

Source: Wong Tung & Partners Ltd

2

3

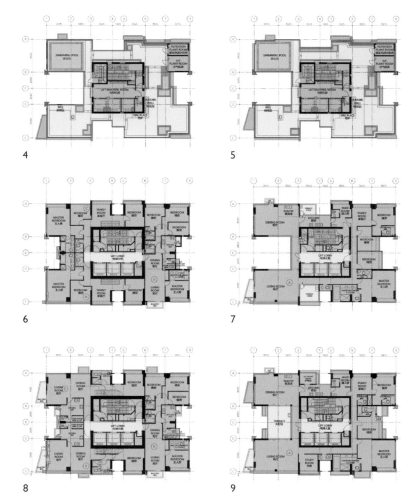

4

5

6

7

8

9

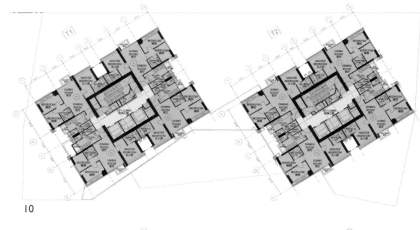

10

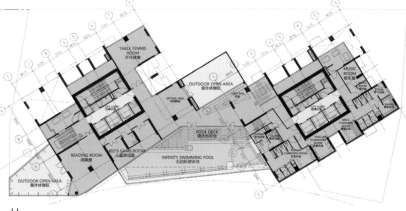

11

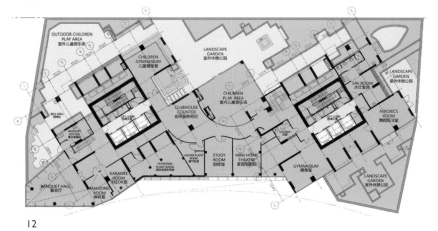

12

700 m
600 m
500 m

hongkong

400 m
300 m
200 m

166 m 543 ft

100 m

I

■ The Enterprise Square 5 is an amalgamation of shopping, entertainment (including an ice-skating rink that sits under a 30-metre-high [98-foot] beehive-shaped atrium), and office spaces that are set at a conspicuous waterfront site of Kowloon Bay. Looking from afar, the 20-storey shopping podium, aptly named MegaBOX, appears to form a single **monolithic box**. To break down the overall mass, 30 different tones of red are introduced to the façade

An expansive circular glass wall cuts through the front elevation, not only to add visual interest to the building, but also to enhance interaction between the inside activity and urban fabric. Perched high above on the shopping podium, the 15-storey twin office towers are clad in glass to reflect their different use, while inviting natural sunlight, as well as glamorous sea views into the interior space. The architectural vocabulary

of the Enterprise Square 5 stands in stark contrast to the urban fabric in Kowloon Bay. While the office towers are rendered transparent, the shopping podium is conceptualised as the massive opaque box in striking red, dominating the waterfront and creating an iconic new landmark.

1 Express escalators connecting the huge atria
2 Circular glass wall of podium facing the urban fabric
3 Section view of mall
4 Typical tower office floor plan

Photography: courtesy Wong Tung & Partners Ltd

Enterprise Square 5 / MegaBOX

Location Hong Kong
Completion 2007
Client Kerry Properties Ltd
Architect Wong Tung & Partners Ltd
Design architect The Jerde Partnership International, Inc.
Structural engineer Siu Yin Wai & Associates Ltd
MEP engineer Meinhardt (M&E) Ltd
Vertical transportation consultant Meinhardt (M&E) Ltd
Façade engineer Meinhardt Façade Technology (HK) Ltd
Cost consultant WT Partnership (HK) Ltd
Landscape architect Belt Collins HK Ltd
Lighting consultant Lightsource International (Asia) Ltd
Other consultants Environmental Resources Management (environmental) • City Planning Consultants Ltd (land) • CL3 Architects Ltd (design) • Ove Arup & Partners Hong Kong Ltd (fire engineer) • Dutton Bray Design Ltd (signage) • Asia Sports Ltd (ice-skating rink)
Main contractor China Overseas Building Construction Ltd
Uses Office, retail
Number of buildings 2

Height 165.56 m (543 ft)
Above-ground storeys 35
Basements 1
Mechanical levels Roof level
Refuge levels 19/F
Site area 12,594 m² (135,560 ft²)
Gross above-ground building area 151,000 m² (1,625,350 ft²)
Gross basement area 6,030 m² (64,906 ft²)
Total gross area 151,000 m² (1,625,350 ft²)
Floor area ratio (FAR)/Plot ratio 12
Gross typical floor area 1,390 m² (14,962 ft²)
Basic planning module 12 m (39 ft)
Total number of elevators 28
Elevator brand Schindler
Number of car parking spaces 764
Number of motorbike spaces 53
Principal structure materials Reinforced concrete

Source: Wong Tung & Partners Ltd

2

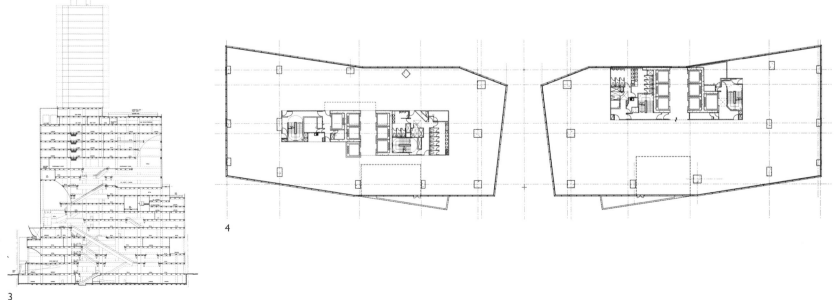

3

4

I

The project is designed to maximise program-specific relationships within the existing urban context. By asymmetrically stacking the hotel tower above the retail podium, the design helps integrate the building's mass with its surroundings. The orientation of the podium entry to the north creates an ideal relationship with the active urban plaza. The hotel tower, sited to the south, provides all rooms with unobstructed views and abundant natural light. The two primary masses of podium and tower are unified by a series of **stepped gardens** that are accessible from the hotel's sky-lobby, ballrooms and dining facilities.

■ The 37-storey Grand Hyatt Chengdu occupies a full city block adjacent to a vibrant public plaza in the central business district of Chengdu. As a mixed-use development, the project integrates a 12-storey shopping centre with a 25-storey hotel. Together, they provide 111,484 square metres (1.2 million square feet) of retail space, 391 guest rooms, and supporting hotel amenities.

Cantilevered glass volumes activate the base of the building, broadcasting digital media to passersby. These contemporary 'retail awnings' provide a continuous rhythm of canopies for pedestrians while further organising the podium's extensive signage and advertising needs.

1 Street view from the southwest
2 Street view from the southeast
3 Exterior overall entry view from the northwest
4 Aerial rendering view of exterior podium rooftop
5 Ground floor plan
6 Typical hotel plan

Credits: 1,2,3 ©1st-image; 4 ©Goettsch Partners

Grand Hyatt Chengdu at Chicony Plaza

166 m | 545 ft

Location Chengdu
Completion 2011
Client Chicony Co.
Architect Goettsch Partners
Associate architect Architectural Design Institute of Sichuan Province
Structural engineer Architectural Design Institute of Sichuan Province
MEP engineers Parsons Brinckerhoff • Architectural Design Institute of Sichuan Province
Vertical transportation consultant Parsons Brinckerhoff
Façade engineer Schmidin Ltd. Façade Technology
Landscape architect P Landscape
Lighting consultant Duo Lighting Design Associates
Other consultants Tonychi and Associates (hotel interior designer) • Glyph Design Studio Inc. (retail interior designer)
Main contractor The Second Construction Co., Ltd. of China Construction Third Engineering Bureau Co., Ltd
Uses Hotel: 56,501 m² (608,172 ft²) [10/F–37/F] • retail/department store: 111,480 m² (1,199,961 ft²) • basement levels 1–2 [1/F–9/F]
Number of buildings 1
Height 166 m (545 ft)

Above-ground storeys 37
Basements 5
Mechanical levels 16/F
Refuge levels 16/F, 25/F
Sky-lobby levels 14/F
Site area 7,993 m² (86,036 ft²)
Gross above-ground building area 139,108 m² (1,497,346 ft²)
Gross basement area 47,841 m² (514,956 ft²)
Total gross area 186,949 m² (2,012,302 ft²)
Gross typical floor area 1,672 m² (17,997 ft²)
Floor area ratio (FAR)/Plot ratio 12.72
Total number of elevators 31
Elevator brands Tytheen, Hitachi, Toshiba
Speed of fastest elevators 3.5 m (11.5 ft)/s
Number of car parking spaces 517
Hotel brand Grand Hyatt
Principal structure materials Concrete

Source: Goettsch Partners

2

3

4

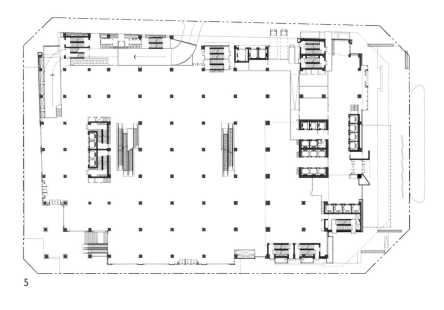

5

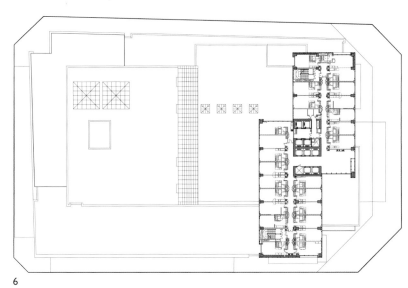

6

■ The architecture of W Guangzhou is a response both to the urban conditions of contemporary Guangzhou, and to the unique program of a compact city hotel and a serviced apartment.

The building is an actual amalgamation of two components: a 317-room boutique hotel and a 160-unit serviced apartment under one single management.

The building flanks a major boulevard along the central axis of the city's new central business district. The two portions are architecturally unified, but at the same time are punctuated in the centre with a large vertical 'window' that allows the inner landscaped park of the urban block to visually and spatially merge with the public street. This compositional gesture brings about an urban permeability that enhances the lighting and air-flow pattern within the district.

Within the unified architectural mass, individual components are given their own expression: the private residential portion (guest rooms and apartments) is clad in dark granite/glass, its scale subtly defined by a matrix of **vertical glass fins**, while the public portion (bar, restaurants and spa) is enclosed in transparent glazed boxes that visually spring out from the dark background and allow the hotel's ambience to radiate into the surrounding neighbourhoods.

With major hotel functions being stacked up vertically by virtue of the compact size of the urban lot, the architecture is an actual embodiment of an intriguing spatial journey from the ground up: a three-dimensional and intertwining sequencing of diverse spatial forms and experience, from the narrow and vertical entrance vestibule, to the spacious, but intimate, reception 'living room', to the transparent bar in the floating glass box, all the way to the green and semi-enclosed swimming pool resting on the building's top.

The architecture of W Guangzhou visually intrigues, and at the same time creates a spatial odyssey that invites exploration and keeps the senses invigorated.

1 Façade modulation articulated by scale of guestrooms
2 View of main façade at dusk
3 Lobby lounge interior
4 Interior of glass façade reflected by the rooftop swimming pool
5 View of entrance from lobby
6 Hotel floor plan (1/F)
7 Hotel floor plan (3/F)
8 Typical hotel guestrooms floor plan

Photography: ©Liky Lam;
Illustrations: ©Rocco Design Architects Limited

W Guangzhou

Location Guangzhou
Completion 2013
Client KWG Property Holding Ltd
Architect Rocco Design Architects Limited
Associate architect Guangzhou Foreview Architect Institute
Structural engineer RBS Architectural Engineering Design Associates
MEP engineer J. Roger Preston Ltd
Vertical transportation consultant Mitsubishi Electric Automation (China) Ltd
Façade engineer Ove Arup & Partners HK Ltd
Project management consultant China Construction Eighth Engineering Division Corp. Ltd
Landscape architect Bensley Design Studios
Lighting consultant Isometrix Lighting + Design Ltd
Other consultants Interior design: Yabu Pushelberg, Glyph Design Studio, A.N.D., Design Wilkes, AFSO
Main contractor China Construction Eighth Engineering Division Corp. Ltd
Uses Hotel reception, wine bar, reading room [1/F] • all-day dining [2/F] • pre-function room, meeting room, ballroom [3/F] • Chinese restaurant [4/F] • Japanese restaurant [5/F] • typical guest rooms [7/F–27/F] • spa [28/F] • sky lounge, swimming pool [29/F] • presidential suite [30/F]

Source: Rocco Design Architects Limited

Number of buildings 1
Height Hotel = 127.5 m (418 ft) • serviced apartments: 169.5 m (556 ft)
Above-ground storeys Hotel: 30 • serviced apartments: 41
Basements 4
Mechanical levels B1/F, B2/F, 21/F, R/F
Refuge levels 21/F
Site area 22,625 m² (243,533 ft²)
Gross above-ground building area 106,504 m² (1,146,399 ft²)
Total gross area Total: 106,504 m² (1,146,399 ft²) [hotel: 73,173 m² (787,628 ft²) • serviced apartments: 33,331 m² (358,772 ft²)]
Floor area ratio (FAR)/Plot ratio 4.7
Gross typical floor area 1,012 m² (10,893 ft²)
Total number of elevators Hotel: 8 guest lifts, 5 service lifts • serviced apartment: 3 guest lifts, 1 service lift
Elevator brand Mitsubishi Electric Automation (China) Ltd
Hotel brand W Hotel
Residence brand W Residence
Residence service brand W Residence Service
Principal structure materials Concrete
Other materials Steel

700 m
600 m
500 m
400 m
300 m
200 m
170 m | 556 ft
100 m

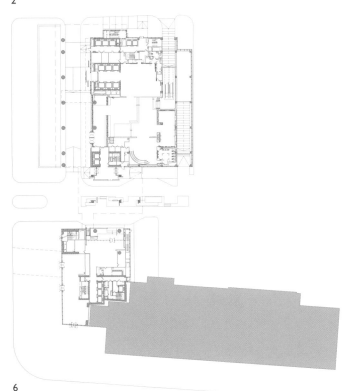

2

3

4

5

6

7

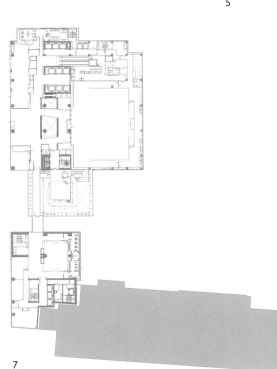

8

1

An undertaking of impressive scale, City Crossing in Shenyang includes the MixC retail and entertainment components, the CR Building, a 70,000-square-metre (753,474-square-foot) office tower, a hotel, as well as residences. The 353-room five-star Grand Hyatt Shenyang hotel is situated opposite the office tower and connects via a winter garden passageway. The design scheme also employs a non-axial pathway to connect and distinguish project components within the development.

More specifically, the multifunctional project is located strategically in Shenyang's **Golden Corridor** – The Youth Street, which is both the financial and political centre of the city. The development has attracted international brands, such as Louis Vuitton, Hermès, Prada, Miu Miu and many other secondary brands to set up their flagship or first stores in Shenyang city. With the opening of the mall in 2011, and the Grade 5A CR Building office tower in 2011, and the Grand Hyatt in 2013, City Crossing in Shenyang has now become a popular meeting point for both business and leisure purposes.

1   The MixC mall's six-storey glass-enclosed winter garden
2   CR Building office tower (left) and the Grand Hyatt hotel (right)
3   The MixC mall main entrance and plaza
4   The MixC mall six-storey glass-enclosed winter garden at night
5   CR Building, typical office floor plan (low-rise)
6   Typical hotel floor plan
7   Hotel sky-lobby floor plan (27/F)

Credits: 1,2,3,4,6,7 ©2013 Hansen / MF Vision; 5 from CR Building leasing brochure (coll. G. Binder)

City Crossing

173 m | 568 ft

Location Shenyang

Completion The MixC mall: 2011 • office tower: 2011 • hotel: 2013

Client China Resources Land (Shenyang) Co., Ltd

Architect RTKL Associates, Inc.

Associate architect China Construction Beijing Architectural Design & Research Institute Ltd (CBADRI)

Structural engineer Arup

MEP engineer Parsons Brinckerhoff Asia

Vertical transportation consultant MVA (Hong Kong)

Façade engineer Arup (Shanghai)

Cost consultant RLB (Hong Kong)

Landscape architect Belt Collins International

Lighting consultant Shenzhen Uconia Co., Ltd

Main contractor China Construction First Building (group) Corporation Ltd

Uses Office: 70,000 m² (753,474 ft²) [office tower] • retail 250,000 m² (2,690,977 ft²) • hotel: 63,000 m² (678,126 ft²) [+ 350 keys] • residential: 105,000 m² (1,130,210 ft²)

Height The MixC mall: 52.4 m (172 ft) • office: 173.3 m (568 ft) • hotel: 148.2 m (486 ft)

Above-ground storeys The MixC mall: 7 • office: 33 • hotel: 29

Basements 3

Mechanical levels The MixC mall: B3/F, B2/F, 7/F • office: B3/F, B2/F, 7/F, 20/F, 34/F • hotel: B3/F, B2/F, 6/F, 24/F, 30/F

Refuge levels Office: 7/F, 20/F • hotel: 6/F, 24/F

Sky-lobby levels 27/F (hotel)

Site area 81,070 m² (872,630 ft²)

Gross above-ground building area Office: 59,800 m² (643,681 ft²) • hotel: 63,000 m² (678,126 ft²)

Gross basement area 11,400 m² (122,708 ft²)

Total gross area 398,000 m² (4,284,036 ft²)

Floor area ratio (FAR)/Plot ratio 5.3

Gross typical floor area 2,025 m² (21,797 ft²)

Basic planning module 3 m (10 ft)

Total number of elevators 28

Speed of fastest elevators 5 m (16 ft)/s

Elevator brand Schindler (China)

Number of car parking spaces 1,630

Hotel brand Grand Hyatt

Principal structure materials Metal, stone, glass

Source: RTKL Associates, Inc.

2

3

4

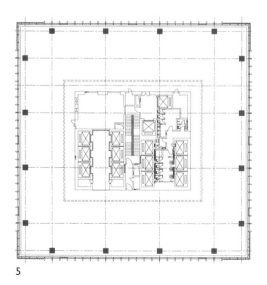

5

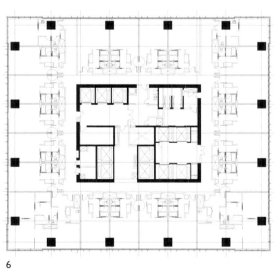

6

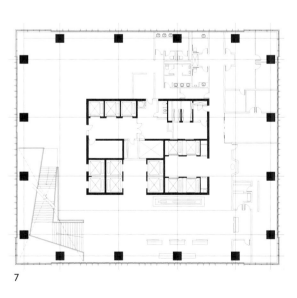

7

■ Under a 'no-reclamation' approach, the government has proposed a visionary blueprint for tomorrow's living in the area surrounding the former Kai Tak International Airport. Occupying the prime vantage point on the southeast Kowloon waterfront, near the former international airport site which now houses the cruise terminal and waterfront promenades, Grand Waterfront comprises five towers of 57 storeys, offering a total of 1,782 units. The site is also located at the hub of the transport networks, next to the pier, bus terminal and a new railway station.

Sporting white cladding that is highlighted with soothing purple and green, Grand Waterfront presents a chic contemporary outlook. The decorative cornice at the pinnacle of each tower is in itself a modern sculpture, blending art into everyday life. Each unit is designed with bay window, balcony, utility platform or roof. The rectangular layout is efficient and versatile. Outside the living room's French windows lies a balcony that floods the room with **natural light**. The spilt design for the balcony and utility platform creates a natural fresh airflow through cross ventilation.

From its waterfront location, the majority of units at Grand Waterfront enjoy different angles of harbour views towards southeast Kowloon, Lei Yu Mun, Hunghom, or across the harbour from Hong Kong Island east to Central.

Linking all towers with the shuttle lift lobby, the glass-ceiling podium concourse basks in greenery on every side. From here there are views of the resort-style swimming pool through the lush vegetation. The development also offers recreation facilities and amenities in a vast sustainable greenery setting.

1   View across the Kowloon waterfront
2   Overview
3   Outdoor pool area
4   Typical floor plan (Tower 6, 6/F–22/F)

Photography: courtesy Dennis Lau & Ng Chun Man Architect & Engineers (HK) Ltd

Grand Waterfront

177 m | 581 ft

Location Hong Kong

Completion 2007

Client Henderson Land Development Company Limited

Architect Dennis Lau & Ng Chun Man Architects & Engineers (HK) Ltd

Structural engineer Stephen Cheng Consulting Engineers Limited

MEP engineer Meinhardt (M&E) Ltd

Project management consultant Henderson Land Development Company Ltd

Cost consultant Davis Langdon & Seah Hong Kong Ltd

Landscape architect Belt Collins Hong Kong Limited

Main contractor Heng Shung Construction Company Ltd

Uses Residential 90,939 m² (978,859 ft²) • retail 12,124 m² (130,501 ft²)
• clubhouse: 4,540 m² (48,868 ft²)

Number of buildings 5

Above-ground storeys 57

Height 177 m (581 ft)

Refuge levels 23/F, 43/F

Sky-garden levels 43/F

Site area 12,126 m² (130,523 ft²)

Gross above-ground area 103,063 m² (1,109,360 ft²)

Total gross area 103,071 m² (1,109,447 ft²)

Floor area ratio (FAR)/Plot ratio 8.5

Gross typical floor area Towers 1, 2, 3, 5: 354–361 m² (3,810–3,886 ft²)
• tower 6: 389–392 m² (4,187–4,219 ft²)

Total number of elevators 30

Elevator brand Fujitec

Number of car parking spaces 279

Number of motorbike parking spaces 30

Principal structure materials Reinforced concrete

Source: Dennis Lau & Ng Chun Man Architects & Engineers (HK) Ltd

2

3

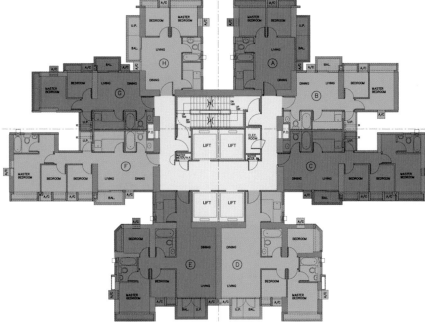

4

Heart of Lake, a 2,000,000-square-metre (21,527,821 square-foot) pedestrian garden city in Xiamen, is planned with the mix of residential building types that make up a city that has evolved naturally: high-rise and mid-rise apartment buildings, townhouses and single-family villas. Xiamen is a major coastal city in China with a pleasant climate with cooler temperatures in the summer months compared to the rest of the province.

The residences, on a 10-hectare (25-acre) site on Huxindao Island, are organised around a hierarchy of landscaped public spaces, a lush green central park, intimate courtyards and stone-paved plazas. Landscaped pedestrian streets lead to the waterfront public park that wraps the peninsula. A highly visible clubhouse serves as a gateway and social centre; the neighbourhood will also include 3,000 square metres

(32,291 square feet) of retail. The project's architectural vocabulary, inspired by both traditional Chinese and Mediterranean architecture, responds to the local climate capturing breezes from the north and takes advantage of local materials and construction techniques.

The project is a model of how to achieve high density in a 21st-century **garden city** by combining point towers with low-to mid-scale buildings. We looked closely at local traditions to discover appropriate organisational strategies, hierarchies of pedestrian streets and pathways, residential types, and public and private landscaped spaces – from civic-scaled parks to private courtyards with their own teahouses. In particular, we looked closely at Gulong Island, a historic European Treaty Port that includes a mix of public and private spaces, highly trafficked markets, and a balance of buildings and streets as a precedent and a utopian model that brings together Chinese and Western sensibilities. One of the

fundamental goals at Heart of Lake is the establishment of a high-density garden city that provides the variety of living options one might find in a traditional city, while conserving land for public use. This has been achieved by creating the hierarchy of building types and, as in New York, locating larger, taller buildings facing the major boulevard parks and single-family courtyard houses and townhouses on side streets where the perimeter blocks create smaller communities.

The project is being implemented in eight total phases. Construction began in 2012; the first three phases (including the gateway clubhouse) have been completed. The total project completion is scheduled for 2018.

1 View from villas looking to towers
2 Exterior view of residential high-rise towers
3 Clubhouse courtyard
4 Residential high-rise ground floor plan
5 Typical residential high-rise floor plan (8/F–25/F)

Photography & illustrations: ©Robert A.M. Stern Architects

Heart of Lake

Location Xiamen

Completion 2018

Client Vanke Real Estate Enterprise Co. Ltd (Shenzhen)

Architect Robert A.M. Stern Architects

Associate architect BIAD (Beijing)

Structural & MEP engineers BIAD (Beijing)

Landscape architects The Olin Studio (Philadelphia, Pennsylvania) • J&D Studio (Shanghai)

Lighting consultant Citelum (Beijing)

Other consultants Robert A.M. Stern Interiors, LLC (New York) [interior design] • Wilson Associates (Shanghai, China) [associate interior design]

Main contractor Xiamen Vanke Real Estate Enterprise Co. Ltd (Shenzhen)

Uses Residential, retail

Number of buildings 8 (high-rise) • 12 (mid-rise)

Height High-rise: 80–180 m (262–590 ft) • mid-rise: 19.5–32.5 m (64–107 ft)

Above-ground storeys High-rise: 22, 31, 37, 47 or 56 • mid-rise: 4, 5 or 9 • clubhouse: 1

Basements 2 (parking)

Refuge levels 2 (below-grade)

Site area 95,098 m² (1,023,626 ft²)

Gross typical floor area [High-rise] 264 flats: 240 m² (2,583 ft²) • 152 flats: 260 m² (2,799 ft²) • 104 flats: 280 m² (3,014 ft²) • 10 penthouses: 270 m² (2,906 ft²) • 6 penthouses: 300 m² (3,229 ft²) • 16 maisonettes: 360 m² (3,875 ft²) • [mid-rise] 62 flats: 250 m² (2,691 ft²) • 16 penthouses: 280 m² (3,014 ft²) • [multifamily] 13 flats: 160 m² (1,722 ft²) • 27 duplexes: 190 m² (2,045 ft²)

Total gross floor area Residential: 196,710 m² (2,117,369 ft²) • commercial: 2,000 m² (21,527 ft²) • clubhouse: 6,000 m² (64,583 ft²)

Total number of elevators 2 passenger elevators & 1 service elevator in each high-rise

Residence service brand Heart of Lake

Principal structure materials Concrete, local granite, stucco, clay tile roofs

Other materials Interior: stone, plaster, speciality finishes, tile

2

3

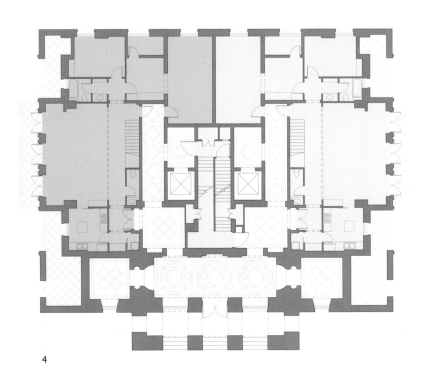

4

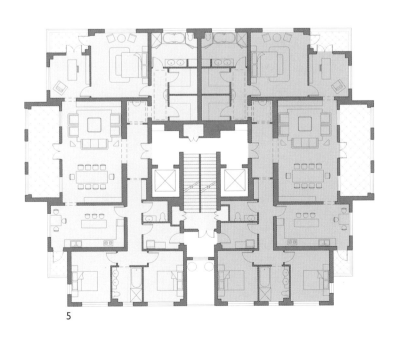

5

1

■ Located in the heart of the city's central business district, Yanlord Landmark is a mixed-use development in what has become a key economic, transport and communication hub in southwestern China. The prominent site – bordered by Renmin Nan Road, a major north–south city axis, on the west and situated between the Sichuan Exhibition Center and the Jin River – allows the complex to function as a landmark and **focal point** within the city.

The project is comprised of three towers containing offices, serviced apartments and a hotel, rising from a retail and entertainment podium.

Phase 1, completed in 2010, includes two towers that anchor the highly visible corners of the northern end of the triangular site and are oriented to maximise uninterrupted views and minimise solar exposure. An office and hotel tower is scheduled for a future phase and has been designed to have commanding 360-degree views.

To balance the developer goals with the client's and city's desires for an architectural landmark, the design team based the tower forms on a simple and efficient floor plate. The simple tower volumes are wrapped in a continuous glass façade, which visually unifies the towers with the podium below, creating a single, cohesive architectural expression. At street level, the façade folds out over the sidewalk, defining major entry points into the complex.

1   Close-up of exterior
2   Street view
3   Rendering of initial overall concept
4   View of plaza
5   Office floor plan, low-rise (7/F–23/F)
6   Office floor plan, high-rise (26/F–39/F)
7   Typical serviced apartments tower floor plan

Photography & renderings: courtesy NBBJ

Yanlord Landmark

Location Chengdu
Completion 2010
Client Yanlord Land Group
Architect NBBJ
Architect of record China Southwest Architectural Design and Research Institute (CSADR)
Structural engineer CSADR
MEP engineer Arup
Vertical transportation consultant Arup
Façade engineer Aurecon
Project management consultant Yanlord Land Group
Cost consultant DLS
Landscape architect EDAW
Lighting consultant Panorama
Other consultants Yuanda Construction Group (façade) • Jones Land LaSalle (property) • Dutton Bray (signage) • Lian Zhitian and CL3 (interior design)
Main contractor Yanlord Land Group
Uses Retail: 44,399 m² (477,907 ft²) [B1/F–5/F] • office tower: 70,360 m² (757,349 ft²) • serviced apartments tower: 49,095 m² (528,454 ft²) • parking: 36,009 m² (387,598 ft²)

Number of buildings 2 + podium
Height Office tower: 180 m (590 ft) • serviced apartments tower: 165 m (541 ft)
Above-ground storeys Office tower: 40 • serviced apartments tower: 40
Basements 3
Mechanical levels 2
Refuge levels 2
Total gross area 212,482 m² (2,287,137 ft²)
Gross typical floor area Office: 2,000 m² (21,528 ft²) • serviced apartments: 1,350 m² (14,531 ft²)
Basic planning module 1.5 m (4.9 ft)
Total number of elevators 14
Speed of fastest elevators 8 m (26 ft)/s
Number of car parking spaces 700
Number of bike parking spaces 370
Hotel brand Frasier Suites
Principal structure materials Steel/concrete composite
Other materials Glass

Source: NBBJ

180 m | 590 ft

2

3

4

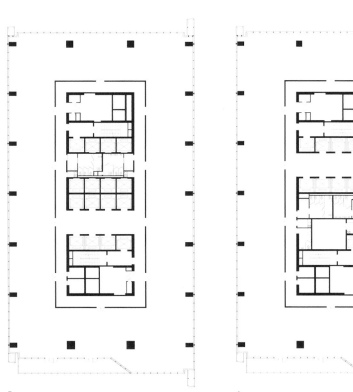

5

6

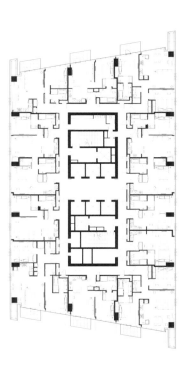

7

1

Manhattan Hill is a high-rise residential development consisting of five 40- to 43-storey towers over a three-level podium that contains retail facilities, a car park and an ultraluxurious clubhouse. The concept of 'metropolitan living' is articulated by two design concepts. Firstly, the towers are twisted to enable each tower to enjoy the harbour views. This creates a nice setback at the street level for new private passageways and allows more streetscape greening. Secondly, it is to design a series of unique spatial experiences linking all the towers at the podium level and providing a unique clubhouse for the residences. The **twisted slab block** arrangement of residential towers avoids overlooking and thus enjoys the best views.

The curved corner glazing of the master bedroom accentuates the panoramic harbour scene, which also makes a distinguished architectural statement for the external elevation. Volumetric (three-dimensional) consideration was taken into account. The breathtaking view of atrium marks the unique ambience of clubhouse; together with the doubled volume cafeteria, indoor swimming pool and gymnasium, spatial elasticity filled with natural lighting and water reflection have been created for the pleasure of residents.

1   Contemporary façade design
2   Overview
3   Typical floor plan (Towers 1 & 2)
4   Typical floor plan (Towers 3, 5 & 6)
5   Ground floor plan
Photography: courtesy Ronald Lu & Partners

Manhattan Hill

186 m | 612 ft

Location Hong Kong
Completion 2007
Clients Sun Hung Kai Properties Ltd • Kowloon Motor Bus Co. Ltd
Architect Ronald Lu & Partners
Structural engineer Siu Yin Wai & Associates Ltd
MEP engineer J. Roger Preston Limited
Project management consultant Sun Hung Kai Properties Ltd
Cost consultant Davis Langdom & Seah HK Ltd
Landscape architect Sun Hung Kai (A&E)
Lighting consultant Guava Hong Kong Limited
Other consultants J. Roger Preston Ltd (M&E) • Davis Langdom & Seah HK Ltd (quantity surveyor)
Main contractor Chun Fai Construction Co. Ltd
Uses Residential (49 floors aboveground), podium of clubhouse, car park & shopping arcade
Number of buildings 4 residential blocks • 3-level retail & car parking podium

Height 186.4 m (612 ft)
Above-ground storeys 49
Basements NIL
Site area 13,030 m² (140,254 ft²)
Gross above-ground building area 98,934 m² (1,064,917 ft²) [domestic] • 19,477 m² (209,649 ft²) [nondomestic]
Total gross area 118,411 m² (1,274,565 ft²)
Floor area ratio (FAR)/Plot ratio 8.304 (domestic) • 1.638 (nondomestic)
Basic planning module 5 towers on a podium
Total number of elevators 26
Elevator brand Mitsubishi
Number of car parking spaces 442
Number of motorbike spaces 45
Principal structure materials Reinforced concrete

Source: Ronald Lu & Partners

2

3

4

5

1

■ Landmark East is a Grade-A high-rise, two-tower office development that rises from a dense urban site in the Kwun Tong district of Hong Kong. Kwun Tong, historically an industrial and light manufacturing district supporting the old Kai Tak airport, is in the process of urban regeneration and Landmark East is the flagship project leading the process.

The slender rectilinear slabs that form the tower volumes are derived from the long narrow plot. The towers respond to the site, rising above the adjacent buildings in a slender, elegantly moving motion reminiscent of bamboo swaying gently in the wind. The idea was to differentiate the buildings from the static neighbourhood in creating a dynamic form that clearly defines the towers from their surroundings.

The rectangular floor plates of both towers provide efficiency and allow side cores to the north. This in turn orientates the office floors to the south, taking advantage of the privileged views of Victoria Harbour and Hong Kong Island beyond. The orthogonal tower forms have been segmented in section creating a series of interlocking **parallelogram slabs**. This arrangement emphasises the sensation of movement and conveys lightness to the towers, forming a strong, dramatic, unified identity for the development.

Efficient floor plans are therefore retained while providing dynamism to what would otherwise be a regular box derived from a rectangular plan. Where the forms interlock additional corner offices are created taking advantage of the valuable harbour and island views. The car parking and loading areas are restricted to the basement of both towers and a podium structure at the base of tower 2. As a result, the remainder of the site is left open to form an elegant and beautifully landscaped public plaza with sculptures gardens and cafes that provide valuable open space for tenant and local residents use.

1   View from Hong Kong Harbour
2   View from west
3   AIA Tower (tower 2)
4   AXA Tower (tower 1) lobby
5   *Man Walking East* sculpture
6   Site plan

Photography: 1 courtesy Arquitectonica; 2 ©Amral Imran; 3, 4 ©Rogan Coles; 5 © William Furniss

Landmark East

Location Hong Kong	**Curtain wall sub-contractor** Permasteelisa Hong Kong
Completion 2008	**Lift sub-contractor** Schindler Lifts
Client Wing Tai Asia	**Uses** Office tower 1: 45,000 m² (484,375 ft²) • Office tower 2: 65,000 m² (699,654 ft²)
Architect Arquitectonica	**Number of buildings** 2
Architect of record Arthur Kwok Architects & Associates Limited	**Height** 191.25 m (627 ft)
Structural engineer Mott Connell	**Above-ground storeys** Tower 1: 43 • tower 2: 43
MEP engineer Thomas Anderson & Partners	**Basements** 2
Façade engineer Mott Connell	**Site area** 8,913 m² (95,938 ft²)
Landscape architect EDAW	**Total gross area** 110,000 m² (1,184,030 ft²)
Lighting consultant Isometrix	**Number of car parking spaces** 449 car park spaces & 49 loading spaces
Other consultants Quantity surveyor: Davis Langdon & Seah • planning: Townland Consultants	**Principal structure materials** Structural System: post-tensioned reinforced concrete • external cladding: unitised aluminum framed curtain wall
Main contractor Paul Y. Engineering Group	

Source: Arquitectonica

191 m | 627 ft

2

3

4

5

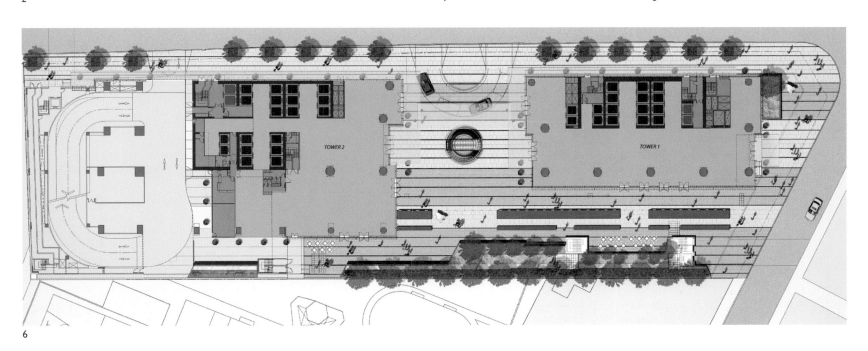

6

This development is a novel bifurcated plan-form that captures a 240-degree arc of harbour and city views. Concentration of floor area in the tall tower reduces bulk and increases permeability at street level.

A private, naturally lit, lift lobby serves each apartment, and the introduction of natural light and views to the lobbies transforms the day-to-day experience of the building. Inside the apartments the 9.5-metre-wide (31-foot) living rooms capture sweeping panoramic views. Semi-duplexes and duplexes offer unusually majestic and spacious high-rise living spaces.

Visually, the soaring stone-clad shear walls of the tower are balanced with a careful **rhythm of windows**, spandrels and fins. In parallel with the efficient planning, the architect conceived the envelope as an original and restrained aesthetic composition of counterpoints; of natural and artificial materials, human and massive scale, all presented in a rational and modern assembly.

The design integrates environmental features to make the property energy efficient and environmentally friendly. Since the initial design stage, the building's environmental suitability was assessed through various techniques, tools and sophisticated computer software applications, including Computational Fluid Dynamics (CFD) and Radiance Simulations. The aspects, such as building disposition, wind microclimates, natural ventilation, natural lighting and other factors were assessed.

A green energy approach has been utilised: a solar thermal system is used for water heating at the clubhouse and T5 fluorescent tubes and LED lights are extensively used in the building for energy conservation. Maintaining good indoor air quality is another important target of the project. To this end, a carbon dioxide monitoring system and active fresh air supply system are installed in the living and dining areas of each residential unit. In addition, a central vacuum cleaning system is also provided. The building has been awarded with HK BEAM Platinum Rating and Quality Building Award.

1   View of the façade's window, spandrel and fin design
2   Overall view
3   Outdoor swimming pool area
4   Living room
5   Master bedroom
6   Typical semi-duplex upper floor plan

Photography & illustrations: courtesy Dennis Lau & Ng Chun Man Architects & Engineers (H.K.) Ltd

39 Conduit Road

192 m | 629 ft

Location Hong Kong
Completion 2009
Client Henderson Land Development Company Limited
Architect Dennis Lau & Ng Chun Man Architects & Engineers (H.K.) Ltd
Structural engineers Stephen Cheng Consulting Engineers Limited
• Leslie E. Robertson Associates
MEP engineer Arup
Façade engineer HS + A Ltd
Landscape architects Scape Design Associates Ltd • AXXA Group Limited
Lighting consultants Lightsource International (Asia) Ltd • Pro-Lit Company Limited
Other consultants KCA International (interior design)

Main contractor Heng Shung Construction Company Limited
Uses Residential
Number of buildings 1
Height 191.57 m (629 ft)
Above-ground storeys 42
Basements NIL
Site area 5,272 m² (56,747 ft²)
Total gross area 18,266 m² (196,613 ft²)
Principal structure materials Reinforced concrete

Source: Dennis Lau & Ng Chun Man Architects & Engineers (H.K.) Ltd

2

3

4

5

6

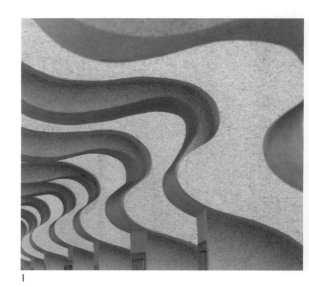

As different cultures have different forms of expression, the different architectural concepts of the Bird's Nest, Water Cube and Pangu Plaza on both sides of the central axis of Beijing manifest a thought-provoking **cultural discourse**.

Light is the basis of being in Western culture. In architecture, it evolved into the precise pairing of physical space expressing a unit with detailed texture. Therefore, the architectural concept of both the Bird's Nest and the Water Cube

is to be a light container, where the space is expressed in the light gradation. In Chinese culture, *chi* is a word that describes the system of existence in every living thing. In architecture, this concept has naturally evolved into a creative concept of the unity of heaven, earth and man, the highest state of being. In Oriental culture, a building is a unit that conveys creative concepts through form that manifests into the perfect combination of heaven, earth and man. The traditional city structure planning of Beijing fully displays this expression. The Pangu Plaza combines five independent buildings into one entity through the stereotypical element of the dragon and expresses the lyrical *chi* and vivacity of Chinese culture. The plaza has turned to tensile aesthetics

that combine form and quality – the magnificent freehand expression of the dragon form and four-in-one complex are symbols for the fusion with heaven; the long and gigantic corridor in the form of a dragon symbolises fusion with earth and the people residing within. Taken together, these elements shape an information field presenting architectural aesthetics unique to Oriental culture.

1 Dragon corridor, made of stone
2 View of Pangu Plaza (left), with Water Cube (centre) and the Bird's Nest (right)
3 Business club
4 Dragon corridor columns (66), with view of dragon's head
5 View of the dragon form
6 Site plan

Photography: courtesy Beijing PANGU Investment Inc., & C.Y. Lee & Partners Architects/Planners

Pangu Plaza

Location Beijing
Completion 2008
Client Beijing PANGU Investment Inc
Architects C.Y. Lee & Partners Architects/Planners
  • Dayuan Architecture Design Consulting (Shanghai)
Structural engineer John A. Martin & Associates, Ltd. (Beijing, China)
MEP engineer Shanghai Arup
Façade engineer PFT
Landscape architect Ecoland
Uses Office (B5/F–39/F) • hotel (B3/F–19/F) • residential (B3/F–19/F)

Number of buildings 5
Height Office: 192 m (630 ft) • hotel: 88 m (288 ft) • residential: 78.6 m (257 ft)
Above-ground storeys 39
Basements 5
Site area 39,360 m^2 (423,667 ft^2)
Gross above-ground building area 299,866 m^2 (3,227,730 ft^2)
Gross basement area 118,618.7 m^2 (1,276,801 ft^2)
Total gross area 418,484.72 m^2 (4,504,532 ft^2)
Principal structure materials Granite, structural steel, aluminium extruded sections, glass

Source: C.Y. Lee & Partners Architects/Planners

2

3

4

5

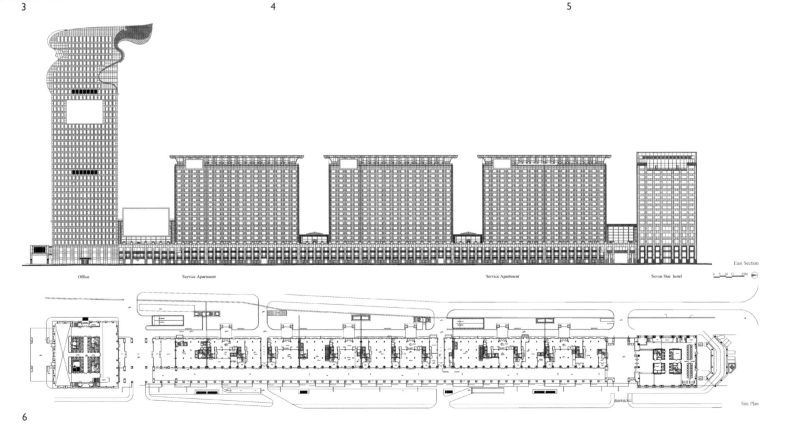

Office   Service Apartment   Service Apartment   Seven Star hotel   East Section

Site Plan

6

1

■ The Grand Hyatt Shenzhen is characterised by its unusual inverted upside-down layout, which positions the front desk and main lobby at the 33rd sky-lobby level, with five restaurants and bars on the rooftop levels 32/F to 38/F and the guestrooms below. This feature is expressed by a 50-metre glass atrium on top of the tower offering **dramatic views** of the region's mountain peaks. At night, the glow of the gently lit restaurants and roof gardens inside the atrium are a beacon on the landscape.

The tower's façade treatment employs a vocabulary of simplicity and elegance, while the architectural language is forward and inspires movement. A series of stainless steel vertical fins highlight the tower's vertical line, while horizontal polished stone spandrels contour the shape into a harmonious, continuous curve.

Three distinctly defined wedges rotated from the centre of the tower create the appearance of a curved façade opening out to views of Hong Kong's mountains and preserved wetlands. The hotel's north elevation has a slightly different façade that distinguishes it from the south façade. Hotel rooms flanking each end and a full-height glass line through the centre of the tower create a perfect balance between the different elements.

Located in the Luohu district, the Grand Hyatt Shenzhen offers 471 rooms, including 53 suites and 48 serviced apartments, and is part of a larger mixed-use urban ensemble – City Crossing – comprising an office tower, three residential towers as well as a MixC mall.

1 Aerial view in context
2 Overall view at night
3 Section plan (full)
4 Main reception at sky-lobby level (33/F)
5 The Snow Kitchen restaurant (32/F)
6 Podium floor plan
7 Ground floor plan

Photography: ©courtesy City Crossing;
illustrations ©RTKL.com

Grand Hyatt Shenzhen

Location Shenzhen	**Above-ground storeys** 42
Completion 2009	**Basements** 3
Client China Resources (Shenzhen) Co., Ltd	**Mechanical levels** 3M/F, 23M/F, 28M/, 39/F–42/F
Architect RTKL Associates, Inc.	**Refuge levels** 18/F
Associate architect CCDI	**Sky-lobby levels** 33/F
Structural engineers CCDI; Arup (top of tower)	**Gross above-ground building area** 72,000 m² (775,001 ft²)
MEP engineer Parsons Brinckerhoff (Asia)	**Floor area ratio (FAR)/Plot ratio** 4.79 (City Crossing site)
Landscape architect Belt Collins	**Total number of elevators** 21
Other consultants Wilson Associates (interior design)	**Hotel brand** Grand Hyatt
Uses Hotel (471 rooms), including 48 serviced apartments & 53 suites	**Principal structure materials** Reinforced concrete shear wall structure
Number of buildings 1	**Other materials** Steel, concrete, stone, glass
Height 193 m (633 ft)	

700 m
600 m
500 m
400 m
300 m
200 m
193 m 633 ft
100 m

Sources: RTKL Associates, Inc.; ha+d 2011, Vol. 1, Issue 1; Grand Hyatt Shenzhen

2

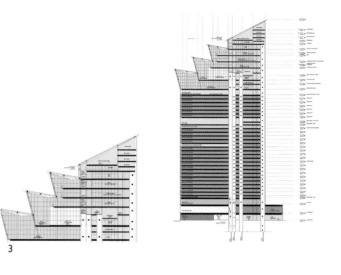

3

4

5

6

7

The Fake Hills development is located on the coastal city of Beihai, in southern China, on an 800-metre-long (2,624-foot), narrow oceanfront site. The fundamental geometry of the scheme combines two common – yet opposite – architectural typologies, the high-rise and groundscraper, producing an **undulating building** typology, resulting in the form of a hill. The geometry of the architecture maximises potential views for the residents; the continuous platform along the roof becomes the public space, with gardens, tennis courts and swimming pools on top of the artificial hills. Each opening in the building allows the sea breezes to pass through and creates ocean views from the interior.

■ The vast majority of development in China's new cities takes the form of residential housing, often standardised and cheap to guarantee a quick return for investment. Is it possible to build high-density, economically viable housing that is also architecturally innovative?

Aiming for a high-density solution and a new landmark for the city, Fake Hills provides a heightened experience of the coastline and an opportunity for unhindered interaction with the city and the vast natural environment that it faces.

1 Construction detail
2 Rendering day view
3 Floor plan (19/F)
4 Model
5 Rendering night view

Renderings: courtesy MAD Architects

Fake Hills

194 m | 636 ft

Location Beihai	**Height** Tower: 194 m (636 ft) • groundscraper: 106 m (348 ft)
Completion 2015	**Above-ground storeys** Tower: 55 • groundscraper: 33
Client Beihai Xinpinguangyang Real Estate Development Co. Ltd	**Basements** 2
Architect MAD Architects	**Site area** 109,203 m² (1,175,451 ft²)
Associate architect Jiang Architects & Engineers	**Gross above-ground building area** 492,369 m² (5,299,816 ft²)
Structural engineer Jiang Architects & Engineers	**Total number of elevators** 34
MEP engineer Jiang Architects & Engineers	**Speed of fastest elevators** 2.5 m (8.2 ft)/s
Uses Residential	**Number of car parking spaces** 2,011
Number of buildings 2	**Principal structure materials** Concrete

Source: MAD Architects

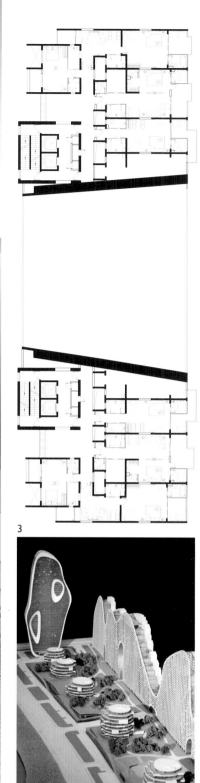

2

3

4

5

1

700 m | 2296 ft

600 m | 1968 ft

500 m | 1640 ft

400 m | 1312 ft

300 m | 984 ft

100 m | 328 ft

dalian

■ Located in China's northeastern coastal city of Dalian, sited fronting the Yellow Sea and adjacent to the large public park of Xinghai Square, the building responds to both its physical and environmental contexts. The tower's **triangular plan** is designed to ensure that all rooms receive southern light, as well as views of the sea and nearby mountain ranges. Additionally, the triangular form helps to minimise the structural impact of the area's uniquely high winds, channelling them to the building's northern corners, where vertical-axis turbines capture the energy and produce electricity year-round. Programmatically, the hotel floors are stacked below the serviced apartment levels, enabling

the core to telescope and creating the architectural 'portal' along the north façade. Internal circulation is exposed on this face to provide corridors with natural daylight and views of the skyline, as well as to assure a consistent lighting profile at night. The top two levels of the tower house the signature restaurant, offering unobstructed views in all directions.

1 Overall view in context
2 Street view from the northeast
3 Overall water view from the southeast
4 Exterior entry view from the northeast
5 View of outdoor restaurant terrace
6 Ground floor plan
7 Typical hotel plan

Photography: ©Goettsch Partners

Grand Hyatt Dalian

Location Dalian

Completion 2014

Client China Resources Land Limited

Architect Goettsch Partners

Associate architect China Architecture Design & Research Institute

Structural engineer RBS Architectural Engineering Design Associates

MEP engineer Meinhardt

Vertical transportation consultant Meinhardt

Façade engineers Goettsch Partners (façade designer) • Meinhardt (façade engineer)

Landscape architect ACLA

Lighting consultant Tino Kwan

Other consultants LTW Design Works (interior design)

Uses Hotel: 54,265 m² (584,103 ft²) [5/F–29/F] • residential/serviced apartments: 18,815 m² (202,523 ft²) [30/F–41/F]

Number of buildings 1

Height 195.4 m (641 ft)

Above-ground storeys 44

Basements 2

Mechanical levels 15/F, 29/F, 41/F (mezzanine levels)

Refuge levels 15/F, 29/F (mezzanine levels)

Site area 15,707 m² (169,069 ft²)

Gross above-ground building area 78,373 m² (843,600 ft²)

Gross basement area 21,527 m² (231,715 ft²)

Total gross area 99,900 m² (1,075,314 ft²)

Gross typical floor area 1,411 m² (15,188 ft²)

Floor area ratio (FAR)/Plot ratio 6.1

Basic planning module 1.2-m (4-ft) curtain wall module; 9.6-m (31.5-ft) bay

Total number of elevators 21

Speed of fastest elevators 6 m (20 ft)/s

Number of car parking spaces 225

Hotel brand Grand Hyatt

Residence service brand Serviced apartments operated by Hyatt

Principal structure materials Concrete

Other materials Composite columns, concrete slab & core

Source: Goettsch Partners

2

3

4

5

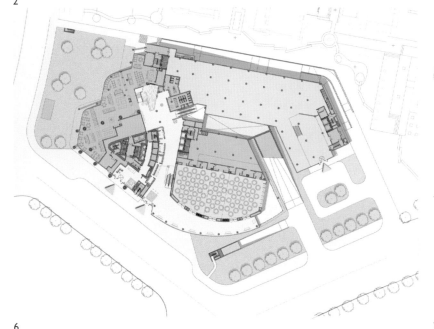

6

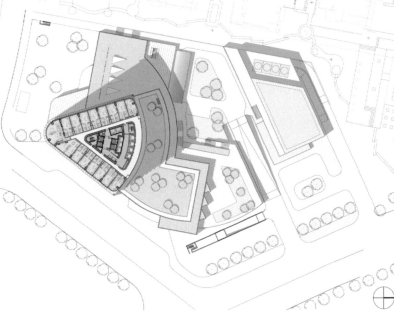

7

1

This development lies between two major southern highways entering Guangzhou (also known as Canton in the West). Guangzhou was a significant maritime port for the historic Silk Road and was the city first sanctioned by the last Qing emperor to trade with the West in the 16th century.

The original masterplan proposed five square office towers on Pearl River. The easternmost headquarters tower was being built when Atkins won an international competition to redesign the masterplan. The challenge was to transform a partly built complex that will also kickstart this redevelopment district while keeping to the same planning guidelines.

Atkins reduced the depth of the four towers and replaced the area on top as bridge sections. Thus the design neatly morphed the four unbuilt towers into two '0' shaped structures to simplify the overall development into a legible image. Thus the complex will appear as two powerful icons of '100' or '001' as seen from the central business district or from the river, respectively. These **symbolic 'windows'** reflect Guangzhou's historic position and continuing success as a trading port.

Exploiting the existing dockland context, Atkins proposes to convert two buildings into cultural and exhibition venues and conceives a new marina focused around a lighthouse to complement the Class A office development.

The middle '0' tower (Lot B) designed by Atkins is 196 metres (643 feet) tall with a spectacular 178-metre-long (584-foot) river view at the top and bottom bridge sections. The opening spans a

record 60 metres (197 feet) and is 150 metres (492 feet) high, helping to preserve river views for future buildings to the north. The podium containing dining and health club facilities provides an all-weather porte-cochère in the wet monsoon climate, as well as a 60-metre-wide (197-foot) vista towards the river.

The green building strategy reduces the towers to only 25 metres (82 feet) deep to allow cross ventilation and views for the individual office units. Vertical frames on the east and west façades and a rooftop trellis shade from the intense subtropical sun. There are also solar cells and a heliport on the roof.

1 Perspective
2 Bird's-eye view of towers (Lots A, B, C, respectively, from right to left)
3 Floor plan (40/F) (Lot B)
4 Typical floor plan (20/F–32/F) (Lot B)
5 Ground floor plan (Lot B)

Renderings: ©Atkins Consultants (Shenzhen) Co., Ltd

Window of Canton

196 m | 643 ft

Location Guangzhou

Completion 2018

Client CCCC Fourth Harbor Engineering Co., Ltd

Architects Atkins Consultants (Shenzhen) Co., Ltd (masterplan; design Lots B & C) • China Shipbuilding NDRI Engineering Co., Ltd (design, Lot A)

Architects of record Architectural Design and Research Institute of Guangdong Province (Lot B) • China Shipbuilding NDRI Engineering Co., Ltd (Lot A)

Structural engineers Arup (Lot B) • China Shipbuilding NDRI Engineering Co., Ltd (Lot A)

MEP engineers Arup (Lot B) • China Shipbuilding NDRI Engineering Co., Ltd (Lot A)

Landscape architect Atkins Consultants (Shenzhen) Co., Ltd

Main contractor CCCC Fourth Harbor Engineering Co., Ltd

Uses Office, commercial

Number of buildings 3

Height 196 m (643 ft)

Above-ground storeys 40

Basements 3

Mechanical levels 33/F

Refuge levels 5/F, 19/F, 33/F

Sky-lobby levels NIL

Site area 88,430 m² (951,852 ft2) • Lots A & B: 51,657 m² (556,031 ft²) • Lot C: 36,773 m² (395,821 ft²)

Gross above-ground building area 136,220 m² (1,466,260 ft²) [Lot B]

Gross basement area 56,580 m² (609,022 ft²) [Lot B]

Total gross area 192,800 m² (2,075,282 ft²) [Lot B]

Floor area ratio (FAR)/Plot ratio Lots A & B: 4.53 • Lot C: 3

Gross typical floor area 4,400 m² (47,361 ft²) [Lot B]

Basic planning module NIL

Total number of elevators 24 (Lot B)

Principal structure materials Steel & concrete (frame core wall structure)

Source: Atkins Consultants (Shenzhen) Co., Ltd

2

3

4

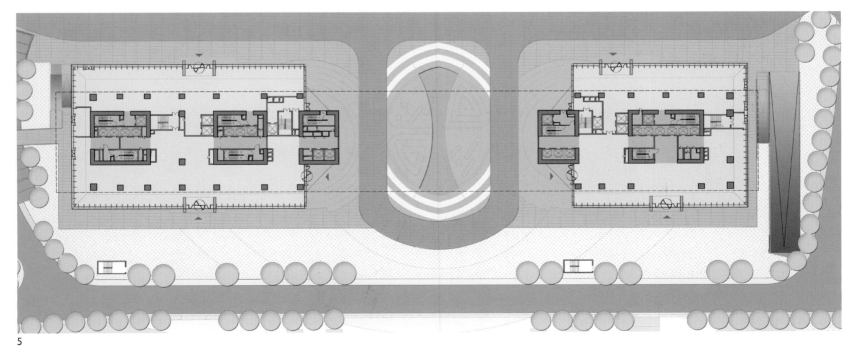

5

The 9,298 square-metre (100,083-square-foot) site of the Oriental Financial Center is located in the central area of LuJiaZui, bounded on the east by YinChengZhong Road, on the south by LuJiaZui Ring Road, and faces water on its west sides.

The Oriental Financial Center is a 198-metre-tall (650-foot), mixed-used office building with 31 storeys above-ground and four storeys underground. The building accommodates 113,382 square metres (1,220,434 square feet) of office, retail, parking, and common space. The ground floor's entry is approached through a series of exterior spaces sheltered by and overlooked by the building's transparent 1st floor. This entry sequence presents visitors with a view of the building's structure and function, and moderates between public and private, appropriately serving as entry point for both the offices above and the retail space below. Offices occupy the space from the ground floor to the 31st floor, with an opening in the northeast corner at the 30th floor, allowing light to penetrate even more deeply into the column of open-air interior space in the building. The first below-ground level houses retail space and the following three floors are reserved for parking and MEP.

The traditional centre core high-rise has proven to be an effective means of building quickly and in large quantities. However, modern office functions, such as finance and services, require increasingly large floor plates with higher population densities. As a result, workers have less access to natural light and air. New and innovative building designs are required to meet the modern demands of the workplace while sustaining our environment and improving worker happiness.

The design proposal considers a new concept for the high-rise, modelling it around an **open-air courtyard** that provides ample light, air and water. The challenge is to adapt a traditionally low-rise plan typology to a modern high-rise building, while simultaneously integrating architectural, structural, mechanical, environmental, and safety systems in a rational and efficient way. The cost of implementing sustainable elements in the design is offset by the increased rentable floor area efficiency of the multiple-core design. This provides a financial mechanism that allows a traditional office developer to pursue an environmental agenda.

1   Looking up through open-air courtyard
2   Rendering overview
3   View of ground-floor entry at street level
4   Sky garden floor plan
5   Typical high-rise floor plan
6   Typical low-rise floor plan
7   Section

Renderings: courtesy Kohn Pedersen Fox Associates

Oriental Financial Center

198 m | 650 ft

Location Shanghai	**Uses** Office, retail
Completion 2014	**Number of buildings** 1
Client Shanghai Cheung Tai Property Development Ltd • Cheung Kong Holdings (developer)	**Height** 198 m (650 ft)
Architect Kohn Pedersen Fox Associates	**Above-ground storeys** 31
Associate architect ECADI, Local Design Institute	**Basements** 4
Structural engineer Meinhardt (Shanghai) Ltd	**Site area** 9,298 m² (100,083 ft²)
MEP engineer P&T International Inc.	**Gross above-ground building area** 80,000 m² (861,113 ft²)
Project management consultant Kohn Pedersen Fox Associates	**Total gross area** 113,382 m² (1,220,434 ft²)
Main contractor China State Construction Engineering Corporation	**Principal structure materials** Composite
Other consultants Rolf Jensen & Associates, Inc. (fire)	

Source: Kohn Pedersen Fox Associates

2

3

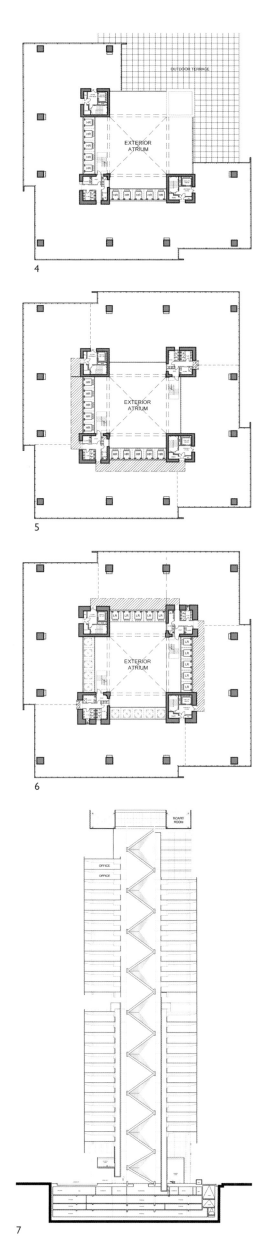

4

5

6

7

1

■ The site for the Wangjing SOHO project is located in the Chaoyang District of northeast Beijing, near the Airport Expressway and between Fourth and Fifth Ring Roads. The area contains the offices of many Chinese start-up companies, as well as global companies, such as Microsoft, Daimler, Caterpillar, Panasonic, Nortel and Siemens. It is conveniently located on the way to the Beijing Capital International Airport and near various metro stations, and is home to a vibrant mix of local and international residents and visitors.

The **fan-shaped** Wangjing SOHO has a central built area that's surrounded by generous green spaces, including a park on the south, and green buffer zones to the north, east and west. The site is bordered to the north by the semicircular Fu Tong West Street, on the east and west by Fu An East and West Streets, and along the south by Wangjing Street. The site layout consists of three towers and various small buildings set in a landscape of rolling green spaces with activity zones and water features.

The composition of the towers also extend into the surrounding landscape with flowing lines that echo the dynamic mountain forms, creating paths of movement and exciting activity zones of shopping and leisure for the people. The lines of movement extend to the perimeter and integrate all the green areas along the north, south, east and west of the site. In-between the main building towers is a 'canyon' of retail shops and activities and several pavilion gate buildings that create shopping streets at ground level. There are two sunken courts in the east and west of the canyon that continue the landscape paths down to the retail concourse below.

The tower entrance lobbies face outwards to the city and welcome visitors into dynamic elegant halls that connect to the office floors and the retail at the second floor and sunken courts. The office floors are open-plan spaces offering natural daylight and continuous panoramic views in all directions.

1 Pedestrian view of northwest Retail Street
2 Aerial view from northwest with pavilion
3 Tower 2 office lobby core
4 Site plan

Credits: 1 ©Jerry Yin; 2 ©SOHO China; 3 ©Xia Zhi; 4 ©Zaha Hadid Architects

Wangjing SOHO

Location Beijing

Completion Towers 1 & 2: 2013 • Tower 3: 2014

Client SOHO China Co., Ltd

Architect Zaha Hadid Architects

Architect of record CCDI

Structural engineers CABR • CCDI (engineer of record)

MEP engineers Arup • CCDI (engineer of record)

Vertical transportation consultant Arup

Façade engineers Arup • Inhabit Group

Project management consultant SOHO China Co., Ltd

Cost consultant SOHO China Co., Ltd

Landscape architect Ecoland

Lighting consultant Lightdesign

Other consultants Ikonik (wayfinding) • Yonsei University (wind) • EMSI (LEED)

Main contractor CSCEC

Uses Retail: below-grade 10,000 m² (107,639 ft²) [B1/F]; above-grade 40,000 m² (430,556 ft²) [1/F–5/F]

Number of buildings 3 towers, 3 pavilions

Height Tower 1: 118 m (387 ft) • Tower 2: 127 m (417 ft) • Tower 3: 200 m (656 ft) • Pavilions 1 & 2: 15 m (49 ft) • Pavilion 3: 6 m (20 ft)

Above-ground storeys Tower 1: 25 • Tower 2: 26 • Tower 3: 44

Basements Total 4: (1 retail, 3 parking/mechanical floors)

Mechanical levels Tower 1: 6/F, 14/F, 23/F • Tower 2: 6/F, 23/F • Tower 3: 15/F, 29/F, 30/F

Refuge levels Tower 3: 15/F, 29/F, 30/F

Site area 115,393 m² (1,242,080 ft²)

Gross above-ground building area Tower 1: 136,384 m² (1,468,025 ft²) • Tower 2: 125,131 m² (1,346,899 ft²) • Tower 3: 125,307 m² (1,348,793 ft²) • pavilions: 5,443 m² (58,588 ft²)

Gross basement area 129,000 m² (1,388,544 ft²)

Total gross area 521,265 m² (5,610,850 ft²)

Floor area ratio (FAR)/Plot ratio 5

Basic planning module 8.4 m (28 ft)

Total number of elevators 35

Speed of fastest elevators 6 m (20 ft)/s

Elevator brand Fujitech

Number of car parking spaces 1,809

Number of bike parking spaces 8,045

Principal structure materials Steel, concrete

Source: Zaha Hadid Architects

2

3

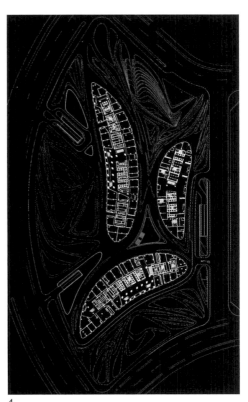

4

l

■ Located in the densest of Hong Kong's neighbourhoods on a site defined by two very different urban contexts, Hysan Place provides a vibrant mix of retail and office spaces that are designed to provide long-term planning flexibility and a synergy between the uses in a form that opens itself to the environment.

The massing of the project is developed as a series of shifting forms, each designed to optimise the internal planning of the uses housed within. These forms are configured to generate vertical gardens over the height of the building, providing multistorey rooftop oases for users and openings for prevailing breezes to pass through the building. Porosity for wind enhances pedestrian comfort at grade and betters the surrounding environment of Causeway Bay beyond the boundary of the site itself.

Sustainable design is fundamental to both the brief and the scheme, resulting in the region's first **LEED Platinum** certified commercial project.

The retail podium accommodates a mix of planning models, with public gathering spaces serving to unify the shopping experience, while providing unique places for activity. Between these two uses sit five semiretail floors that are configured with internal planning flexibility in mind to allow long-term re-use between retail and office functionalities.

l   Close-up of bridge (sky lobby)
2   Aerial view
3   Street view
4   View of retail interiors
5   Typical office floor plan
6   Sky-lobby floor plan
7   Level 7 floor plan
8   Level 4 floor plan
9   Ground floor plan

Photography: 1,2,3 ©Grischa Ruschendorf; 4 ©Tim Griffith

Hysan Place

204 m | 669 ft

Location Hong Kong
Completion 2012
Client Hysan Development Company Limited
Design architect Kohn Pedersen Fox Associates
Executive architect Dennis Lau & Ng Chun Man Architects & Engineers (HK) Ltd
Structural engineer Meinhardt Ltd
MEP engineer Parsons Brickerhoff Asia
Façade engineer ALT Cladding
Landscape architect Urbis
Lighting consultant Lighting Planners Associates
Other consultants Arup (sustainability & LEED) • Davis Langdon & Seah • Shen Milsom Wilke (acoustic) • Graphia Brands (signage) • Benoy (retail interiors)

Main contractor Gammon Construction • Permasteelisa • Gartner
Uses Retail, office
Number of buildings 1
Height 204 m (669 ft)
Above-ground storeys 36
Basements 4
Site area 66,520 m² (716,000 ft²)
Gross above-ground building area 66,511 m² (715,918 ft²)
Number of car parking spaces 86
Principal structure materials Composite

Source: Kohn Pedersen Fox Associates

2

5

6

7

8

9

3

4

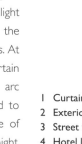

The inspiration for this project comes from the relic discovered in San Xing Dui, Chengdu – the Yu Zhang, known as the **jade ornament**. Combining the relic's culture and shape, the building's design uses a lot of the arcs similar to the jade ornament. Standing at just over 200 metres (656 feet) tall, the building stands comfortably without the hindrance of a podium below. Surrounded by square office blocks, the building height combines with the arcs and curves, making the structure stand out as a magnificent landmark.

The tower comprises offices, hotels and amenities. The building is divided into four main functions, namely five floors of basements, seven floors of lobbies, meeting and conference rooms and restaurants, 24 floors of low- and high-rise office space and 14 floors of five-star hotel rooms. The oval-shape planning, positioned diagonally on the site, provides an unobstructed 180-degree view. The main tower block, together with the New Century building on the west side, creates a harmonious dialogue between the two buildings. The main street, Dongda Avenue (East Avenue), is angled towards the south, enabling the main façade to face the busy downtown, demonstrating a welcoming gesture.

The façade design uses the notion of different planes on the glass curtain walls, which create a light and shadow effect, enhancing the richness in the façade elements. At the same time, the glass curtain walls and steel structure's arc shape of the building are used to strengthen the idea and shape of the jade ornament. During the night, lighting effects enhance the steel structure arc shape of the building, highlighting the unique forms of the building.

1 Curtain wall detail
2 Exterior north view
3 Street view
4 Hotel lobby interior
5 Ground floor plan
6 Office floor plan (high-rise)
7 Hotel lobby floor plan
8 Typical hotel guestrooms floor plan

Photography: ©Ming Lai Architects, Inc.

Minyoun Financial Plaza

206 m | 676 ft

Location Chengdu
Completion 2012
Client Minyoun Group
Architect Ming Lai Architects, Inc.
Associate architect Chengdu Sina Smith Group
Architect of record Ming Chi, Lai
Structural engineer Fanarchi Architectural Design & Consultant Co.
MEP engineer Chengdu Sina Smith Group
Main contractor China Construction Second Engineering Bureau Ltd
Uses Office (8/F–31/F) • hotel (33/F–47/F) • amenities (1/F–7/F) [lobbies, meeting & conference rooms & restaurants]
Number of buildings 1
Height 206 m (676 ft)
Above-ground storeys 47
Basements 5
Mechanical levels B1/F

Refuge levels 16/F, 32/F
Sky-lobby levels 35/F
Site area 6,394.98 m² (68,834 ft²)
Gross above-ground building area 92,773.1 m² (998,601 ft²)
Gross basement area 28,021.7 m² (301,623 ft²)
Total gross area 120,794.8 m² (1,300,224 ft²)
Floor area ratio (FAR)/Plot ratio 14.5
Gross typical floor area 1,891.6 m² (20,361 ft²)
Total number of elevators 21
Speed of fastest elevators 6 m (20 ft)/s
Number of car parking spaces 470
Number of bike parking spaces 215
Hotel brand Minyoun Royal Hotel
Principal structure materials Composite (concrete, steel)
Other materials Low-E glass curtain wall

Source: Ming Lai Architects, Inc.

2

3

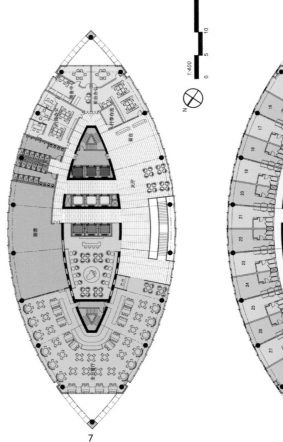

4

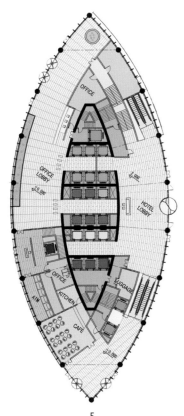

5

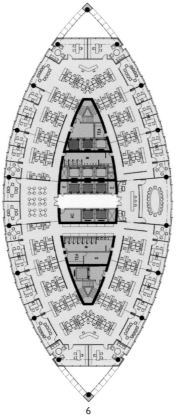

6

7

8

1

■ Xiamen, a southeastern coastal city located approximately halfway between Hong Kong and Shanghai, occupies a large island and surrounding mainland areas. Situated on one of the last waterfront parcels facing Xiamen's historic Gulangyu Island, the Eton Center integrates dense, high-quality residential and hotel development with retail and public amenities.

The site – adjacent to the harbour, the central business district, and the main street leading from the water deep into the city – enjoys tremendous views of the sea and nearby historic Gulangyu Island. The project contains a five-star hotel and ballroom, serviced apartment and retail.

The design connects the site to the surrounding city fabric, a pedestrian-friendly area with narrow streets. In response, porous retail podiums define a recessed central courtyard and onsite public plazas. Two major elements rise vertically above: an 17-storey hotel and a 47-storey, 210-metre-tall (689-foot) serviced apartments tower, both curved as if **carved by water**. The horizontally proportioned, waterfront hotel

maximises sea views; spanning a high breezeway at ground level, it creates a large entry portal for the hotel lobbies and frames views out towards the sea. The curved residential tower, rising slightly inland, also takes advantage of the extraordinary views.

To introduce urban vitality and a sense of place into Xiamen Eton Center, the retail and hotel/ballroom programs are split among the residential and hotel buildings, with pedestrian bridges connecting them. These linkages encourage cross-pollination between the two buildings, as shoppers traverse the central courtyard at grade level, and as hotel guests cross at the 4/F and 5/F into the ballroom and meeting spaces in the residential building. With the pedestrian bridges fully glazed, the movement is apparent to people on the street and the surrounding buildings, lending a sense of dynamism to the public spaces.

Additionally, both buildings feature a 'thick' façade, which, while simple in concept and construction, operates at high levels of climatic and architectural performance: deep extrusions at the edge of each floor plate not only shade the interior from Xiamen's strong sunlight, but also conceal the air-conditioner condenser units. This strong horizontal banding gives the development its unique visual identity and a presence on the Xiamen skyline. At the same time, it provides a clean architectural solution to the perennial challenge of avoiding the visual clutter of mechanical units on the exterior of residential buildings – even as it decreases the load on those units.

1   Bird's-eye view in context
2   View across from waterfront
3   Podium floor plan (1/F)
4   Podium floor plan (6/F)
5   Hotel floor plan (16/F)
6   Residential tower floor plan, high-rise floors
7   Residential tower floor plan, low-rise floors

Renderings: courtesy NBBJ

Xiamen Eton Center

210 m | 689 ft

Location Xiamen
Completion Under construction 2014
Client Eton Properties
Architect NBBJ
Associate architect Architecture Design Institute IPPR (Xiamen) Engineer Co., Ltd
Structural engineer H&J International, PC
MEP engineer J Roger Preston Ltd
Façade engineer ALT Limited
Landscape architect NBBJ
Lighting consultant NBBJ
Other consultants NBBJ (interior design) • EW Cox (BMU) • RWDI (wind tunnel)
Main contractor CSECS Third Engineering Bureau
Uses Residential (serviced apartments), hotel, ballroom, retail
Number of buildings 2

Height Residential tower: 210 m (689 ft) • hotel: 87.3 m (286 ft)
Above-ground storeys Residential tower: 47 • hotel: 17
Basements 4
Mechanical levels 6/F, 18/F, 34/F, roof
Refuge levels 6/F, 18/F, 34/F
Site area 19,480 m² (209,681 ft²)
Gross above-ground building area 139,943 m² (1,506,334 ft²)
Gross basement area 72,866 m² (784,323 ft²)
Total gross area 212,829 m² (2,290,872 ft²)
Floor area ratio (FAR)/Plot ratio 7.2
Gross typical floor area Residential tower: 1,840 m² (19,805 ft²) • hotel: 3,000 m² (32,291 ft²)
Total number of elevators 12
Hotel brand Eton
Principal structure materials Concrete

Source: NBBJ

2

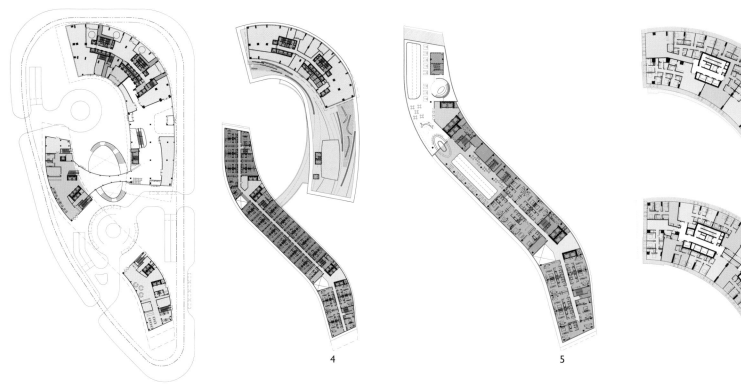

3

4

5

6

7

■ TaiKoo Hui is a landmark mixed-use development situated on a prime location in Tianhe District, Guangzhou, China. The state-of-the-art integrated program includes a retail centre; office towers; a five-star, 287-key Mandarin Oriental Hotel with serviced apartments; a cultural centre; associated ancillary facilities for car parking, loading and unloading docks; mechanical and electrical plants, and equipment; and related management and service facilities. The principle components are connected by an open-air landscaped public plaza, which incorporates a sculpture garden and public access to the cineplex, F&B outlets and entertainment facilities.

The project is connected with subterranean pedestrian tunnels to the Metro 3 train line's underground station, located on Tianhe Road.

The site is organised with the four main buildings (the three towers and the cultural center) located at each corner of the site. The retail area sits at the centre, forming the **kernel** of the development, tying all the components together naturally.

The three towers are placed at angles – orienting themselves to allow clear views, and maximise open space and natural light into the heart of the site. The office towers have shared drop-offs with the retail podium, while the hotel and cultural centre have dedicated drop-offs. The retail podium is accessed via four entrances at the east, south and west, via customised glazed entrances, and to the north by a shared covered drop-off. The covered drop-off provides convenient access to the hotel ballroom and lobby, the cultural center and the basement car parking.

1   Swire office tower (T1) & HSBC bank tower (T2)
2   Overall view from Tianhe Road
3   Typical office floor plan
4   Typical hotel floor plan

Photography: ©Cathy Lee @ Arquitectonica

TaiKoo Hui

212 m | 695 ft

Location Guangzhou

Completion Office: 2011 • retail mall: 2011 • hotel: 2013

Client Swire Properties

Architect Arquitectonica

Associate architect LWK Architects

Architect of record Guangzhou Design Institute

Structural engineer Thornton Tomasetti Engineers

MEP engineer Meinhardt (M&E)

Vertical transportation consultant Meinhardt

Façade engineers Meinhardt Façade Technology • Hugh Dutton Associates (design consultant)

Project management consultant Swire Properties

Cost consultant Davis Langdon & Seah International

Landscape architect ArquitectonicaGEO

Lighting consultant L'Observatoire International

Other consultants Arquitectonica (interior design retail) • Tony Chi (interior design hotel) • Shen Milson & Wilke Ltd (acoustic) • Graphia (graphics & signage) • RWDI (wind tunnel) • The MVA Group (traffic) • Metro Design Institute: 2nd Railway Survey & Design Institute • Guangzhou Design Institute (site survey)

Source: Arquitectonica

Main contractor China State Construction

Uses Retail podium: 129,300 m² (1,391,773 ft²); L3 podium roof level called 'The Garden' • Swire office tower (T1): 99,900 m² (1,075,314 ft²) • HSBC bank tower (T2): 61,100 m² (657,674 ft²) • Mandarin Oriental Hotel & Residences: 61,300 m² (659,827 ft²); 233 rooms, 30 suites & 24 serviced apartments • cultural centre: 60,300 m² (649,063 ft²); 1,000 seats

Number of buildings 5

Height Swire office tower (T1): 212 m (695 ft) • HSBC bank tower (T2): 165 m (541 ft) • Mandarin Oriental Hotel: 128 m (419 ft) • retail podium: 14 m (45 ft) • cultural centre: 58.7 m (192 ft)

Above-ground storeys Swire office tower (T1): 40 • HSBC bank tower (T2): 29 • Mandarin Oriental Hotel: 28 • retail podium: 2 (2 below-grade, 2 above-grade &1 roof level) • cultural centre: 10

Basements 4 (2 retail, 2 parking & MEP)

Mechanical levels On refuge levels & tower top

Refuge levels Swire office tower (T1): 16/F, 29/F • HSBC bank tower (T2): 20/F • Mandarin Oriental Hotel: 5/F, 16/F, 27/F

Sky-lobby levels NIL

Site area 48,954 m² (526,936 ft²)

Gross above-ground building area Swire office tower (T1): 97,700 m² (1,051,634 ft²) • HSBC bank tower (T2): 57,800 m² (622,154 ft²) • Mandarin Oriental Hotel: 53,400 m² (574,792 ft²) • retail podium: 36,900 m² (397,188 ft²) • cultural centre: 41,200 m² (443,473 ft²)

2

Gross basement area 163,700 m² (1,762,052 ft²)

Total gross area 453,300 m² (4,879,280 ft²)

Floor area ratio (FAR)/Plot ratio 9.2

Gross typical floor area Swire office tower (T1): 2,500 m² (26,909 ft²) • HSBC bank tower (T2): 2,250 m² (24,218 ft²) • Mandarin Oriental Hotel: 1,750 m² (18,836 ft²) • cultural centre: 5,800 m² (62,430 ft²)

Basic planning module 1500 curtain wall module

Total number of elevators 75

Number of car parking & motorbike parking spaces 718 spaces + 42 loading docks

Number of parking bike spaces 450

Hotel brand Mandarin Oriental Hotel

Principal structure materials Structure: concrete, steel • exterior walls/cladding: glass, Low-E, metal

3

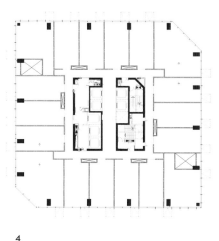

4

1

■ The Xiamen Financial Centre is a 49-storey-high office tower in Xiamen, forming the major group of towers in the new central business district (CBD). The tower's iconic sculptural form was inspired by natural ice formations and its design creates an outstanding and striking image and showcases Gravity's scope for aesthetic experimentation. The folding façades also help to disguise its mass in a tight urban site.

The **glass 'iceberg'** tower has an elevated lobby that takes the occupant to the escalator alongside the civic square on its south and brings them up to second floor, which enjoys direct sea views to the east. With a sky clubhouse on the 15th floor and an observation deck on the top floor, occupants are able to enjoy the panoramic sea views on different levels.

A large sunken plaza on the south of the building next to the civic square brings in natural lighting and ventilation to the basement's shopping arcade. The basement shops and car park have been integrated into a massive underground pedestrian and car park network in the CBD underground. It becomes an important node that connects all the adjoining development and provides convenience pedestrian access to the seashore.

1 Looking up from main entrance
2 Southwest view along the street
3 Typical office floor plan (Zone 2)
4 Lobby floor plan (2/F)
5 Double-column lobby space
6 System of folding surfaces morphs into canopy and elevated lobby structure

Photography & Illustrations: courtesy Gravity Partnership Ltd

Xiamen Financial Centre

Location Xiamen
Completion 2013
Client Xiamen Land Development Company
Architect Gravity Partnership Ltd
Architect of record Xiamen BIAD Architectural Design Ltd
Structural engineer Xiamen BIAD Architectural Design Ltd
MEP engineer Xiamen BIAD Architectural Design Ltd
Façade engineer Arup Façade Engineering
Project management consultant C&D Real Estate Co., Ltd
Cost consultant C&D Real Estate Co., Ltd
Landscape architect Gravity Green Ltd
Lighting consultant BIAD Lighting Design Studio
Main contractor China State Construction Engineering Corporation Ltd
Uses Office: 84,200 m² (906,321 ft²) [1-49/F] • retail: 3,988 m² (42,926 ft²) [B1/F–1/F] • parking: 18,693 m² (61,329 ft²) [B3/F–B1/F]
Number of buildings 1
Height 212.65 m (698 ft)

Above-ground storeys 49
Basements 3
Mechanical levels 4/F, 16/F, 32/F
Refuge levels 16/F, 32/F
Site area 7,876 m² (84,776 ft²)
Gross above-ground building area 89,058 m² (958,612 ft²)
Gross basement area 50,444 m² (542,975 ft²)
Total gross area 139,502 m² (1,501,587 ft²)
Floor area ratio (FAR)/Plot ratio 10.971
Gross typical floor area 1,956 m² (21,054 ft²) [25/F]
Total number of elevators 18
Speed of fastest elevators 6 m (19 ft)/s
Elevator brand Mitsubishi
Number of car parking spaces 260
Principal structure materials Composite of steel & reinforced concrete
Other materials Stone, aluminum, glass

Source: Gravity Partnership Ltd

2

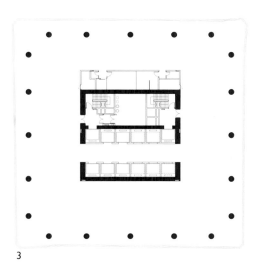

3

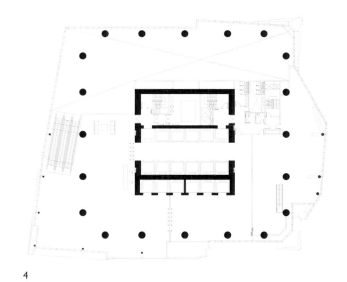

4

5

6

1

Rising in the new development district of the ancient Chinese city of Suzhou, these are the headquarters of the Suzhou Broadcasting System, the city's only broadcaster. The building is a multifacility complex incorporating offices, shops, a hotel, serviced apartments and other amenities.

The city of Suzhou is historically important to China. The design was chosen from an international competition between five companies that best showcased how to pursue the theme of modernity of Suzhou culture. The winning concept features this historical culture in a contemporary fashion, and this project's design aims to embody **creativity and tradition** by using traditional materials and modern motifs.

The main tower, the location of the broadcasting company offices, adopts a modern glass curtain wall. The façade has projecting elements to provide shading and give a sense of scale – the projecting pattern was designed to express the beauty of traditional Suzhou culture.

The hotel is located in the smaller tower. The façade on this tower has a wickerwork pattern of curved, perforated black panels to create a relaxing space for the hotel guests. These black metal panels also reflect the shapes and colours of traditional Suzhou tiles.

Sandwiched between these two opposing buildings is the Media Square, which is covered by a softly curving glass roof. The image of the glass roof is that of traditional Suzhou silk being draped between two rods on either side.

Water and gardens are also highlights of life in Suzhou and the water landscaping around the buildings has been incorporated into waterways and ponds to reflect this bond between a new development and the history of Suzhou.

1 Office building atrium
2 Bird's-eye view
3 Level 1 floor plan
4 Typical floor plan

Renderings: ©Nikken Sekkei

Modern Media Plaza

215 m | 705 ft

Location Suzhou
Completion 2015
Client Suzhou Broadcasting System
Architect Nikken Sekkei Ltd
Structural & MEP engineers Nikken Sekkei
Façade engineer ShenYang YuanDa Enterprise Group
Project management consultant Savills Plc
Cost consultant Shanghai Shen Yuan engineering Cci Capital Ltd
Landscape architect Suzhou Industrial Park Design & Research Institute Co., Ltd
Lighting consultant Leuchte Lighting Consultants
Other consultants Asiantime Beyond Design Consultant Co, Ltd (outdoor signage design)
Main contractor Zhongyifeng Construction Group Co, Ltd
Uses Office, hotel, media studio, commercial, retail
Number of buildings 2 (twin towers)
Height Office: 214.8 m (705 ft) • hotel: 164.9 m (541 ft)
Above-ground storeys Office: 42 + PHF • hotel: 38
Basements 3

Mechanical levels Office: 17/F, 31/F, PH/F • hotel: 8/F, 23/F
Refuge levels Office: 17/F, 31/F • hotel: 8/F, 23/F
Sky-lobby levels 42/F (in the office building)
Site area 37,749 m² (406,327 ft²)
Gross above-ground building area Office: 91,935 m² (989,580 ft²) • hotel: 71,724 m² (772,031 ft²) • media studio: 41,637 m² (448,177 ft²) • commercial: 9,301 m² (100,115 ft²) • retail: 2,180 m² (23,465 ft²)
Gross basement area 106,948 m² (1,151,179 ft²)
Total gross area 323,724 m² (3,484,536 ft²)
Gross typical floor area Office 2,345 m² (25,241 ft²) • hotel: 1,757 m² (18,912 ft²)
Total number of elevators Office: 24 • hotel: 18
Speed of fastest elevators Office: 240 m (787 ft)/min • hotel: 150 m (492 ft)/min
Elevator brand KONE
Number of car/bike parking spaces 1,374+14/1,600
Hotel brand Hilton Hotel
Residence service brand DoubleTree by Hilton
Principal structure materials Steel reinforced concrete

Source: Nikken Sekkei Ltd

2

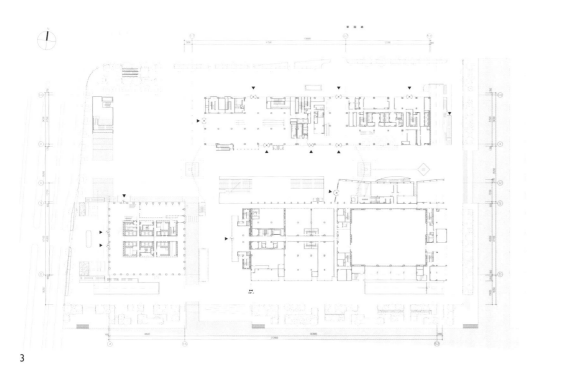

3

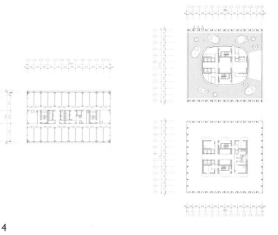

4

■ This project has added two 49-storey-high office towers to the historic Shanghai Shipyard Site. The Agricultural Bank of China and China Construction Bank will set their headquarters in the new towers at the Riviera TwinStar Square. The design of the office towers forms a gateway in the shape of a ship that is aligning with the axis of a slipway, and leads to Celebration Park on the waterfront. The spectacular site fronts the Huangpu River and the historic Bund, and the slipway will be restored for use as a new museum.

The development also includes the Mandarin Oriental Hotel, Spa & Residences. The hotel will be Mandarin's flagship in Shanghai, with an 18-storey tower of 362 rooms and a world-class spa. The Mandarin Oriental Residences is an adjacent 18-storey tower of luxury residences to be serviced by the hotel.

The project is occupied by two very different types of businesses, an investment company and a hotel, so the design is for the symmetrical towers to be about balance, order, and stability – the buildings' interdependence sends the message of mutual union and respect for each business.

Two stone and glass towers rise in tandem, forming a gateway to the Huangpu River. As they face each other, their façades curve dramatically to form an imaginary space that frames the skies and the city skyline. Their **nautical symmetry** will convey memories of the ships that were once launched from the now relocated Shanghai Shipyards. The Mandarin Oriental Hotel, Spa & Residences are in a companion pair of smaller glass towers that rise on adjacent land closer to the river. Their transparency and undulating forms recall the waves generated by the ships and complement the overall composition. The towers were designed to glow from within with a special lighting scheme for the inner curves at the centre to be lit to emphasise the distinctive shape and monumental scale of the space.

The hotel and serviced apartments are quite different. Intentionally, they're more dynamic in contrast with the static, stable composition of the offices. The buildings simulate junk sails or even waves: one curves up and the other down, avoiding symmetry. They are not aligned but instead are at angles to each other, and they are glassy, transparent and suspended off the ground, compared with the more solidly anchored stone and glass expression of the offices. Their curvatures are horizontal in profile, contrasting with the vertical curves of the offices. The contrast is intentional: two different uses, two different scales.

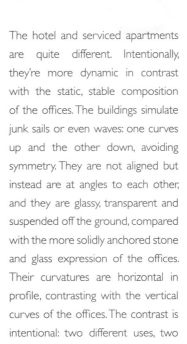

1 Close-up of façade, Riviera TwinStar Square
2 Overall view of north façade, Riviera TwinStar Square
3 Overall view from the Bund
4 Lobby, Mandarin Oriental Hotel
5 Building entry, Riviera TwinStar Square
6 Ground floor plan

Credits: 1,2,3,5 ©Rogan Coles; 4 courtesy Mandarin Oriental Hotel Group

Riviera TwinStar Square and Mandarin Oriental Pudong Shanghai

216 m | 708 ft

Location Shanghai

Completion Office: 2011 • hotel: 2013

Client Shanghai Rui Ming Real Estate Company [Joint venture between CITIC Pacific Limited and China State Shipbuilding Corporation (CSSC)]

Architect Arquitectonica

Architect of record East China Architectural Design & Research Institution (ECADI)

Structural engineer Arup

MEP engineers J. Roger Preston • Parsons Brinckerhoff

Vertical transportation consultants J. Roger Preston • Parsons Brinckerhoff

Project management consultant Shanghai Rui Ming

Landscape architect Belt Collins

Lighting consultants Brandston Partnership • Light Directions

Other consultants ECADI (civil) • Campbell Shillinglaw Lau (acoustic) • Shanghai Point High-rise Equipment (building maintenance) • Arup (curtain wall) • Belt Collins (fountains/water features) • Graphia (graphics & signage) • Shanghai Urban Planning & Design Institute (traffic) • Shanghai Tongji University (wind tunnel)

Main contractor Shanghai Construction (Group) General Co.

Uses Offices (both towers): 200,000 m² (2,152,782 ft²) • Mandarin Oriental Hotel & Residences: 110,000 m² (1,184,030 ft²)

Number of buildings 4

Height Office tower 1: 216 m (708 ft) • office tower 2: 216 m (708 ft) • Mandarin Oriental Hotel, tower 1: 77 m (252 ft) • Mandarin Oriental Residences, tower 2: 75 m (246 ft)

Above-ground storeys Office tower 1: 49 storeys • office tower 2: 49 storeys • Mandarin Oriental Hotel, tower 1: 21 storeys • Mandarin Oriental Residences, tower 2: 19 storeys

Basements Office tower 1: 4 below-grade levels • office tower 2: 4 below-grade levels

Mechanical levels Office towers: 16/F, 17/F, 33/F, 34/F • Mandarin Oriental Hotel, tower 1: between 2/F & 3/F • Mandarin Oriental Residences, tower 2: between 2/F & 3/F

Refuge levels Office tower: 16/F, 33/F

Site area Total 42,440 m² (456,820 ft²) • office: 26,290 m² (282,983 ft²) • hotel & residences: 16,150 m² (173,837 ft²)

Gross above-ground building area Office tower 1: 100,000 m² (1,076,391 ft²) • office tower 2: 100,000 m² (1,076,391 ft²) • Mandarin Oriental Hotel & Residences: 110,000 m² (1,184,030 ft²)

Source: Arquitectonica

2

3

4

5

Gross basement area Office towers: 91,086 m² (980,441 ft²) • hotel & residences: 47,613 m² (512,502 ft²)

Floor area ratio (FAR)/Plot ratio Office towers: 28.7 • hotel & residences: 17.67

Gross typical floor area Office towers: 2,090–2,405 m² (22,496–25,887 ft²) • hotel: 1,547 m² (16,651 ft²) • residences: 1,215 m² (13,078 ft²)

Total number of elevators Office tower 1: 22 • office tower 2: 22 • hotel: 8 • residences: 6

Speed of fastest elevators 6 m (19 ft)/s

Elevator brand Hitachi

Number of car parking spaces Offices: 1,003 • hotel & residences: 319

Number of bike parking spaces Offices: 2,500 • hotel & residences: 450

Hotel brand Mandarin Oriental Hotel Group

Residence service brand Mandarin Oriental Hotel Group

Principal structure materials : Structure: reinforced concrete • exterior walls: glass curtain wall with stone frame • interiors: stone, glass, stainless steel

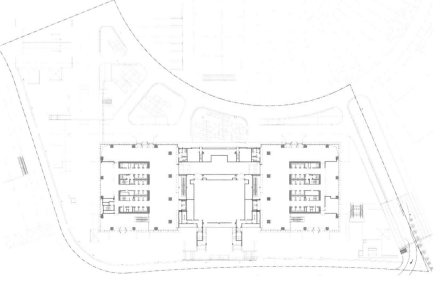

6

1

The skyscraper has evolved as an economically efficient way to provide flexible, functional and well-illuminated workspaces for dense populations of professionals. Since the early 20th century, however, air conditioning and electric lighting have served as modern solutions to increasing demand without giving thought to environmental consequences or energy shortages. Today the skyscraper needs to evolve into a new sustainable species. It must retain highly developed qualities such as flexibility, daylight, views, density and general usability while exercising new and untested attributes.

Seen from the city, the Shenzhen Energy Headquarters structure will appear as a classic shape with an **organic pattern**. A folded curtain wall shades the building from the sun and creates a comfortable interior climate. The folds create special niches and unique spaces inside the office floors as well as on street level around the building. The traditional curtain wall glass façade has a low insulation level and leaves offices overheated by direct sunlight.

The result, excessive air-conditioning consumption as well as the need for a heavy glass coating that makes the view seem permanently dull and grey. By combining maximum daylight exposure with minimal sunshine exposure and using integrated ways of limiting the need for cooling, the Shenzhen Energy Headquarters serve as a model for the 21st-century skyscraper and energy headquarters.

1   Overall view
2   Modified curtain wall
3   Aerial view
4   Staff activity floor plan (5/F)

Renderings: ©BIG – Bjarke Ingels Group / Glessner Group; illustration: ©BIG – Bjarke Ingels Group

Shenzhen Energy Headquarters

218 m | 715 ft

Location Shenzhen

Completion Under construction

Client Shenzhen Energy Company

Architect BIG

Other consultants Arup • Transsolar • SADI Shenzhen • Front • MOCAPE • SED • Aurecon • KMZM

Use Office, retail, conference, dining, gardens

Number of buildings 2

Height Large tower: 218 m (715 ft) • small tower: 116 m (381 ft)

Above-ground storeys Large tower: 44 • small tower: 20

Site area 142,000 m² (1,528,475 ft²)

Total gross area 96,000 m² (1,033,335 ft²)

Principal structure materials Concrete main structure, aluminium, glass façade

Source: BIG

2

3

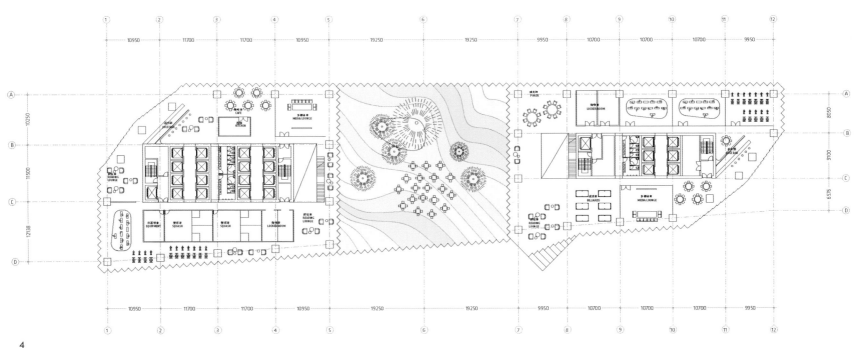

4

The building masses are located with open views to the sea from the sites behind, so that each building shares the beautiful surrounding natural resources. The commercial towers are dispersed so that there are interesting outdoor spaces of different scale and function, yet they still form a pedestrian network in-between the building masses which connect to the coastline.

■ The C&D complex consists of a 49-storey main office tower, the headquarters of the C&D group, and commercial blocks of high-end retail stores. The complex is in a prominent seashore landmark location of the future CBD of Xiamen, with panoramic views over the coastline.

The central plaza opens to an entrance to the sunken retail arcade, bringing in natural light and ventilation to the vast underground pedestrian network. This multilevel pedestrian network also doubles as an axis for the site, dissecting the 200-metre-long (656-foot) site into a readable, accessible size.

The multi-faceted building façade breaks from the traditional, regular rectangular form. By tapering at both ends, the towers' **sculptural forms** and verticality are exaggerated while leaving more open space at street level. The 'diamond-like' form reflects the client's strong corporate identity, yet an efficient and rectilinear office space remains.

The project creates an anchor point for the pedestrian network system in the new CBD and welds to the surrounding buildings in urban scale.

1   Close-up of façade
2   Street view from northeast
3   Main lobby
4   Internal street view
5   Typical office plan
6   Tower section

Photography & illustrations: courtesy Gravity Partnership Ltd

C&D International Tower

219 m | 719 ft

Location Xiamen
Completion 2013
Client Xiamen C&D Corporation Ltd
Architect Gravity Partnership Ltd
Architect of record Shanghai Institute of Architectural Design & Research Co., Ltd
Structural engineer Shanghai Institute of Architectural Design & Research Co., Ltd
MEP engineer Shanghai Institute of Architectural Design & Research Co., Ltd
Façade engineer Arup Façade
Project management consultant Xiamen C&D Real Estate Co., Ltd
Cost consultant Xiamen C&D Real Estate Co., Ltd
Landscape architect Gravity Green Ltd
Lighting consultant Brandston Partnership Inc.
Interiors consultant HASSELL
Main contractor China Construction Third Engineering Bureau Corp. Ltd
Uses Retail 45,435 m² (489,058 ft²) [B1-8/F] • office 81,338 m² (875,514 ft²)[1-49/F]
Number of buildings 4

Above-ground storeys 49
Height 219.4 m (| 719.8 ft)
Basements 3
Mechanical levels 15/F, 31/F, 48/F
Refuge levels 15/F, 31/F, 48/F
Site area 21,748 m² (234,093 ft²)
Gross above-ground building area 126,395 m² (1,360,504 ft²)
Gross basement area 54,500 m² (586,633 ft²)
Total gross area 180,895 m² (1,947,137 ft²)
Floor area ratio (FAR)/Plot ratio 5.63
Gross typical floor area 1,932 m² (20,795 ft²) [25/F]
Total number of elevators 16
Speed of fastest elevators 6 m (19.7 ft)/sec
Elevator brand Mitsubishi
Number of car parking spaces 918
Principal structure materials Composite of steel and reinforced concrete

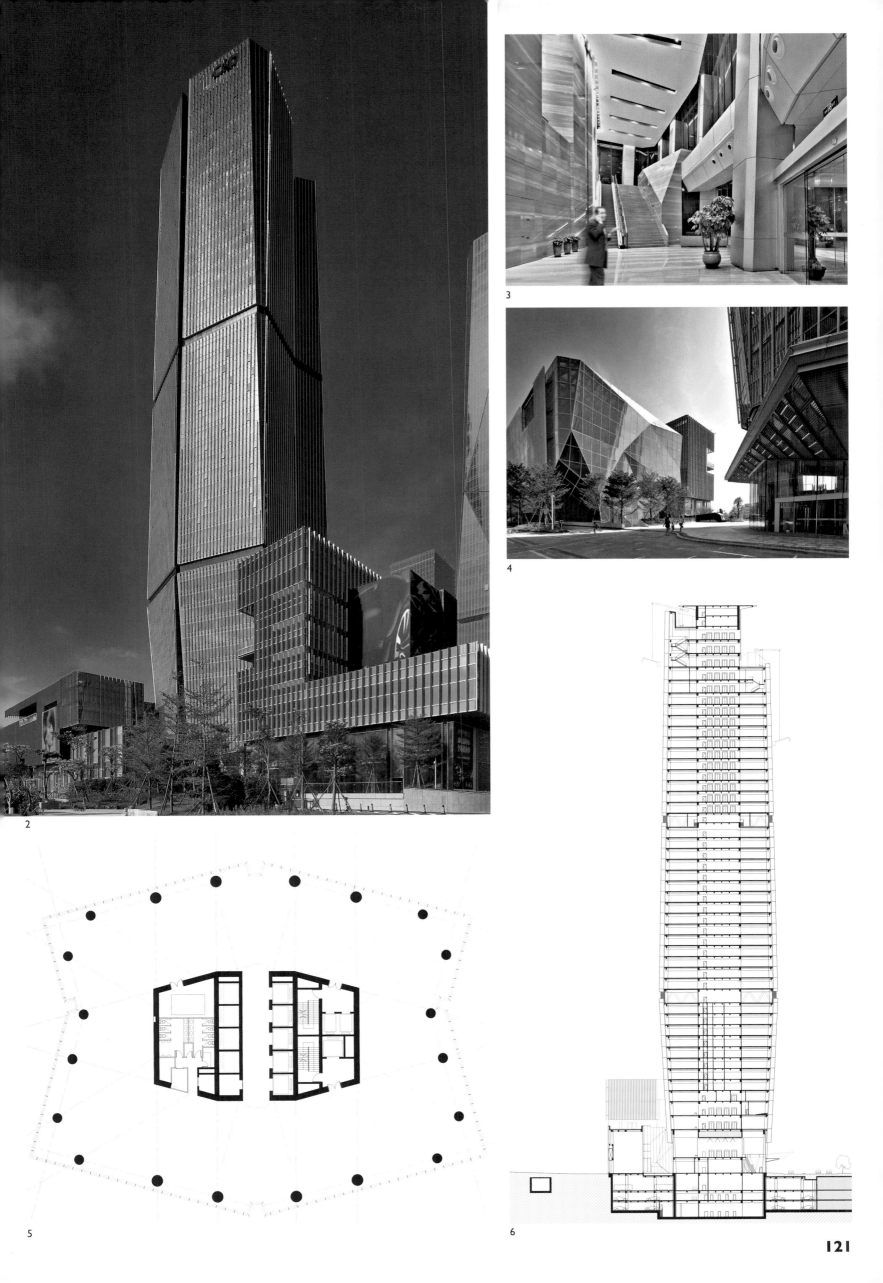

2

3

4

5

6

1

■ One City is a vibrant urban centre between the mountains and the waterfront of Yantian, the seaside district of the bustling city of Shenzhen. This mixed-use development is set in a large park and will include residential buildings in a variety of scales, office towers, a hotel and retail. With easy access to mass transit, One City promotes **car-free living** in a green, resort-like environment.

PCPA designed seven towers for One City, including its signature mixed-use tower, the tallest in the development. The buildings and public spaces of One City are arranged along a linear park that runs from the bay to a large plaza adjacent to Yantian's cultural centre and government centre. Towers are placed to take advantage of views to the bay and Hong Kong Islands.

Sheathed in lightly reflective glass, the 51-storey signature tower is taller and more formally expressed than its neighbours. Vertical elements of the curtain wall – aluminium mullions with a pearlescent white finish – project at the ground level to form the entrance. This seamless canopy leads to a double-height lobby clad in frosted glass. The tower will include a 300-room Hyatt hotel, offices and retail.

The residential towers, service apartment towers and SoHo townhouses of One City share an architectural language to unify the development and provide a background for the signature tower. The other buildings have curving glass façades and wave-like aluminium sunshades. Terraces, roof gardens and balconies bring residents outdoors to enjoy cool breezes from the bay.

The SoHo townhouses frame the pair of residential towers, 30 and 35 storeys tall. A landscaped plinth that includes pools and small pavilions links the townhouses and the residential towers.

1 Overall view in context
2 Aerial view of signature tower
3 Typical office floor plan
4 Typical hotel floor plan

Photography & illustrations: ©Pelli Clarke Pelli Architects

One City

220 m | 722 ft

Location Shenzhen
Completion 2017
Client Vanke Real Estate Co., Ltd (Shenzhen)
Architect Pelli Clarke Pelli Architects
Associate architect HS Architects
Structural engineer HS Architects
MEP engineers HS Architects • Parsons Brinckerhoff
Vertical transportation consultant Parsons Brinckerhoff
Façade engineer ECO Building Façade Technologies Ltd
Landscape architects AECOM • Design Workshop
Lighting consultant LDPI
Uses Hotel, office, residential, retail

Number of buildings 8
Height 219.9 m (722 ft)
Above-ground storeys Total: 51 (office: 7/F–28/F • hotel: 30/F–48/F)
Basements 2
Mechanical & refuge levels 16/F, 29/F, 33/F
Sky-lobby levels 31/F
Site area 137,600 m² (1,481,114 ft²)
Gross above-ground building area Hotel: 55,000 m² (592,015 ft²)
Total gross area 345,370 m² (3,717,531 ft²)
Principal structure materials Concrete

Source: Pelli Clarke Pelli Architects

2

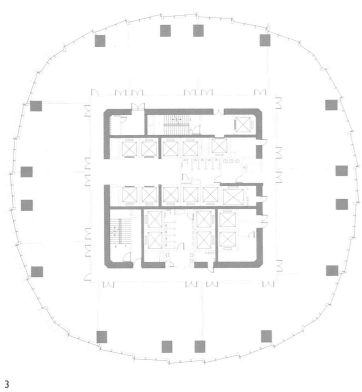

3

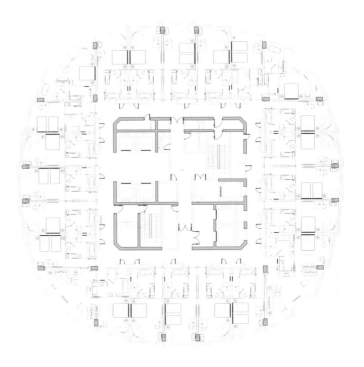

4

123

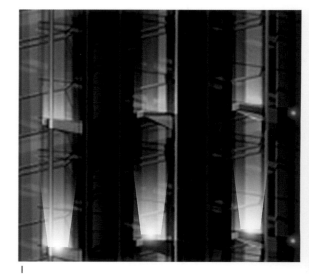

1

■ This project is located south of Hong Kong Road, north of Haifeng Road, east of the Golden Square, and west of the Equatorial Convention Centre. It is 500 metres (1,640 ft) from the Shinan government district, only 500 metres (1,640 ft) from the southwest side of 'Wusi Square', in the heart of Qingdao's central business district.

Coming into the 21st century, Qingdao saw rapid urban development, and one of the city's highlights was the 2008 Olympic Games' sailing competition. On this occasion, Qingdao needed to show its charm and style to the world and we were tasked to build a landmark building to demonstrate the city as a **sailing capital**.

The building's design follows two major themes. The first is its distinctive architectural characteristics: the main building is presented as a beautiful sail of Qingdao, to greet the arrival of the 2008 Olympic Games' sailing competition – a curved building form pointing to the blue sea, making a vivid sailing image. The façade is constructed with metal frame and glass; it's simple and makes a strong, contemporary statement. The second major theme follows technological and ecological aspects by the application of high-tech materials and eco-technologies to create a highly efficient and pleasant human habitation; a work space where it is easy to both work and rest. By scattering green eco-spaces throughout the building, a comfortable internal microclimate is created, making it a perfect combination of natural ecology and building technology.

1 Glass curtain wall with light
2 Overall view showing the building's curved façade
3 Overall view of the structure's curved, sail-like characteristics
4 Typical office floor plan
5 Site plan

Renderings & photography: courtesy C.Y. Lee & Partners Architects/Planners

Farglory International Plaza

223 m | 732 ft

Location Qingdao
Completion 2011
Client Farglory Group
Architects C.Y. Lee & Partners Architects/Planners • Dayuan Architecture Design Consulting (Shanghai)
Associate architect LDI
Structural engineer LDI
MEP engineer LDI
Vertical transportation consultants C.Y. Lee & Partners Architects/Planners • Dayuan Architecture Design Consulting (Shanghai)
Façade engineers C.Y. Lee & Partners Architects/Planners • Dayuan Architecture Design Consulting (Shanghai)
Project management consultant Farglory Group
Cost consultant Farglory Group
Landscape architects C.Y. Lee & Partners Architects/Planners • Dayuan Architecture Design Consulting (Shanghai)
Uses Multipurpose podium, office, residential, hotel

Number of buildings 1
Height 223 m (732 ft)
Above-ground storeys 42
Basements 5
Mechanical levels B1/F, 15/F, 27/F
Refuge levels 15/F, 27/F
Site area 13,414.2 m² (144,389 ft²)
Gross above-ground building area 96,084 m² (1,034,239 ft²)
Gross basement area 42,405 m² (456,443 ft²)
Total gross area 138,489 m² (1,490,683 ft²)
Floor area ratio (FAR)/Plot ratio 7.16
Gross typical floor area 1,836.3 m² (19,765 ft²)
Total number of elevators 21
Speed of fastest elevators 8 m (26 ft)/s
Number of car parking spaces 907
Principal structure materials Structural steel, glass curtain

Source: C.Y. Lee & Partners Architects/Planners

2

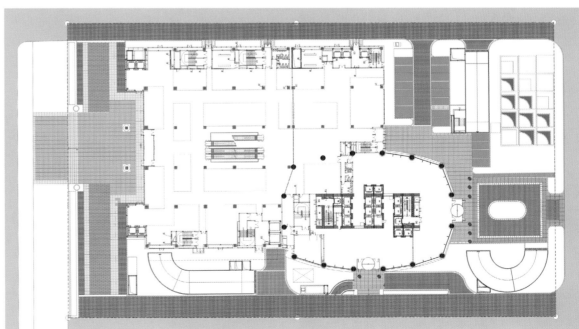

3

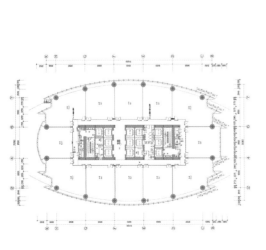

4

5

I

Shanghai's Hongkou district is located across the Huangpu and Suzhou Rivers and across from the skyscrapers of the Lujiazui district. If Lujiazui is interpreted as the 'modern' quarter of the city then Hongkou can be seen as a 'historic' quarter. Indeed, with its many historic buildings and traditional markets, Hongkou preserves a rich historical context.

Nikken Sekkei sought to build in this historic part of the city, not in the historic style, but with a modern 228-metre-high (748-foot-high) skyscraper and low-rise commercial building complex. 'Modernity' should not be reduced to the antithesis of 'history'. In a district like Lujiazui where the entire urban environment that surrounds it is new, structures built as the antithesis of 'history' could be made to work

well, and in fact can be an attraction, distinguishing the character of the **urban fabric** from other parts of the city. But to build modern structures amid the historical context as a simplistic, confrontational contrast to history would put up barriers and isolate the two from each other. Such actions result in discontinuities, yet are a method often employed in large-scale development projects. Instead, this design embraces Hongkou's history, townscape, and idiosyncrasies, seeking to create a seamless urban fabric responsive to changing times, in which history and modernity are sometimes set in harmony, sometimes in pleasant contrast.

In creating the low-rise commercial spaces, the concept interpreted in modern terms the traditional neighbourhood lanes (lilong) running among old apartment houses and came up with clustered forms composed of divided volumes with an elaborate three-dimensional network of lanes in various hierarchies. The high-rise office space has natural ventilation openings in its glazing and features the abstraction of traditional townscape scale despite its high-rise structure.

1   Close-up view of exterior with ventilation devices
2   View of lower level from street
3   Overview
4   View at night
5   Ground floor plan
6   Typical floor plan

Credits: 1,3,4 ©Nacasa & Partners Inc;
2 ©Nishikawa advertisement photograph office

CITIC Plaza

228 m | 748 ft

Location Shanghai
Completion 2010
Client HiTime Corporation
Architect Nikken Sekkei Ltd
Architects of record Shanghai Institute of Architectural Design & Research • Shanghai Mingkong International Design Co., Ltd
Structural & MEP engineers Nikken Sekkei
Landscape architects Studio Correnttori • Inc. A-I-SHA Architects
Lighting consultant A-I-SHA Architects
Main contractor Shanghai No.4 Construction Company Limited Company
Uses Office (tower) • retail (podium)
Number of buildings I tower + retail podium
Height 228 m (748 ft)
Above-ground storeys 47 + 2 penthouses

Basements 3
Mechanical levels 16/F, 27/F, 38/F
Refuge levels 16/F, 27/F, 38/F
Site area 15,535 m² (167,217 ft²)
Gross above-ground building area 10,131 m² (109,049 ft²)
Gross basement area 37,876 m² (407,694 ft²)
Total gross area 137,996 m² (1,485,376 ft²)
Floor area ratio (FAR)/Plot ratio 6.44
Gross typical floor area 2,098 m² (22,582 ft²)
Basic planning module 1.5 m (4.9 ft)
Total number of elevators 22 (tower)
Number of car parking spaces 330
Principal structure materials Steel framing & concrete core for tower; podium is a mix of reinforced concrete & steel

Source: Nikken Sekkei Ltd

2

3

4

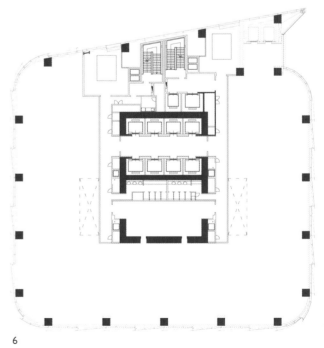

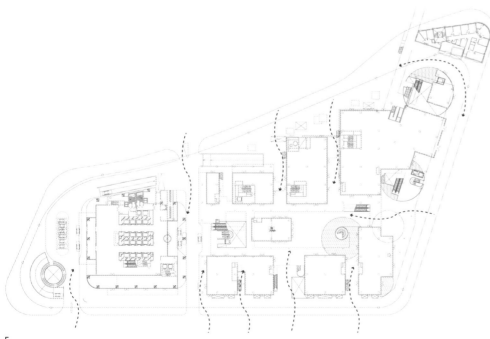

5

6

700 m

600 m

500 m

■ The site enjoys both the southwest views towards the urban green zone of Beijing and the northeast views towards Da Wang Jing Park. Since the site is surrounded by green space, the design concept is to incorporate the green area into a first-class commercial environment. It aims to provide an architectural space that consists of commercial and leisure facilities.

400 m

The site consists of three plots, located at the intersection of the Airport Expressway and Fifth Ring Road of Beijing; it's the main gateway connecting Beijing downtown and the airport. With its **organic design**, the project would become a new landmark of the Da Wang Jing area and Beijing. The high-end business environment – with a consistent design in terms of massing, form and space across the site – aims to enhance the city's new look.

300 m

The design also focuses on the integration of green area, urban space and internal connection between the three plots. The dynamic massing strategy enhances the circulation flow in and out of the site. The openness between the buildings acts as urban open spaces penetrating through the architecture. The dynamic form connects and merges the architecture, urban space and public space. The unique design contributes to the better city space for Beijing.

1 Plaza area
2 Aerial view
3 Meirui office ground floor plan
4 Meirui office floor plan (10/F)
5 Kuntai serviced apartment floor plan (42/F–51/F)
6 Kuntai serviced apartment floor plan (3/F–12F)

Renderings: courtesy Aedas

Da Wang Jing Plot #2

228 m | 748 ft

200 m

Location Beijing
Completion 2015
Client Beijing Qianjing Real Estate Development Co., Ltd
Architect Andrew Bromberg of Aedas
Local design institute China Building Technique Group Co., Ltd
Structural engineer Arup
MEP engineer Parsons Brinckerhoff
Vertical transportation consultant MVA
Façade engineer Inhabit, Schmidlin
Cost consultant WT Partnership
Lighting consultant ADCAS
Uses Offices, serviced apartments, exhibition centre
Number of buildings 6 (5 towers and 1 exhibition centre)

100 m

Height Meirui offices: 217.15 m (712 ft) • AVIC offices: 219 m (718 ft) • Kuntai offices: 155.5 m (510 ft) • Kuntai serviced apartments: 228 m (748 ft) • Kaifei offices: 169.7 m (556 ft) • Kuntai exhibition centre: 24 m (78 ft)
Above-ground storeys Meirui offices: 42 • AVIC offices: 44 • Kuntai offices: 32 • Kuntai serviced apartments: 55 • Kaifei offices: 37 • Kuntai exhibition centre: 3

Basements 5
Mechanical levels 42/F, 32/F, 55/F
Refuge levels 13/F, 27/F, 16/F, 32/F, 15/F, 27/F, 41/F, 22/F
Sky-lobby levels 10/F, 24/F, 36/F
Site area Total 305,509.98 m² (3,288,482 ft²); consists of 3 plots: 618#: 29,866.1 m² (321,476 ft²) • 623#: 10,301.9 m² (110,888 ft²) • 626#: 22,563.5 m² (242,871 ft²)
Gross above-ground building area Total 391,878 m² (4,218,139 ft²) • Meirui office: 80,000 m² (861,112 ft²) • AVIC offices: 91,482 m² (984,704 ft²) • Kuntai offices: 53,000 m² (570,487 ft²) • Kuntai serviced apartments: 76,109 m² (819,230 ft²) • Kaifei offices: 80,000 m² (861,112 ft²) • Kuntai exhibition centre: 11,333 m² (121,987 ft²)
Gross basement area 180,000 m² (1,937,503 ft²)
Total gross area 571,878 m² (6,155,643 ft²)
Height 228 m (748 ft)
Floor area ratio (FAR)/Plot ratio 618# 7 • 623# 1.1 • 626# 7.6
Gross typical floor area Offices: 3,623 m² (38,997 ft²) • serviced apartments: 1,422 m² (15,306 ft²)
Total number of elevators 45
Speed of fastest elevators 7 m (23 ft)/s
Number of car/bike parking spaces 1508/1300
Principal structure materials Concrete, steel

Source: Aedas

2

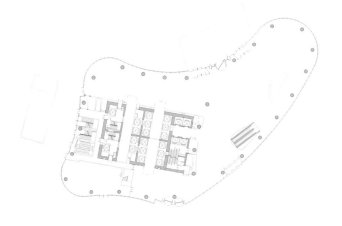

3

4

5

6

1

The former Shanghai Longhua Airport along the main river in Shanghai was in use until the middle of the 20th century. The area is now being redeveloped as a twin tower scheme. The twin towers besides the old runway are to form an imaginary gate and comprise a **wind-oriented design**. The design started in 2009 and is to be completed in 2016.

During the design phase it had been noted that all runways in Shanghai are oriented in parallel directions. The reason is simple: during landing and take-off a plane is most stable when it flies with or against a head wind, thus these runways were oriented in the direction of the prevailing winds of Shanghai. Importantly, the project includes an airline company office, as well as pilot simulation and training facilities.

In the course of working through the history and geography of this area, it was decided that the prevailing southeasterly wind should be made the key planning philosophy.

The twin towers are designed by modelling two phoenix birds as the motif, varying each tower's height to avoid uniformity. Such asymmetrical composition may be compared to Oriental beauty, as typified by calligraphy and the art of flower arrangement. This sense of beauty coincides with the site's correlation with the river and distance views from the towers. Likewise, in each tower a plural number of planes form the crest in a wrapping way. This configuration is also analysed

with engineering technologies and fed back to the configuration from the viewpoints of wind and structural dynamics. The towers soar above the other two low-rise buildings. At their base, the tower façade opens up as if opening their wings. The façade flows over the tower podium creating a rich half-open space. In this way, the wind simultaneously directs the form of the design, and the design helps to direct the wind to follow the tower's forms.

1 View through to tower podium
2 Overview from the southeast
3 Bird's-eye view in context
4 Tower W floor plan (20/F)
5 Tower X floor plan (20/F)

Renderings & Illustrations: ©Nikken Sekkei Ltd

Longhua Twin Towers

231 m | 758 ft

Location Shanghai
Completion 2016
Client Shanghai Longhua Airport Group Company
Architect Nikken Sekkei Ltd
Architect of record SIADR
Structural engineer Nikken Sekkei Ltd
MEP engineer Nikken Sekkei Ltd
Main contractors Tower W: Shanghai Construction No7 • Tower X: China Construction Company
Uses Tower W: retail (-1/F); conference hall (1/F–3/F); office (4/F–36/F); hotel (38/F–52/F) • Tower X: retail (-1/F–3/F); office (4/F–39/F) • low-rise towers (a): aviation government office; (b) retail (-1/F–8/F)
Number of buildings 4: 2 towers + 2 low-rise
Height Tower W: 231 m (758 ft) • Tower X: 200 m (656 ft) • low-rise towers (a) 75 m (246 ft); (b) 55 m (18 ft)
Above-ground storeys Tower W: 52 • Tower X: 39 • low-rise towers: (a) 15; (b) 8

Basements 3
Mechanical levels Tower W: 5/F, 21/F, 37F • Tower X: 14/F, 24/F
Sky-lobby levels Tower W: 50/F • Tower X: 39/F
Site area 72,209 m² (777,251 ft²)
Gross above-ground building area Tower W: 179,105 m² (1,927,870 ft²) • Tower X 139,640 m² (1,503,072 ft²)
Gross basement area 194,407 m² (2,092,580 ft²)
Total gross area 513,152 m² (5,523,522 ft²)
Gross typical floor area 2,400 m² (25,833 ft²)
Basic planning module 9.6 m (31.5 ft)
Elevator brand Various
Number of car parking spaces 2,750
Number of motorbike & bike parking spaces 5,000
Hotel brand Rocco Forte Hotel Group (UK)
Principal structure materials Steel reinforced concrete
Other materials Steel (for skirt skin of towers)

Source: Nikken Sekkei Ltd

2

3

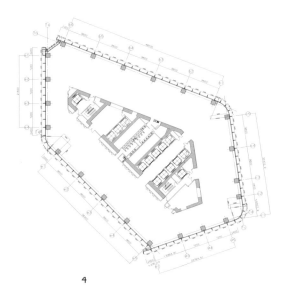

4

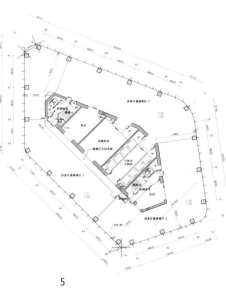

5

1

The faceted form of Kingtown International Tower (KIC) is an evolution of integrated architectural, structural, and mechanical systems. **Diagonal braces** that wrap the tower from top to base define the external envelope; reductions in structural materials achieved through this system were on the order of 20 percent. The envelope is coupled with a second, internal glass façade, creating an integrated cavity that contains the diagonal structure. The cavity space, vented to the outside, helps the tower to respond to the extreme heat of Nanjing's 'stove city' environment by establishing a thermally insulating buffer zone around all conditioned spaces. Further cavity wall performance benefits include improved HVAC system performance, lower MEP systems first costs and lower MEP optimisation costs, and increased daylighting and better comfort and acoustics in interior spaces.

Inside, a system of translucent and opaque screens focuses light down a 27-storey atrium, defining a glowing room that is the hallmark of the hotel experience. Glass balconies, placed periodically within the cavity, provide a desirable amenity to upgraded rooms. The project also includes a small retail component and an innovative housing form, characterised by skip/stop access, thru block units and operable sunshades that provide privacy and solar control.

1   Close-up of faceted exterior form
2   Overall view of intergrated cavity wall–braced tower
3   View of interior of 27-storey-high atrium
4   Diagram showing air movement
5   Setting at base of tower
6   Axonometric diagram
7   Typical hotel floor plan

Photography: ©Tim Griffith
Illustrations: ©SOM

Kingtown International Tower (KIC)

232 m | 761 ft

Location Nanjing
Completion 2014
Client Jiangsu Golden Land Real Estate Development Co., Ltd
Architect Skidmore, Owings & Merrill LLP (SOM)
Architect of record Nanjing Design Institute
Structural engineer SOM
MEP engineer WSP
Vertical transportation consultant Edgett Williams (escalators & elevators)
Project management consultant SOM
Landscape architect SWA
Lighting consultant Brandston Partnership, Inc.
Other consultants CS Caulking Co. Inc (exterior maintenance) • CMS Collaborative (water feature) • Charles Group (retail)
Main contractor Wuhan Construction Engineering Group Co., Ltd (Nanjing)
Uses Hotel: 40,000 m² (430,556 ft²) • office: 50,000 m² (538,195 ft²) • retail (in podium): 52,400 m² (564,029 ft²) • residential (in podium): 20,200 m² (217,431 ft²)
Number of buildings I
Height 232 m (761 ft)

Source: Skidmore, Owings & Merrill LLP (SOM)

Above-ground storeys 56
Basements 2
Mechanical levels 28/F, 29/F
Refuge levels 29/F
Sky-lobby levels 32/F (hotel)
Site area 24,500 m² (263,716 ft²)
Gross above-ground building area 168,000 m² (1,808,337 ft²)
Gross basement area 52,000 m² (559,723 ft²)
Total gross area 220,000 m² (2,368,060 ft²)
Floor area ratio (FAR)/Plot ratio 6.0
Gross typical floor area 1,840 m² (19,806 ft²)
Basic planning module 4 m (13 ft)
Total number of elevators 20
Speed of fastest elevators 5 m (16 ft)/s
Number of car parking spaces 637
Number of bike parking spaces 2,069
Hotel brand Fairmont
Residence brand Fairmont
Residence service brand Fairmont
Principal structure materials Concrete with perimeter steel bracing system

2

ATRIUM LINER

CORE

STRUCTURAL FRAME

INNER SHELL

DIAGONAL BRACING

OUTER SHELL

6

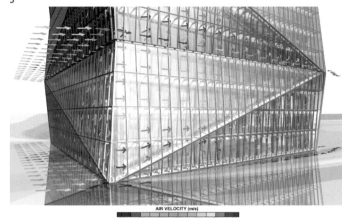

3

4

5

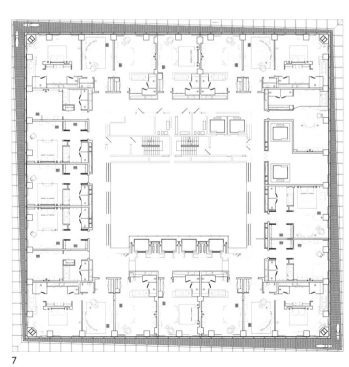

7

133

The CCTV headquarters aims at an alternative to the exhausted typology of the skyscraper. Instead of competing in the race for ultimate height and style within a traditional two-dimensional tower 'soaring' skyward, CCTV's loop poses a truly three-dimensional experience, culminating in a 75-metre (246-foot) cantilever. The building is visible from most of Beijing.

CCTV's form facilitates the combination of the entire process of TV-making in a loop of interconnected activities. Two towers rise from a common production studio platform, the Plinth. Each tower has a different character: Tower 1 serves as the editing area and offices, and the lower Tower 2 is dedicated to news broadcasting. The towers are joined by a cantilevering bridge for administration, the Overhang.

The innovative structure of the building is the result of long-term collaboration between European and Chinese architects and engineers. The forces at work within the structure are rendered visible on the façade: a web of triangulated steel tubes – diagrids – that, instead of forming a regular **pattern of diamonds**, become dense in areas of greater stress, looser and more open in areas requiring less support. The façade itself becomes a visual manifestation of the building's structure.

The self-supporting hybrid façade structure features high performance glass panels with a sun shading of 70 percent open ceramic frit, creating the soft silver-grey color that gives the building a surprisingly subtle presence in the Beijing skyline.

The main lobby, in Tower 1, is an atrium stretching three floors underground, and three floors up. It has a direct connection with Beijing's subway network, and will be the arrival and departure hub for the 10,000 workers inside CCTV headquarters. Connected to the lobby, 13 production studios perform the main function of the building: TV making.

The CCTV headquarters also facilitates an unprecedented degree of public access to the production of China's media; a Public Loop takes visitors on a dedicated path through the building, revealing everyday studio work as well as the history of CCTV and culminating at the edge of the cantilever, with spectacular views towards the CBD, the Forbidden City and the rest of Beijing.

1 View looking upwards
2 Overview
3 Plan (1/F)
4 Section

Credits: 1 ©OMA / photography by Philippe Ruault; 2 ©OMA / photography by Iwan Baan; 3,4 ©OMA

CCTV

234 m 767 ft

Location Beijing
Completion 2012
Client China Central Television (CCTV)
Architect OMA
Associate Architect and Engineer East China Architectural Design & Research Institute (ECADI)
Structural engineer Arup
MEP engineer Arup
Vertical transportation consultant Lerch, Bates & Associates, London
Façade engineer Front Inc, New York
Cost consultant Zhou Zhijun, Zhou Weiming
Landscape architect Inside/Outside, Amsterdam
Lighting consultant Lighting Planners Associates, Tokyo

Other design consultants DHV • DMJMH+N • Ducks Scéno • Sandy Brown Associates • Romano Gatland NY • 2x4,NY
Uses Administration 64,200 m² (691,043 ft²) • multipurpose 54,900 m² (590,938 ft²) • news production 65,800 m² (708,265 ft²) • broadcasting 31,800 m² (342,292 ft²) • program production 105,400 m² (1,134,516 ft²) • staff facilities 30,000 m² (322,917 ft²) • parking 61,500 m² (661,980 ft²) • service building 15,000 m² (161,458 ft²)
Number of buildings 1
Height 234 m (767 ft)
Above-ground storeys 54
Site area 20 hectares (49.42 acres) in new CBD
Building CCTV area 473,000 m² (5,091,329 ft²)
Total gross area 599,548 m² (6,453,481 ft²)
Principal structure materials Steel, concrete

Source: OMA

2

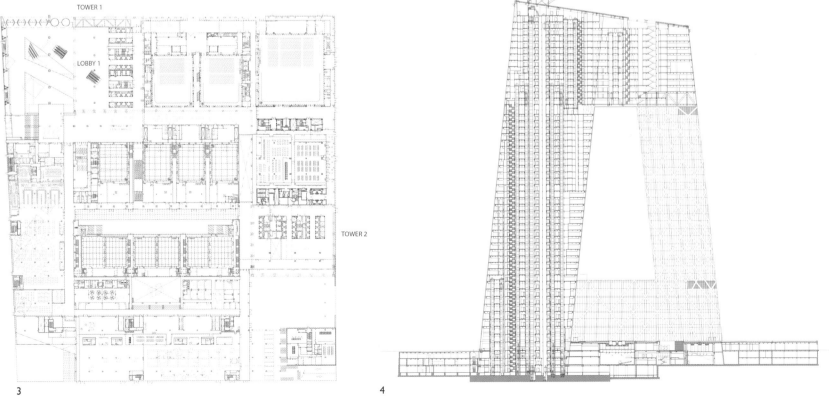

TOWER 1

LOBBY 1

TOWER 2

3

4

■ The existing 37-storey Jinling Hotel became a true public landmark in the center of Nanjing when it was completed in 1982. It was the then-tallest building in mainland China and become a source of pride for the people of Nanjing.

Recognising the need for new, contemporary and extended accommodation, the hotel held a design competition to establish a land use and development strategy. The winning proposal by P&T houses the new extension with all associated facilities in a single, 57-storey-tall Asia Pacific Tower. A **podium structure** related and linked to the existing hotel houses new, extensive banqueting facilities, restaurants and a health club with an indoor swimming pool on its roof. The remainder of the mid-city site is allocated to circulation and extensively landscaped gardens.

The square tower is essentially divided into two sections. The 370 new rooms and suites of the hotel's five-star extension are provided on the top floors of the tower and are reached directly by express lifts. An exclusive lounge located above the guest rooms tops the tower.

Grade A offices are formed below the hotel, extending over 30 typical floors, featuring spacious and column-free office accommodation. The hotel entrance and lobby and the office foyer are at street level and are adjoined by a grand multistorey-high entrance hall.

The tower is clad with white aluminium panels in combination with double-glazed, tinted windows and the podium in lined with beige Brazilian granite throughout.

Basement levels extending over the whole site contain car parking, loading and unloading and back-of-house hotel facilities. Basement 1 features an extensive retail arcade lined with shops and restaurants, and is linked to an adjoining mass transit station, providing easy and convenient access for visitors and workers alike.

1 Aerial view at night
2 View from south
3 Office A floor plan
4 Typical hotel guest room floor plan

Photography & illustrations: P&T Group

Asia Pacific Tower

242 m | 794 ft

Location Nanjing
Completion 2014
Client New Jinling Hotel Co., Ltd
Architect P&T Group
Architect of record Jiangsu Provincial Architectural D&R Institute Ltd
Structural engineer P&T Architects & Engineers Ltd
MEP engineer Jiangsu Provincial Architectural D&R Institute Ltd
Façade engineers Beijing Jangho Curtain Wall Co., Ltd (façade contractor) • Meinhardt Facade Technology (Shanghai) Ltd (façade consultant)
Project management consultant Jinling Hotel Corporation Ltd
Landscape architect Nanjing Institute of Landscape Architecture Design & Planning Ltd
Lighting consultant Shanghai Citelum Lighting Design Co. Ltd
Other consultants Chhada Siembieda Leung Ltd (interior design) • Watermark Associates Designers & Consultants Ltd (signage)
Main contractor China State Constructions Engineering Corporation
Uses Hotel accommodation 51,451 m² (553,813 ft²) [41-55/F] • office 63,720 m² (685,876 ft²) [6-21/F, 23-38/F] • hotel supporting facilities 7,923 m² (85,282 ft²) [56-57/F] • bank 267 m² (2,873 ft²) [2-3/F] • basement back of house and retail arcade 15,717 m² (169,176 ft²) [B1/F] • basement car park 26,192 m² (281,928 ft²) [B2/F & B3/F]
Number of buildings 1

Source: P&T Group

Height 242 m (794 ft)
Above-ground storeys 57
Basements (number of levels) 3
Mechanical levels 5/F, 22/F, 39/F, 40/F
Refuge levels 5/F, 22/F, 39/F
Sky-lobby levels 56/F
Site area Total 16,039 m² (172,642 ft²): new development 13,300 m² (143,160 ft²) • existing development 2,739 m² (29,482 ft²)
Gross above-ground building area 123,361 m² (1,327,846 ft²)
Gross basement area 41,909 m² (451,104 ft²)
Total gross area 165,270 m² (1,778,951 ft²)
Floor area ratio (FAR)/Plot ratio 7.69
Gross typical floor area 2,000 m² (21,527 ft²)
Basic planning module 9M structural grid
Total number of elevators 23
Number of car parking spaces 510
Hotel brand Jingling Hotel
Principal structure materials Concrete & steel (composite)
Other materials Aluminum, glass, local granite

2

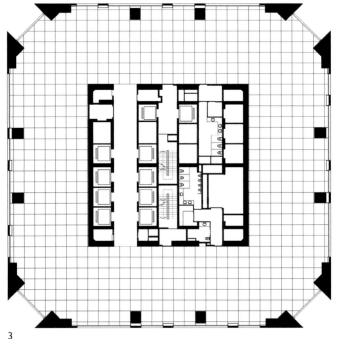

3

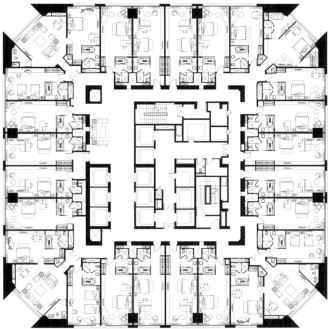

4

1

■ The Q.1 project is a mixed-use program of retail, office and hotel serviced apartment facilities. The site is located at the heart of the business district of Qingdao and sits along its main thoroughfare, Hong Kong Road. The project is a single slender tower of 242 metres (794 feet), with its most prominent side facing the municipal building to its west. This tower comprises two storeys of retail, 19 storeys of office and another 19 storeys of duplex hotel service apartments, together with five storeys of building service and amenities. Because of its unique configuration, this 64-storey building, which includes the 19 duplex upper levels, requires only 45 elevator stops. At its base, a solid edifice rises with a stone façade containing the retail and office floors, which are designed to achieve maximum efficiency through an orthogonal layout. A sculpted curvilinear frame of glass and steel rises from the base and folds to contain elegant serviced apartments with magnificent views. From the outside, the two distinct geometric forms appear engaged with one another while the glass façades at both ends of the tower extend to the ground to create a visually balanced and interesting composition.

The tower assumes the shape of **an arc** that opens out to embrace the Yellow Sea. A full-height glass façade at each floor allows for uninterrupted views of the sky and water. The arc of the hotel tower provides the greatest length of the tower, running east to west, and favours views not only to the south but southwest to the city as well. The duplex design of each unit allows for a double-height space in each living room, resulting in dramatic views and light, while the bedroom is located at the mezzanine floor, facing north to the mountains beyond. Natural cross-ventilation is ensured in each unit. On the 25th level a sky garden, swimming pool and clubhouse provide luxury amenities for the serviced apartment guests and clubhouse members. Lush planting and landscaping at street level and at pool-deck level will bring essential visual relief to the building façade.

1 Clubhouse terrace (25/F)
2 Overview
3 Typical duplex apartment floor plan
4 Clubhouse floor plan (25/F)
5 Typical office floor plan (3/F–24/F)
6 Ground floor plan
7 Office lobby interior
8 Serviced apartment lobby interior
9 Typical duplex residence interior

Renderings & illustrations: courtesy
Pei Partnership Architects, LLP

Q.1

242 m | 794 ft

Location Qingdao

Completion 2015

Client Qingdao Taishan Real Estate Development

Architect Pei Partnership Architects, LLP

Associate architect Qingdao Tourism Design Institute, Qingdao

Structural engineers Weidlinger Associates, New York • Jiang Architects and Engineer, Shanghai • Qingdoa Tourism Design Institute, Qingdao

MEP engineers Parsons Brinckerhoff Engineering Technology Co. Ltd, Hong Kong • Qingdao Tourism Design Institute, Qingdao

Civil engineer Qingdao Tourism Design Institute

Geotechnical Qingdao Tourism Design Institute

Façade consultant Hiersemenzel & Associates

Landscape architects SWA

Lighting consultant Visionova

Interiors consultants INC Architecture & Design PLLC (hotel) • Incorporated (apartments) • Pei Partnership Architects, LLP (office)

Main contractor China Railway Construction Engineering Co

Uses Retail • office • duplex hotel serviced apartments

Number of buildings 1

Height 242 m (794 ft)

Above-ground storeys 64 (including 19 duplex upper levels)

Basements 5

Site area 5,593.3 m² (60,206 ft²)

Total gross area 107,150 m² (1,153,353 ft²)

Speed of fastest elevators 6 m (20 ft)/sec

Number of car parking spaces 426

Principal structure materials Composite, steel, glass

Source: Pei Partnership Architects, LLP

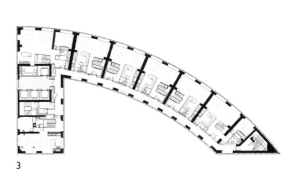

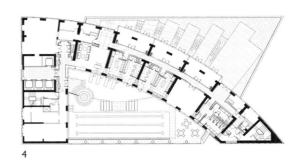

3

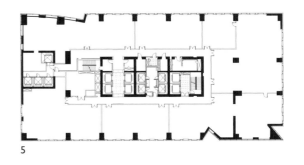

4

5

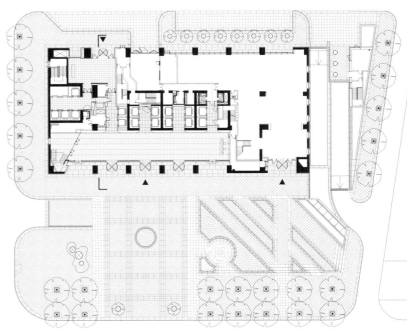

6

2

7

8

9

The external curtain wall façade was carefully designed with a combination of clear glass, glass fritting and sun-shading features. Devised as a unitised cladding system, the clear double-glazing unit with Low-E coating was specifically designed for energy conservation.

A subtle manipulation of the square floor plans creates variations on the façade. Indents are established to reduce the overall massing of the building form. The refuge floors serve as sky parks, and the corners of these floors have been accentuated with perforated metal louvres that give shading to these double-height spaces.

The top of the tower contains areas for plants and is similarly clad by metal louvres that represent the crown of the building. This feature can be specially lit at night and forms a beacon within the urban skyline.

■ R&F Center is a high-rise office tower in the new central business district of Guangzhou. The design concept took reference from China's historical **jade vase**. The square-shaped form signifies formality and elegance, while maximising the building's efficiency and flexibility. It provides 122,000 square metres (1,313,197 square feet) of office space, 20,000 of which (the top 10 floors) are for the client's head office. The building was designed to be translucent and glow under natural lighting while retaining a similar quality at night, achieving remarkable aesthetics for the end users and significant energy efficiency.

The tower is designed as a central core building to maximise planning efficiency and structural stability in seismic conditions. However, for the R&F head office, the core has been specially designed to allow for a central atrium space to be formed within, which links all the different departments and functions with dedicated lifts and open staircases.

1 Light shaft above internal atrium
2 Exterior view
3 Floor plans
4 Section diagram

Photography: courtesy Aedas

R&F Center

242 m | 795 ft

Location Guangzhou	**Use** Offices
Completion 2007	**Number of buildings** 1
Client Guangzhou R&F Properties Co., Ltd	**Height** 242.3 m (795 ft)
Architect Aedas	**Above-ground storeys** 54
Local design institute Guangzhou Residential Architectural Design Institute	**Gross basement area** 34,000 m² (365,973 ft²)
Structural engineer Guangzhou R&F Properties Co., Ltd	**Total gross area** 123,207 m² (1,326,189 ft²)
MEP engineer Parsons Brinckerhoff Asia	**Principal structure materials** Concrete, steel

Source: Aedas

2

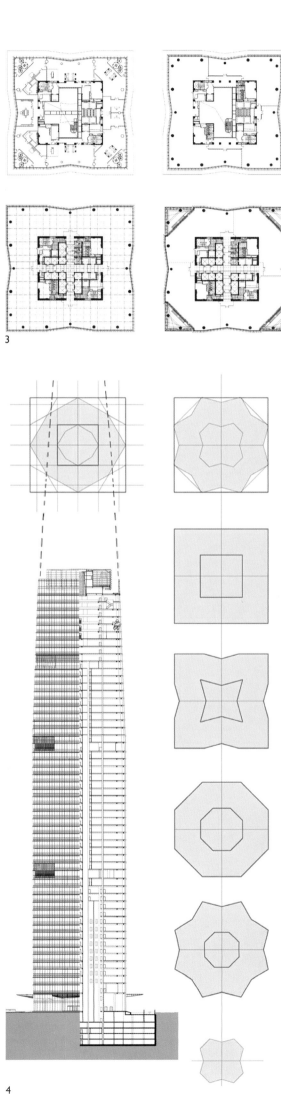

3

4

1

The site is located in the JieFangBei financial zone of Yuzhong District of Chongqing, west of Wuyi Road, east of Xinhua Road. The shape of the site is irregular: the eastern part of the site is more than 10 metres (33 feet) higher than the western part.

The scheme consists of three interconnected massing and a podium, which includes office, hotel, conference, dining, shopping and other functions. The height of the tower is 245 metres (804 feet) and there is a 3-metre-wide (10-foot) cantilever glass swimming pool and a sky garden at the 53rd floor (at 230 metres [755 feet]).

The entrance to the office and the hotel faces the main street. A commercial inner-street and pedestrian network – along with platforms, steps and plazas around the buildings – makes the exterior space as a whole. Six basement levels are used for mechanical equipment, car parking and cargo storage.

The curtain wall of the building façades meets the energy-saving requirements with medium-grey transparent glazing and dark-grey **metal vertical mullions**. The vertical lines of the curtain wall emphasise the height and straight verticality of the ultrahigh skyscrapers and give a concise, transparent image of the building. Moreover, the interiors share good views of both the natural scenic beauty of the confluence of three rivers and the urban landscape of Chongqing.

The landscape design includes platforms, steps, plazas, flowing water and many other elements reflecting the terrain. Native plant varieties and tall trees are planted in the square. A vertical garden system has been adopted across a section of the podium's façade, hanging as a 'green tapestry' within Chongqing's ultrahigh urban density.

1   Close-up of façade curtain wall
2   South perspective
3   View from the west
4   East perspective
5   Ground floor plan
6   Typical hotel guest rooms floor plan
7   Hotel lobby floor plan (51/F)

Photography & illustrations: courtesy Tanghua Architects Shenzhen Co., Ltd

245 m | 804 ft

The Westin Chongqing Liberation Square

Location Chongqing
Completion 2014
Client Chongqing Forebase Industrial Investment (Holding) Co. Ltd
Architect Tanghua Architects Shenzhen Co., Ltd
Structural MEP engineers Chongqing Architectural Design Institute P.R. China
Façade engineer Shenzhen Catic Curtain Wall Engineering Co., Ltd
Landscape architect Metrostudio
Lighting consultant Lutron Electronics Co., Inc.
Other consultants CCD/Cheung Chung Design (HK) (interiors)
  • Architecture:Innovative Ltd (acoustics)
Main contractor MCC Huaye Resources Development Co., Ltd (NCMCC)
Uses Hotel, office, retail, commercial
Number of buildings 3
Height 245.30 m (804 ft)
Above-ground storeys 54
Basements 6

Source: Tanghua Architects Shenzhen Co., Ltd

Mechanical levels 13/F (56.7 m [186 ft]) • 33/F (137.9 m [452 ft]) • 49/F (201.6 m [661 ft]) • roof (212.8 m [698 ft])
Refuge levels 13/F (56.7 m [186 ft]) • 33/F (137.9 m [452 ft]) • 49/F (201.6 m [661 ft])
Sky-lobby levels 51/F (212.8 m [698 ft])
Site area 12,957 m² (139,468 ft²)
Gross above-ground building area A area: 112,675 m² (1,212,823 ft²) • B area: 18,000 m² (193,750 ft²) • C area: 23,168 m² (249,378 ft²)
Gross basement area 40,785 m² (439,006 ft²)
Total gross area 205,904 m² (2,216,332 ft²)
Floor area ratio (FAR)/Plot ratio 15.89
Total number of elevators 60
Speed of fastest elevators 6 m (20 ft)/s
Elevator brand Schindler
Number of car parking spaces 810
Hotel brand Westin
Principal structure materials Reinforced concrete frame, steel space frame
Other materials Glass, stone, aluminium

2

3

4

5

6

7

1

The Shenzhen Stock Exchange is conceived as a physical materialisation of the virtual stock market: it is a building with a **floating base**, representing the stock market — more than physically accommodating it. Typically, the base of a building anchors a structure and connects it emphatically to the ground. In the case of this project, the base, as if lifted by the same speculative euphoria that drives the market, has crept up the tower to become a raised podium.

SZSE's raised podium is a three-storey cantilevered platform floating 36 metres (118 feet) above the ground, with one of the largest office floor plates per floor and an accessible landscaped roof. The raised podium contains all the exchange's functions, including the listing hall and all stock exchange departments. In its elevated position, it 'broadcasts' the virtual activities of the city's financial market, while its cantilevers crop and frame views of Shenzhen. The raised podium also creates a generous public space at ground level for what is typically a secure, private building.

The raised podium (framed by a robust three-dimensional array of full-depth steel transfer trusses) and the tower are combined as one structure, with the tower and atrium columns providing vertical and lateral support for the cantilevering structure. The tower is flanked by two atria — voids that connect the ground directly with the public spaces inside the building. SZSE executive offices are located just above the raised podium, leaving the uppermost floors leasable as rental offices and a dining club.

The generic square form of the tower obediently blends in with the surrounding homogenous towers. However, the building's façade is different: it wraps the robust exoskeletal grid structure supporting the building in patterned glass. The texture of the glass cladding reveals the construction technology. The neutral colour and translucency of the façade change with weather conditions, creating a crystalline effect. The deep façade has recessed openings that passively reduce the amount of solar heat gain entering the building, improve natural daylight and reduce energy consumption. (SZSE is designed to be one of the first 3-star green rated buildings in China.)

The Shenzhen Stock Exchange is a financial center with civic meaning. Located in a new public square at the meeting point of the north–south axis between Mount Lianhua and Binhe Boulevard, and the east–west axis of Shennan Road, Shenzhen's main artery, it engages the city not as an isolated object, but as a building to be reacted to at multiple scales and levels — at times appearing massive and at others intimate and personal.

1 Façade
2 Overall view
3 Landscaped rooftop garden
4 Floor plan (46/F)
5 Floor plan (33/F)
6 Floor plan (15/F)
7 Floor plan (13/F)
8 Floor plan (10/F)
9 Floor plan (9/F)
10 Floor plan (8/F)
11 Floor plan (3/F)
12 Floor plan (1/F)

Photography & illustrations: 1-3 ©OMA/ photography by Philippe Ruault; 4-12 ©OMA

Shenzhen Stock Exchange

Location Shenzhen
Completion 2013
Client Shenzhen Stock Exchange
Architect OMA
Local design institute SADI (architecture & engineering)
Structural engineer Arup
MEP engineers Arup (design development) • SADI (construction documentation)
Vertical transportation consultant Arup
Façade engineers Arup • Front Inc.
Landscape architect Inside Outside
Lighting consultant Arup
Other consultants DHV Building and Industry (level acoustic) • 2x4 (signage & graphics) • L&B (quantity surveyor) • Arup (fire, services, project management, building physics, building intelligence, geotechnics)

Uses Office
Number of buildings 1
Height 245.8 m (806 ft)
Site area 39,000 m² (419,792 ft²)
Gross above-ground building area 180,000 m² (1,937,504 ft²)
Gross basement area 85,000 m² (914,932 ft²)
Total gross area 265,000 m² (2,852,436 ft²)
Gross typical floor area 16,000 m² (172,222 ft²)
Principal structure materials Steel, concrete
Other materials Glass

Source: OMA

2

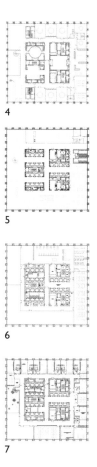

4

5

6

7

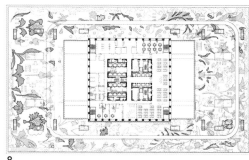

8

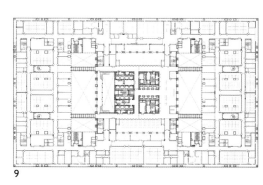

9

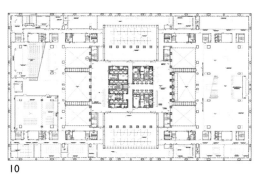

10

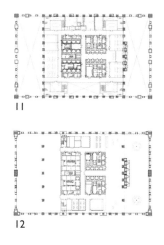

11

12

3

Beijing Yintai Centre is located on a very prominent site in the heart of Beijing's central business district. Designed to enhance the Beijing skyline, Yintai Centre is a comprehensive mixed-use complex that rises from a water garden park at its base. The three towers are square in form and are studies in simple, straightforward design. The mixed-use residential hotel tower is the focal point of the project, flanked by twin office towers. The residential tower features an opulent five-star Park Hyatt hotel with elegant guestrooms, luxury apartments and serviced apartments.

A large cube majestically crowns the residential tower, recalling a **Chinese lantern**. By day, the cube acts as a stately symbol of ancient Chinese architecture, and by night, it shines brilliantly as a beacon marking the site. Express elevators sweep guests to the top of the building, the hotel registration area, which is located within this 'lantern'. Providing spectacular views of Beijing, the 'lantern' houses other public hotel functions as well, such as a bar, lounge and a restaurant.

The podium base of the project includes an upscale retail food outlet, speciality retail shops, several restaurants, meeting room facilities, both Grand and Junior ballrooms, a fitness centre and an enclosed pool. These functions are connected to expansive retail areas in the first basement by a series of escalators and elevators.

A landscaped roof garden ties the three towers together above the podium, connecting the garden to the meeting rooms by bridges. The inclusion of nature in the project's design provides people a sense of tranquility within the city. Rather than attempting to copy a traditional Chinese garden in a modern, formal and rather symmetrical space, elements of a historic Chinese garden are incorporated in a symbolic way. The cool greenery and the sound of water create a welcome antithesis to the urban surroundings; also serving to highlight the forms of the architecture – an artificial entity – against nature's attributes. The lush

roof garden, with its stone paved terrace and pavilion, serves as a sanctuary for tenants and a splendid venue in which to host special events and functions catered by the hotel.

Vehicular access to the site is through a large monumental space under the podium that gives each tower its own sense of grand entry. Supported by majestic circular columns, this covered courtyard is graced by natural light. The site overall is abundantly landscaped and the extensive use of water features is unique to the site, separating it from the congestion of the surrounding roadways. The complex's human-scaled gardens and water features and architectural details suggest the depiction of ancient Chinese architecture in a contemporary way.

1 Chinese lantern–inspired detail
2 Overall view at night
3 Podium rooftop
4 Bar lounge floor plan
5 Hotel lobby floor plan
6 Guestrooms floor plan
7 Apartments floor plan
8 Serviced apartments floor plan
9 Ground floor plan (lobby)

Credits: 1–3 ©Paul Dingman; 4–9 ©John Portman & Associates

Beijing Yintai Centre

Location Beijing
Completion 2008
Client Beijing Yintai Property Co., Ltd
Architect John Portman & Associates
Local architect China Electronics Engineering Design Institute (CEEDI)
Structural engineers John Portman & Associates • LeMessurier Consultants
MEP engineers Newcomb & Boyd • Parsons Brinckerhoff
Vertical transportation consultant Lerch Bates & Associates
Façade engineer Evans Heintges Architects
Project management consultants John Portman & Associates • Bovis Lend Lease
Landscape architects Arnold Associates (main landscape & roof garden design concepts) • Place Media (final design) • SUPER POTATO (final roof garden design)
Interior design Remedios Siembieda, Inc.
Main contractor Beijing Urban Construction Group (BUCG)
Uses Centre tower: hotel, serviced apartments, luxury apartments, retail, restaurants, health club • two side towers: office

Number of buildings 3
Height Centre tower: 249.9 m (820 ft) [residential] • two side towers 186 m (610 ft) [office]
Above-ground storeys Centre tower: 63 [usable: 57] • 2 side towers: 42
Basements 4
Mechanical levels 6: 4/F, 17/F, 33/F, 34/F, 47/F, 56/F [center tower]
Site area 31,629 m² (340,451 ft²)
Gross above-ground building area 118,519 m² (1,275,728 ft²) [center tower]
Gross typical floor area 160 m² (1,722 ft²) [center tower]
Basic planning module 5 m (16 ft) [center tower]
Number of car parking spaces 1,692 cars (67 spaces at ground level, the rest below-grade)
Number of bike parking spaces 1,500
Hotel brand Park Hyatt
Principal structure materials Concrete beams, slabs, columns • shear walls: reinforcing steel, structural steel, steel floor deck • unitised curtain wall
Other materials Granite, glass

Source: John Portman & Associates, Inc.

2

3

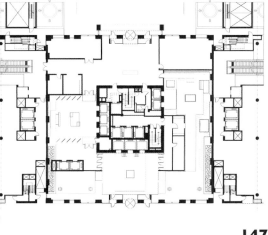

4

5

6

7

8

9

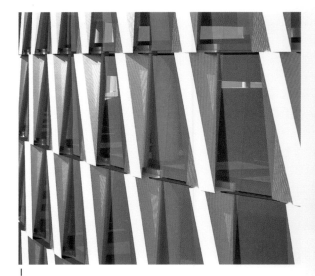

■ The mixed-use Raffles City Hangzhou development is located near the Qiantang River in Hangzhou, the capital of Zhejiang province, located 180 kilometres (112 miles) southwest of Shanghai. With a city population of 1.69 million, Hangzhou is one of China's most renowned and prosperous cities and is well known for its beautiful natural scenery, particularly in the West Lake area.

This project incorporates retail, offices, strata apartments and hotel facilities and marks the site of a cultural landscape within the Quianjiang New Town area.

The philosophy behind the Raffles City Hangzhou concept is to integrate mixed-use in an urban context by focussing on where the urban context meets the landscape of the city. In the design of the towers the urban element of the project twists towards the landscape, while the landscape aspect, in turn, twists towards the urban context, thereby effecting the incorporation and consolidation of these separate elements in one **formal gesture**.

It is a project that communicates both with the architecture and within the context of Hangzhou as a city. At a height of 60 storeys it will present views both to and from the Qiantang River and West Lake areas. Raffles City Hangzhou will be at the core of the Qianjiang New Town area and contribute to the recognition of this area as a new destination in the city; the building itself will form a link in the chain of events and attractions in Hangzhou, complementing the West Lake area and the city's commercial centre.

An inclusive approach to sustainability is an important part of this architect's design philosophy. The incorporation of natural ventilation principles and the ways in which materials are employed all work in sync with one another to lower the energy and material demands of the building. Urban sustainability is also an important consideration in the design – the project is seeking the Gold certification from the LEED Green Building rating system. The program mix creates a dynamic, continuous 24/7 cycle of activity, a hub for business conduct, a new destination for visitors and residents alike and will become an all-in-one destination for working, living, leisure and entertainment.

1 Façade close-up (rendering)
2 Street view
3 SOHO apartment floor plan (high zone, 58/F), T1
4 SOHO apartment floor plan (low zone, 34/F), T1
5 Serviced apartment floor plan (21/F), T1
6 Office floor plan (11/F), T1
7 Rendering of corner
8 Retail interior
9 Retail interior
10 Exploded axonometric diagram overview

Renderings: Raffles City, Hangzhou, China, 2016, ©UNStudio

Raffles City Hangzhou

Location Hangzhou

Completion 2016

Client CapitaLand China

Architect UNStudio

Associate architect China United Engineering Corporation, Hangzhou

Structural engineer Arup

MEP engineers Arup • SAIYO, Shanghai (interior)

Vertical transportation consultant Arup

Façade engineer Meinhardt Façade Technology

Project management consultant Capitaland

Cost consultant Davis Langdon & Seah Consultancy, Shanghai

Lighting consultants ag Licht, Bonn • LEOX Design Partnership, Shanghai

Other consultants TOPO Design Group. LLC, Shanghai (landscape) • Arup (fire, LEED) • MVA (traffic)

Main contractors Shanghai Construction No.4 Group Co. Ltd • Gartner + Yuanda (façade)

Uses Retail: 110,000 m² (1,184,030 ft²) [B1/F–7/F] • T1 office: 17,880 m² (192,459 ft²) [7/F–19/F] • T1 serviced apartments: 18,765 m² (201,985 ft²) [21/F–31/F] • T1 SOHO apartments: 25,426 m² (273,683 ft²) [33/F–59/F] • T2 office: 26,225 m² (282,283 ft²) [7/F–24/F] • T2 hotel: 28,766 m² (309,634 ft²) [8/F, 9/F, 27/F–50/F] • T2 strata apartment: 7,555 m² (81,321 ft²) [51/F–57/F]

Source: UNStudio

Number of buildings 2 towers, 1 podium

Height Towers: 250 m (820 ft) • podium 50 m (164 ft)

Above-ground storeys 60

Basements 3

Mechanical levels T1: 7/F, 17/F, 17M/F, 32/F, 46/F, 60/F • T2: 9/F, 25/F, 27M/F, 51/F, 58/F

Sky-lobby levels T1 [serviced apartments]: 21/F • T2 [hotel]: 26/F, 27/F

Site area 40,355 m² (434,377 ft²)

Gross above-ground building area Towers + podium (total): 283,567 m² (3,047,984 ft²) • T1: 87,500 m² (941,842 ft²) • T2: 97,600 m² (1,050,558 ft²) • podium: 99,384 m² (1,069,760 ft²)

Gross basement area 109,182 m² (1,175,225 ft²)

Total gross area 392,867 m² (4,228,785 ft²)

Floor area ratio (FAR)/Plot ratio 7.03

Gross typical floor area 1,200–2,500 m² (12,916–26,910 ft²)

Total number of elevators T1: 12 • T2: 18

Speed of fastest elevators 6 m (20 ft)/s

Elevator brand Mitsubishi

Number of car parking spaces 1,952

Number of bike parking spaces 1,892

Principal structure materials Steel, concrete

Other materials Façade: glass, aluminium

2

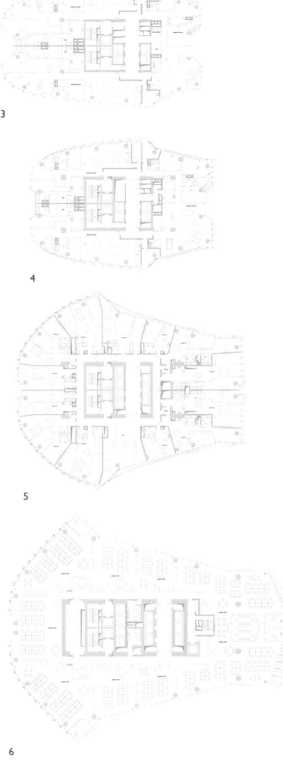

3

4

5

6

7

8

9

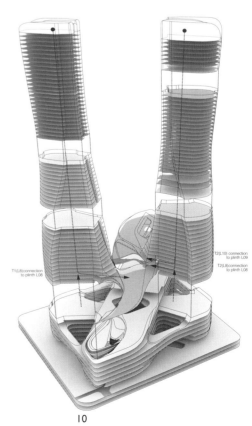

10

The new corporate headquarters for Tencent in the Nanshan District in Shenzhen represent a vision for a new working environment. The towers will help take this company to new levels of innovation and efficiency, project a powerful brand image to the world, and indicate the future of high-performance design, and which will become a global benchmark for high-rise corporate headquarters.

The underlying concept for the design is to create a **vertical campus** for Tencent. This tower symbolically represents the connections of the far corners of the internet and becomes a physical structure that links the employees of the company together in a more effective way than the traditional high-rise building. The structure also becomes an urban link by forming a visual gateway to the Shenzhen High-tech Industrial Park (SHiP). The 'links' are three bridges containing shared functions and which connect the two office towers. These shared functions found in the link bridges help to promote more community, communication and chance encounters within the vertical campus.

The company's brand as a global leader is also reflected through the environmental stewardship this building represents. This was achieved by creating a design founded on the principles of passive design. Each element in the building is designed to respond intelligently to climatic conditions, such as solar and wind patterns, provide views of nature and to the sea, give access to natural light and ventilation, offer easy access to mass transport and minimise waste.

1   Lobby interior
2   View from street intersection at dusk
3   Southeast view from Binhai Road
4   Main entrance view
5   Site plan
6   Section diagram

Renderings: courtesy NBBJ

Tencent Binhai Tower

Location Shenzhen
Completion 2016
Client Tencent Holdings Limited
Architect NBBJ
Architect of record Tongji Architects (Shenzhen)
Structural engineer AECOM (Shenzhen)
MEP engineer WSP (Shenzhen)
Vertical transportation consultant Arup (London)
Façade engineers Inhabit (Hong Kong) • Thorton Tomasetti
Cost consultant WTP
Landscape architect NBBJ
Lighting consultant NBBJ
Other consultants Atkins (Shenzhen) [sustainability] • Arup (Shenzhen) [traffic]
    • atelier ten (New York/San Francisco) [sustainability]
Main contractor China State Construction Engineering
Uses Culture link (meeting, exhibition, retail, cafeteria) [1/F–5/F] • health link (gym, training,
    conference room, special function, employee service) [22/F–26/F] • knowledge link (conference,
    Tencent College, library) [35/F–37/F] • general offices [7/F–20/F, 27/F–33/F, 38/F–50/F]

Number of buildings 2
Height North: 250 m (820 ft) • south: 192 m (630 ft)
Above-ground storeys 52
Basements 4
Mechanical levels 6/F, 21/F, 34/F, 40/F, roof
Refuge levels 6/F, 21/F, 34/F, 47/F
Sky-lobby levels 24/F, 25/F, 35/F, 36/F
Site area 18,650 m² (200,747 ft²)
Gross above-ground building area 277,218 m² (2,983,950 ft²)
Gross basement area 68,352 m² (735,735 ft²)
Total gross area 344,570 m² (3,708,920 ft²)
Floor area ratio (FAR)/Plot ratio 14.28
Total number of elevators 53
Number of car parking spaces 930
Number of bike parking spaces 282
Principal structure materials Composite

Source: NBBJ

3

4

2

5

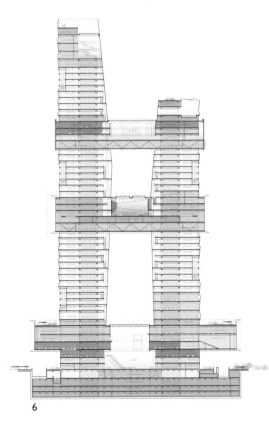

6

■ Wenzhou continues to develop as a vital urban city on the eastern seaboard of China's mainland. The Lucheng District of Wenzhou has undergone a great transformation as a residential district, situated around the newly constructed public Bailuzhou Park (25 hectares [62 acres]). The site of the new Faith Trust Plaza and Cullinan (also known as Wenzhou Zhixin Plaza) mixed-use project is envisioned as the centrepiece for this district.

Guided by sensitivities to program, place and site, Faith Trust Plaza is inspired by a classical architectural sensibility. Formally, the strong bold geometries of the three individual components and the site are positioned based on the exposures of the triangular site and their relationship to the urban context.

The office/hotel tower anchors the project at the apex of the triangular block. The square tower is sited in a circular reflecting pool defined by the entry drive to the office and hotel lobbies. Rising to a height of 255 metres (837 feet), it becomes an urban marker; a symbol on the skyline. Its vertical height is accentuated through the re-entrant corners and the bold expressed vertical mullions of the four identical planar façades. These surfaces rise vertically and slowly peel away from the tower volume, opening up at the top of the tower like a **flower petal** opening to the sky, providing a unique and memorable identity on the Wenzhou skyline.

Contrasting the verticality of the office/hotel tower, the triangular podium is decidedly horizontal. Fronting onto Feixia Road, the tower forms a strong edge on Bailuzhou Park. The surfaces of this element are delineated by strong horizontal mullions on the city side, acting as sunshades to the retail spaces.

Materially, the office/hotel tower and the podium are delineated with almost monolithic glazed surfaces. Contrasting this, Cullinan (the residential tower) is more solid. The small footprint, governed by the program of one home per floor, results in a slender tower, the surfaces of which develop as a composition of solid and void, open and closed, glazed and open terraces. These exterior surfaces extend beyond the top of the tower, enclosing a rooftop garden and event space, giving this element its own unique but secondary image on the skyline.

The total composition is held together and anchored in an urban landscape, yet extends the open landscape of the adjacent park through the site.

1   View of retail from street level
2   Overall view over retail
3   Northeast to southwest section through signature tower
4   Signature tower ground floor plan
5   Typical office floor plan
6   Atrium roof plan

Renderings: ©John Portman & Associates

---

255 m | 837 ft Faith Trust Plaza and Cullinan

Location Wenzhou
Completion 2016
Client Zhixin Real Estate Development Co., Ltd
Architect John Portman & Associates
Associate architect Wenzhou Architectural Design & Research Institute
Structural engineer John Portman & Associates
MEP engineer Newcomb & Boyd
Vertical transportation consultant Fortune Shepler Saling
Façade engineer ALT
Landscape architect AECOM
Fire protection consultant RJA
Uses Centre tower: hotel 40,000 m² (430,556 ft²) • office: 59,000 m² (635,071 ft²) • below-grade: hotel back-of-house, parking, commercial & building services: 63,450 m² (682,970 ft²) • two side towers: residential & retail
Number of buildings 3
Height Faith Trust Plaza: 255 m (837 ft) • Cullinan: 189.5 m (622 ft)
Above-ground storeys Faith Trust Plaza: 53 • Cullinan: 49

Basements 2.5
Mechanical levels 12/F, 33/F, 53/F
Refuge levels 12/F, 33/F
Sky-lobby levels 34/F
Site area 45,709 m² (492,008 ft²)
Gross above-ground building area Faith Trust Plaza: 118,519 m² (1,275,728 ft²) • Cullinan: 27,000 m² (290,626 ft²) • retail mall: 15,000 m² (161,459 ft²)
Gross basement area 63,450 m² (682,970 ft²)
Total gross area 204,450 m² (2,200,681 ft²)
Floor area ratio (FAR)/Plot ratio 3.88
Gross typical floor area Office: 1,960 m² (21,097 ft²) • hotel: 1,618 m² (17,416 ft²)
Number of car parking spaces 1,100
Total bike parking spaces area 3,000 m² (32,292 ft²)
Hotel brand Westin
Principal structure materials Faith Trust Plaza: concrete structure with glass curtain wall • Cullinan: concrete structure with glass & stone curtain wall

Source: John Portman & Associates

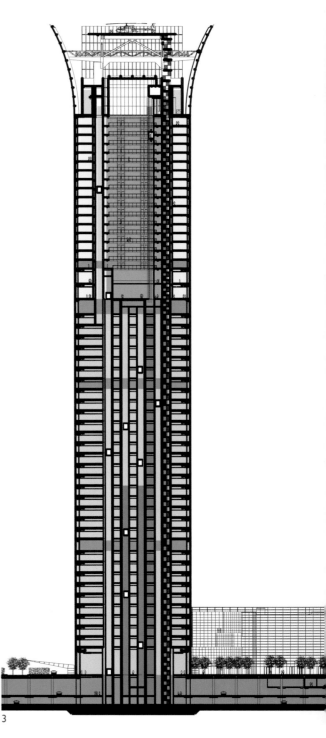

2

3

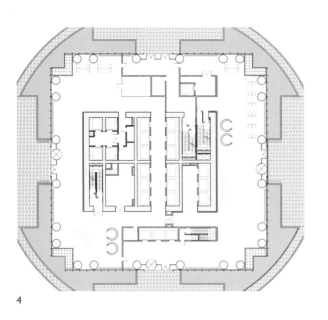

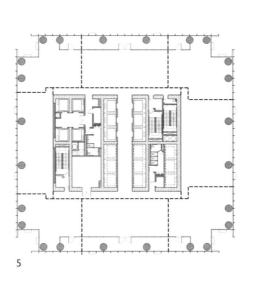

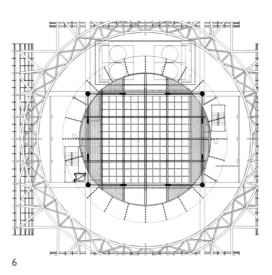

4

5

6

I

While the visual impact of the project is distinctive, the buildings are actually very straightforward in their composition. The towers' vertical members consist of concrete service-core shear walls and columns, with the columns typically spaced 6 metres (20 feet) apart. The curved tops are constructed from steel tubes in a space-frame configuration with aluminium egg-crate to span the entire roof. The standardised glass panels of the curtain wall make up the curve of the towers yet use no curved glass. Full-perimeter glass canopies offer protection to the walkways around the towers' bases. At the pedestrian levels, clear glass is used wherever possible for maximum transparency, allowing for the seamless flow between interior and exterior space.

The focal point of the plaza is *Lotus*, a public art sculpture by John Portman. The sculpture features a pair of soaring 32-metre-tall (105 feet) **red metal columns** from between which emerges a 7-metre-diameter (23-foot) glass-and-stainless-steel lotus-shaped form that is cantilevered 4.5 metres (15 feet) above the plaza pavers. By night, the work is conceived as an urban chandelier. By day, with its petals refracting the sunlight, it is a sparkling piece of public art. The sculpture also provides a transition from the massive office towers down to the human scale at ground level.

■ Featuring two slender office towers set into a sunken plaza that offers dining and retail establishments, the Fortune Finance Center (FFC) sets the benchmark for future development within the new central business district of Hangzhou. The positioning of the towers takes on a sculptural feel. As the top of one building sweeps up, its peak flows into the rising summit of the other, creating a dynamic energy between the sloping roofs of the two towers. The way the towers rise out of the lower-level plaza distinguishes the design from a typical tower/podium scheme.

1 View of the red metal obelisks of the *Lotus* sculpture from rear
2 View of tower top façades with peaks
3 Rendering of interplay between the tower roofs
4 Looking up towards towers from plaza
5 Typical lower levels office floor plan [east tower]
6 Typical lower levels office floor plan [west tower]
Following pages (left to right):
7 Tower façades reflecting sunlight at dusk
8 Overall view in context at night
Credits: 1,2,4,7,8 ©Michael Portman; 3,5,6 ©John Portman & Associates

258 m | 846 ft

Fortune Finance Center

Location Hangzhou	**Number of buildings** 2
Completion Buildings 2011 • plaza 2012	**Height** 258 m (846 ft) [west tower] • 188 m (617 ft) [east tower]
Client Zhejiang Te Fu Long Real Estate (west tower) • Construction Bank of China (east tower)	**Above-ground storeys** West tower: 52 • east tower: 36
Architect John Portman & Associates	**Basements** 3
Associate architect Shanghai Architectural Design & Research Institute (SIADR)	**Site area** 34,384 m² (370,106 ft²)
Structural engineers John Portman & Associates (design) • SIADR	**Gross basement area** 49,845 m² (536,527 ft²)
MEP engineer SIADR	**Total gross area** 210,000 m² (2,260,421 ft²)
Vertical transportation consultant Fortune Shepler Saling	**Floor area ratio (FAR)/Plot ratio** 9.35
Façade engineers RA Heintges & Associates (design) • Beijing Jangho Curtainwall Co. Ltd (material suppliers)	**Total number of elevators** East tower: 12 passenger elevators in 2 zones + 2 service elevators • west tower: 15 passenger elevators in 3 zones (double-deck) + 2 service elevators
Landscape architect Arnold Associates	**No of double-deck elevators** 15
Lighting consultant Randy Burkett Lighting Design	**Number of car parking spaces** 526
Developer Zhejian Te Fu Long Real Estate	**Total bike parking space area** 5,400 m² (58,125 ft²) [approximately]
Main contractor China State Construction Engineering Corporation	**Principal structure materials** Cast-in-place concrete, structural steel framing
Uses Office 66,499 m² (715,789 ft²) [west tower] • office 47,254 m² (508,638 ft²) [east tower] • retail: 3,920 m² (42,195 ft²)	**Other materials** Insulating glass, spandrel glass, sandblasted laminate glass with mirror backing, aluminium & glass unitised tower curtain wall

Source: John Portman & Associates

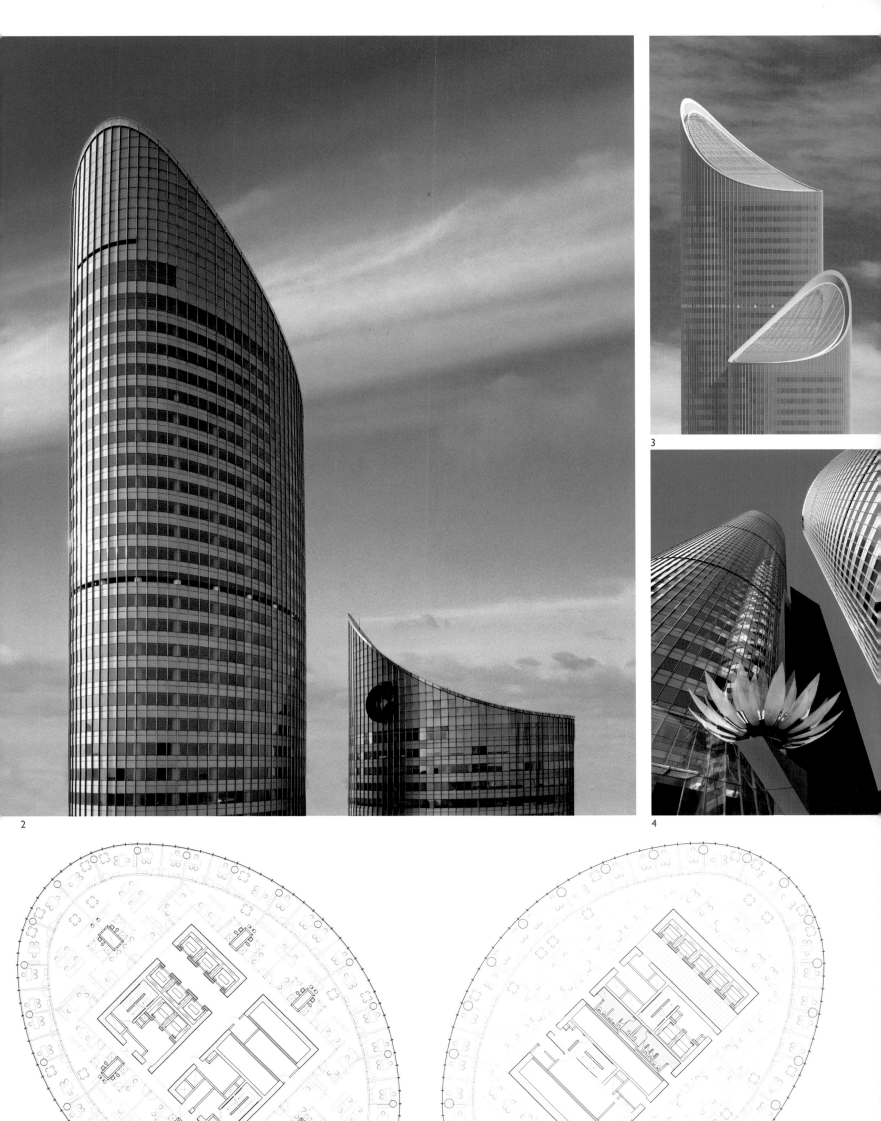

2

3

4

5

6

155

Grand Lisboa, Macau, is original – the boldly sculpted Grand Lisboa is the antithesis of the 'veneered box' template that dominates contemporary casino development. The rich and sensual form of the tower embodies the region's unique vitality and spirit, and the daring and flamboyant exuberance of modern Macau.

An inspiration for the **feathered form** of the hotel superstructure was the head-dress of a Brazilian showgirl's carnival costume, itself a reflection of the Portuguese influence shared by Macau and South America. The plumes also evoke a blossoming lotus flower, the official emblem of the Macau Special Administrative Region.

A grand public foyer occupies much of the ground floor and the whole frontage of the building. The foyer announces respectively the casino and hotel reception lobbies. The casino gaming area (30,000 square metres [322,917 square feet]) is arranged across three double-height floors in the podium dome and a basement hall. The gaming dome is poised above a 6-metre (20-foot) glass wall and the dramatically cantilevered entrance portals of the Grand Foyer. At night the brilliant mosaics of the dome envelope (itself reminiscent of a Fabergé egg) are animated by a programmable LED display that forms a vivid, changing and massive electric artwork.

A glazed parabolic sky dome – a true eagle's nest offering an unsurpassed and majestic venue in Macau – surmounts the lavish five-star hotel.

The realisation of this pioneering building maximises the speed and rationality of design and construction. The local construction industry was tasked to deliver an unprecedented building within reasonable time and cost. The design was also tailored to facilitate construction on a very compact urban site in the heart of the city. The structure is a combination of conventional reinforced concrete, composite deck and steel. The curtain wall façade and cladding assemblies were all manufactured in southern China.

1 Curved circular interior of casino
2 Exterior view
3 Podium ground floor plan
4 Typical tower floor plan

Photography: courtesy Dennis Lau & Ng Chun Man Architects & Engineers (HK) Ltd

258 m | 846 ft

Grand Lisboa

Location Macau

Completion 2008

Client Sociedade de Turismo e Diversões de Macau, S.A.

Architect Dennis Lau & Ng Chun Man Architects & Engineers (HK) Ltd

Structural engineer Maunsell Structural Consultants Ltd

MEP engineer Parsons Brinckerhoff (Asia) Ltd

Façade engineer Merry Ocean Façade Technologies Ltd

Cost consultant Davis Langdon & Seah Hong Kong Ltd

Lighting consultant ISL/Light Direction

Other consultants Khuan Chew & Associates (KCA) International Ltd (interior designer) • Alan Chan Design Co. (interior designer) • SM&W (AV consultant) • Westwood Hong & Associates Ltd (acoustic) • Food Service Consultants Ltd (kitchen)

Main contractor Hip Hing Engineering (Macau) Co. Ltd

Uses Podium (G/F–3/F): hotel facilities, retail outlets, gaming • tower (5/F–43/F): guestrooms, gaming, restaurant • basement (B1/F–B4/F): parking, loading dock, staff facilities & back-of-house, mechnical rooms, gaming

Number of buildings 1

Above-ground storeys 48

Height 258 m (846 ft)

Basements 4

Mechanical levels Basement: 2 • 4/F, 16/F, 30/F

Refuge levels 4/F, 15/F, 29/F

Sky-lobby levels 31/F

Site area 11,626 m² (125,141 ft²)

Total gross area 169,654 m² (1,826,140 ft²)

Floor area ratio (FAR)/Plot ratio 11.65

Gross typical floor area 1,750 m² (18,837 ft²)

Total number of elevators 36

Elevator brand Schindler

Number of car parking spaces 338

Number of motorbike parking spaces 549

Hotel brand Grand Lisboa

Principal structure materials Reinforced concrete, composite deck, steel

Source: Dennis Lau & Ng Chun Man Architects & Engineers (HK) Ltd

2

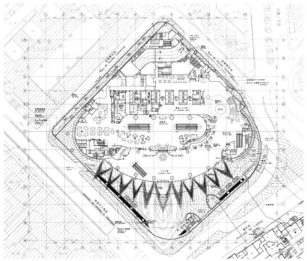

3

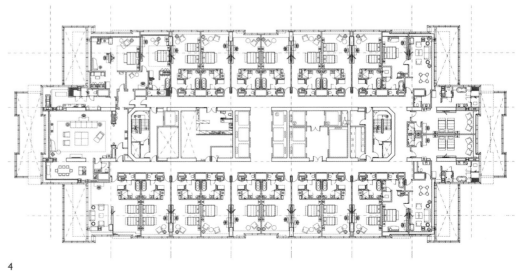

4

The Shanghai IFC (International Finance Center) is one of the most significant developments in Pudong, China's most important financial and commercial centre. This LEED Gold project – consisting of three towers, a shopping mall, and a public plaza – is a central element of Pudong's skyline. Viewed from the Bund, Shanghai's historic riverfront promenade, the development assumes a distinctive presence among the city's landmarks.

The project includes two towers, 48 and 56 storeys, each with approximately 140,000 square metres (1.5 million square feet) of floor area for office and hotel use. The China headquarters of HSBC occupies more than half of the south tower, which also includes the 290-room Ritz-Carlton Shanghai, Pudong, with commanding views of the central city. A third tower, 24 storeys tall, contains serviced apartments, complete banquet and conference facilities, a fitness centre and a swimming pool.

The towers share a common architectural language. Starting with elegant, rectilinear forms clad in a vertically grained glass-and-stainless-steel curtain wall, the towers are sculpted by shearing off corners and edges, creating **crystal-like shafts** that gesture toward one another, creating a single composition from two buildings. Where the edges are sliced away, a horizontally grained interior is revealed.

A four-level podium houses approximately 55,000 square metres (592,000 square feet) of retail, restaurants, and support spaces for the hotels. Below-grade is a cinema complex, retail, a 1,800-space car park and connections to the subway. Tunnels and sky bridges conveniently provide pedestrian connections to the adjoining sites. The project's ground plane is an urban park, extensively landscaped and punctuated with fountains, gardens, sitting areas, and open courts that integrate with the below-grade retail level.

1   Night perspective of retail entrance
2   Overall view
3   Interior of IFC mall
4   Typical hotel floor plan
5   Typical office floor plan
6   Site plan

Photography: ©Tim Griffith; illustrations: ©Pelli Clarke Pelli Architects

---

260 m | 853 ft

Shanghai IFC

Location Shanghai

Completion 2011

Client Sun Hung Kai Properties Ltd

Architect Pelli Clarke Pelli Architects

Associate architect P&T Group

Architects of record East China Architectural Design & Research Institute (ECADI) • P&T Group

Structural engineer Maunsell Structural Consultants

MEP engineer Parsons Brinckerhoff

Façade engineer ALT

Cost consultant Davis Langdon & Seah

Landscape architects Design Land Collaborative • DLQ Design (HK) Ltd • EDAW|AECOM

Lighting consultant Lighting Planners Associates

Main contractor Shanghai Construction

Uses North tower – lobby/retail: 4 floors: 5,152 m² (55,456 ft²); office: 46 floors: 124,748 m² (1,342,776 ft²); parking: 1,800 spaces below-ground • south tower – base lobby/hotel functions: 4 floors; office: 29 floors; HSBC headquarters: 23 floors; The Ritz-Carlton Shanghai, Pudong hotel (290 rooms): 15 floors • IFC Residence – guest amenities: 7 floors; serviced apartments: 16 floors; number of rooms: approx. 400

Number of buildings 4

Height North tower: 260 m (853 ft) • south tower: 250 m (820 ft) • IFC Residence: 85 m (279 ft) • IFC mall: 30 m (98 ft)

Above-ground storeys North tower: 56 • south tower: 48 • IFC Residence: 24 • IFC mall: 4

Basements North tower: 5 • south tower: 5 • IFC Residence: 5 • IFC mall: 5

Mechanical levels North tower: 5/F, 21/F, 22/F, 39/F, 40/F, 55/F, 56/F • south tower: 5/F, 20/F, 21/F, 22/F, 38/F, 39/F, 40/F, 56/F, 57/F, 58/F • IFC Residence: 4/F • IFC mall: 4/F

Refuge levels North tower: 5/F, 22/F, 39/F • south tower: 5/F, 20/F, 38/F

Sky-lobby levels North tower: N/A (shuttle transfers 30/F, 43/F) • south tower: 52/F

Site area 64,406 m² (693,260 ft²)

Gross above-ground building area 355,000 m² (3,821,188 ft²)

Gross basement area 248,451 m² (2,674,304 ft²)

Source: Pelli Clarke Pelli Architects

2

3

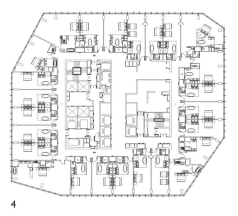

4

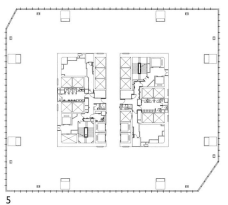

5

Total gross area 603,451 m² (6,495,492 ft²)

Floor area ratio (FAR)/Plot ratio 5.5

Gross typical floor area 2,500 m² (26,910 ft²)

Basic planning module 9 m (30 ft)

Total number of elevators North tower: 37 • south tower: 40

Speed of fastest elevators 8 m (26 ft)/s (north tower)

Elevator brand KONE

Number of car parking spaces 1,800

Hotel brand Ritz-Carlton

Residence brand IFC Residence

Residence service brand IFC Residence

Principal structure materials Steel

Other materials Concrete

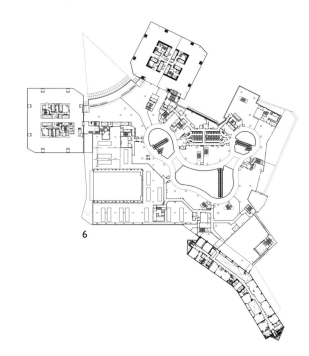

6

1

The tower, in form, configuration and articulation acknowledges and echoes the design of the existing buildings with inclined façade planes and curved corners, yet it is scaled, articulated and refined to reflect its importance. It's clad in a full curtain wall, with articulated fins, all finished in silver coloured aluminium and reflective glass in double-glazing units, making a taut and **elegant skin** carefully wrap the sculpture tower.

■ Located at the Third Ring Road in Beijing's CBD, opposite the iconic CCTV Headquarters, this new Grade A office tower is the last and final component of the prestigious Fortune Plaza project. It completes a development that already features offices, apartments, a five-star hotel and retail space.

As Beijing's second-tallest building at its completion in 2014, the tower provides prestige office accommodation above its spacious entrance foyer. Set in this prime location and within a large and extensively landscaped park, the building is also linked to the MTR via a retail arcade below-ground.

The main entrance lobby (finished in imported granite and marble) is enclosed by a clear glass screen, which links it visually and physically to the extensive park outside. Enriched with water walls and artwork, it provides an appropriately scaled and articulated, elegant foyer to the tall tower. Column-free office space with a generous floor- to-ceiling height provides exclusive office accommodation.

A sky-lobby is formed on the 32nd floor and is served by six express lifts to guarantee high efficiency. Car parking and mechanical plant rooms are housed in the basement structure, which extends over the whole site and is linked to the existing, adjoining provisions.

1   Corner treatment of curtain wall
2   Northeast elevation
3   Section plan
4   Sky-lobby floor plan

Renderings: courtesy P&T Group

267 m | 876 ft

Fortune Financial Center

Location Beijing
Completion 2014
Client Xiang Jiang Xing Li Estates Development Ltd
Architect P&T Group
Associate architect CERI Ltd
Structural engineer Arup
MEP engineer PBA
Vertical transportation consultant PBA
Façade engineer SCHMIDLIN
Project management consultant HKI China Land Ltd
Cost consultant WT Partnership
Landscape architect ACLA
Lighting consultant Philip
Other consultants LEED – EMSI
Uses Offices & retail
Number of buildings 1

Above-ground storeys 60
Height 267 m (876 ft)
Basements 4
Mechanical levels 11/F, 26/F, 41/F
Refuge levels 11/F, 26/F, 41/F
Sky-lobby levels 32/F
Site area 13,582 m² (146,195 ft²)
Gross above-ground building area 151,585 m² (1,631,647 ft²)
Gross basement area 24,296 m² (261,520 ft²)
Total gross area 175,881 m² (1,893,167 ft²)
Floor area ratio (FAR)/Plot ratio 11.2
Gross typical floor area 2,550 m² (27,448 ft²)
Total number of elevators 40
Speed of fastest elevators 6 m (20 ft)/sec
Number of car parking spaces 296
Principal structure materials Steel, concrete, glass

Source: P&T Group

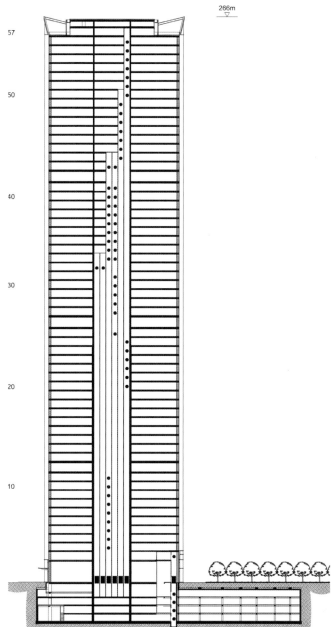

3

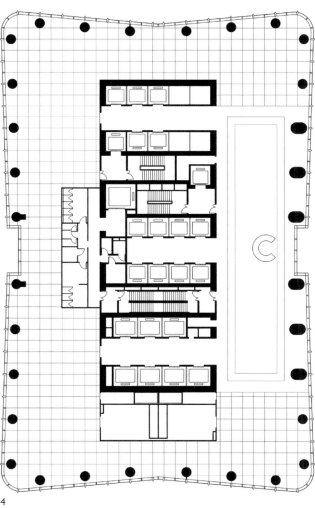

4

Forming part of the Kowloon Station development at Union Square, the 270-metre-tall (886-foot) twin towers here house the Cullinan apartments. Designed by Wong & Ouyang, the two towers also comprise the W Hotel and the Harbourview Place Suites.

The variety of accommodation assigned to The Cullinan twin towers and the integration with the retail component in the podium presented some unique planning challenges requiring innovative solutions. The issues of access and identity were perhaps the most prominent. All vehicular traffic to Union Square is directed to an elevated road system on the west side of the site. To create an arrival experience that compliments the scale of both towers, forecourts were carved out of the podium on either side of the towers at this level. These became the shared, formal arrival courts and drop-off points for both towers and the retail mall. Large 40-metre-tall (131-foot) **glass boxes** at the foot of the towers mark the entrances to the W Hotel in the south tower and apartments in the north tower. These contrast well with the horizontal expression of the podium retail mall façades, giving each element its own presence.

An internal road system leads from these drop-offs up to the upper landscaped podium deck where a separate double-height covered drop-off between the towers serves as a more protected and private arrival area. From here, the individual lobbies that serve the various apartment 'zones' and the residents' recreation facilities are accessed through a unique landscaped 'street'. Clad with an energy efficient double-glazed unitised curtain wall system, the twin towers are characterised by a modern, clean-lined aesthetic, making these hotel and apartment buildings able to stand apart from their neighbours and to enjoy the panoramic sea views on the prominent face of Union Square.

1   View of hotel at night
2   Overall view
3   Floor plan (high zone)
4   Floor plan (middle zone 2)
5   Floor plan (middle zone 1)
6   Harbourview Place suites drop-off
7   Section

Renderings & illustrations: courtesy Wong & Ouyang (HK) Ltd

270 m | 886 ft

The Cullinan

Location Hong Kong
Completion 2008
Client Sun Hung Kai Properties
Architect Wong & Ouyang (HK) Ltd
Structural engineer Arup
MEP engineer J. Roger Preston Limited
Façade engineer Meinhardt Façade
Project management consultant Harbour Vantage Management Ltd
Cost consultant WT Partnership
Landscape architect Belt Collins Associates
Lighting consultant Lighting Planners Associates, Isometrix
Other consultants Steve Leung & Associates, AFSO (interior design)
Main contractor Sanfield Building Contractors Ltd
Uses Residential, serviced apartments, hotel
Number of buildings 2
Height 270 m (886 ft)
Above-ground storeys 68

Basements 1
Refuge levels Cullinan I: 12/F, 39/F, 65/F [T21] • Cullinan II: 12/F, 39/F, 65/F [T20]
Site area 135,403 m² (1,457,466 ft²)
Gross above-ground building area Cullinan I: 69,513 m² (748,232 ft²) [T21] • Cullinan II: 24,258 m² (261,111 ft²) [T20]
Total gross area 93,771 m² (1,009,342 ft²)
Floor area ratio (FAR)/Plot ratio 7.893 (domestic)
Gross typical floor area Cullinan I: 1,300 m² (13,993 ft²) [T21] (mid zone) • Cullinan II: 590 m² (6,351 ft²) [T20] (mid zone)
Total number of elevators Cullinan I: 20 [T21] • Cullinan II: 7 [T20]
Speed of fastest elevators Cullinan I: 6 m (20 ft)/s [T21] • Cullinan II: 5 m (16 ft)/s [T20]
Elevator brand Hitachi (Cullinan I), Fujitec (Cullinan II)
Number of car parking spaces 175
Hotel brand W Hotel
Residence service brand Harbourview Place
Principal structure materials Reinforced concrete
Other materials Double-glazed curtain wall, aluminium cladding

Source: Wong & Ouyang (HK) Ltd

2

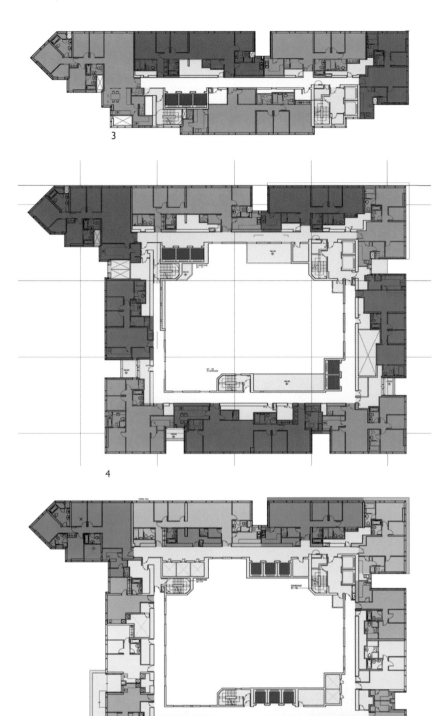

3

4

5

6

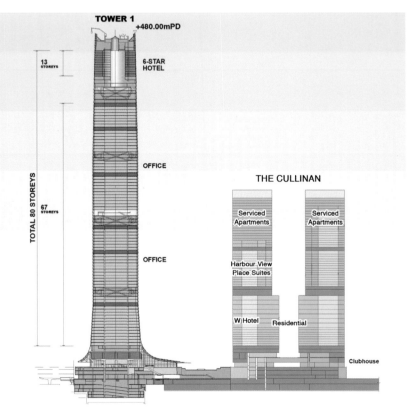

TOWER 1

+480.00mPD

13
STOREYS

6-STAR
HOTEL

OFFICE

THE CULLINAN

67
STOREYS

TOTAL 80 STOREYS

OFFICE

Serviced
Apartments

Serviced
Apartments

Harbour View
Place Suites

W Hotel

Residential

Clubhouse

7

■ The Chengdu International Commerce Centre (CDICC) is a mixed-use development featuring 280-metre-high (919-foot) twin towers serving as the **eastern gateway** into the heart of Chengdu as well as the anchor to the Dongda Street neighbourhood – a financial district and home to international corporation headquarters.

CDICC encompasses 1.3 million square metres (13,993,084 square feet) of office, retail, hotel, serviced apartments and residential program. It exemplifies the principles of smart development growth, urbanism, and sustainability through its LEED Silver certified design.

The development creates a continuous underground connection that links the Metro station through basement retail all the way to the Shahe riverside and Tazhishan Park. The development creates layers in the urban fabric by creating elevated public spaces on the roof of a commercial retail podium. This connection creates both an indoor and outdoor experience with boutique shops and al fresco dining and cafes along the length of this

development. The Skynet above the podium roof creates an elegant and functional space allowing al fresco dining under its canopy and festive celebrations. As an architectural form, it elegantly weaves the sleek towers together, as if the tower façade flows seamlessly down and along the length of the podium.

1 Aerial view of office towers
2 View along Dongda Street showing city gateway
3 Typical office floor plan

Renderings: courtesy Gravity Partnership Ltd

Chengdu ICC

Location Chengdu

Completion Site A: 2014 • Site B: 2017 (estimated)

Client Long Global Investment (Chendu) Limited • Joint Venture Partners: Sung Hung Kai Properties Limited, Henderson Land Development Company Limited and The Wharf (Holdings) Limited

Architect Gravity Partnership Ltd.

Architect of record China Southwest Architectural Design and Research Institute Corp. Ltd

Structural engineer Ove Arup & Partners (Shenzhen)

MEP engineer Meinhardt (M&E) Ltd

Vertical transportation consultant Meinhardt (M&E) Ltd

Façade engineer Hiersemenzel & Associates

Project management consultant Gravity Partnership Ltd

Cost consultant Langdon & Seah China Limited

Landscape architects Sales office: Gravity Green Ltd
• Sites A & B: Belt Collins International (HK) Ltd.

Lighting consultant Lighting Planners Associates

Other consultants [Sites A & B] Interiors: Ronald Lu & Partners (Hong Kong) Ltd.
• retail planning: Aedas Ltd. • sales office (interior): Draughtzman; Cream Architecture

Main contractors Site A: Sichuan No.6 Construction Co., Ltd. • Site B: China Construction Third Engineering Bureau Group Co. Ltd

Source: Gravity Partnership Ltd

Uses Residential: 698,770 m² (7,521,497 ft²) • office: 382,839 m² (4,120,845 ft²) • retail: 184,651 m² (1,987,567 ft²) • hotel: 38,254 m² (411,762 ft²) • refuge: 32,721 m² (352,206 ft²) • basement: 588,872 m² (6,338,565 ft²) • other: 62,925 m² (677,319 ft²)

Number of buildings Site A: 11 • Site B: 13 • Site C: 26

Height [Site A] (residential) 95–125 m (311–410 ft); (clubhouse) 8 m (26 ft) • [Site B]: (office) 210 m (689 ft) & 280 m (919 ft); (retail) 10.6–25.5 m (35–84 ft); (residential) 150 m (492 ft) • [Site C]: (office) 160 m (525 ft) & 280 m (919 ft); (hotel) 120 m (394 ft); (retail) 12 m (39 ft) & 18 m (59 ft); (residential) 11–150 m (36–492 ft)

Above-ground storeys [Site A]: (clubhouse) 1; (residential) 27–39 • [Site B]: (office) 44 & 57; (retail) 2–5; (residential) 42 & 43 • [Site C]: (hotel) 30; (office) 30 & 57; (retail) 2 & 3; (residential) 3–48

Basements Site A: 2 • Site B: 5

Mechanical levels Tower B-01: 6/F, 17/F, 30/F, 45/F, roof • Tower B-02: 6/F, 18/F, 31/F, roof

Refuge levels [Site A] Tower A-1#: 18/F • Tower A-2#: 18/F • [Site B] Tower B-01# (office): 6/F, 17/F, 30/F, 45/F • Tower B-02# (office): 6/F, 8/F, 31/F • Towers B-05#, B-06# (residential): 13/F, 28/F • Towers B-07#, B-08# (residential): 13/F, 29/F

Sky-lobby levels Site B-01#: 31/F, 32/F

Site area 205,514 m² (2,212,134 ft²)

Gross above-ground building area 1,347,303 m² (14,502,249 ft²)

Gross basement area 641,729 m² (6,907,513 ft²)

Total gross area 1,989,032 m² (21,409,762 ft²)

2

Floor area ratio (FAR)/Plot ratio 6.1

Gross typical floor area [Site A]: (residential) 360–740 m² (3,875–7,965 ft2); (clubhouse) 1,100 m² (11,840 ft²) • [Site B]: (office) 2,103–2,631 m² (22,636–28,320 ft²); (residential) 860–1,255 m² (9,257–13,509 ft²); (retail) 600–3,394 m² (6,458–36,533 ft²) • [Site C]: (office) 1,400 m² (12,917 ft²) & 2,800 m² (30,139 ft²); (retail) 570–4,524 m² (6,135–48,696 ft²); (hotel) 950–1,800 m² (10,226–19,375 ft²); (residential) 241–821 m² (2,594–8,837 ft²)

Basic planning module Site B-01#, 02# (office): 12 m (39 ft)

Total number of elevators Site A: 28 • Site B: 131

Number of double-deck elevators Site B: 4

Speed of fastest elevators Site A: 2.5 m (8 ft)/s • Site B: 7 m (23 ft)/s

Elevator brands Site A: Kone • Site B: TBC

Number of car parking spaces Site A: 1,505 • Site B: 10,902

Number of bike parking spaces Site A: 94 • Site B: 2,423

Residence brands Site A: SIRIUS • Site B: The ARCH CHENGDU

Residence service brand Kai Shing Management Services Limited

Principal structure materials Reinforced concrete

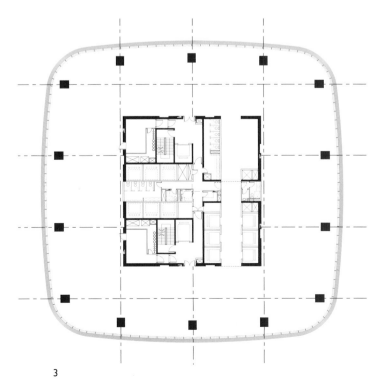

3

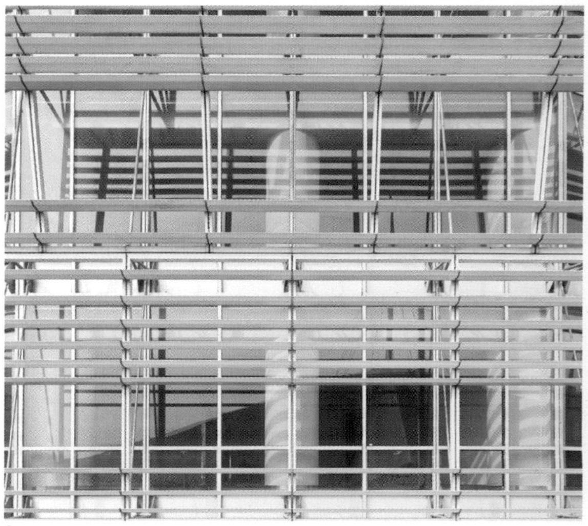

■ At 280 metres (919 feet) in height, this new mixed-use development in Zhengzhou is one of the tallest buildings in western China (as at when this book went to press). Advanced environmental technology, such as a building envelope that reduces solar heat gain and allows the tower to breathe, makes it appropriate to the climate of Zhengzhou.

A **solar reflector** – specifically designed through an intensive series of daylighting studies to maximise the amount of natural light – accentuates the atrium in the 416-room JW Marriott Hotel Zhengzhou (opened in 2014) located in the upper levels. The surfaces of the atrium are finished to help drive light deep within. The atrium is equipped to modulate light levels, based on the available light provided by the reflector, through a series of light-sensing dimmer switches. This feature enables the atrium to consume less energy and generate less heat throughout the year.

The hotel atrium also features a unique, smart control system that utilises an internal stack effect and external wind pressure to achieve a well-ventilated environment. The smart control system operates in different modes to move large volumes of fresh air through the indoor environment using natural forces.

1 Close-up of exterior
2 Overall view at night
3 View of solar reflector
4 Looking up at exterior building envelope
5 Typical office floor plan
6 Typical hotel floor plan

Credits: 2,3,4 SOM | ©Si-ye Zhang; 1,5,6 courtesy SOM

280 m | 919 ft

Millenium Royal Plaza

Location Zhengzhou
Completion 2013
Client Greenland Group
Architect Skidmore, Owings & Merrill LLP (SOM)
Associate architect TK
Architect of record East China Architectural Design & Research Institute (ECADI)
Structural engineer SOM
MEP engineer SOM
Wind engineer RWDI
Landscape architect SWA Group
Lighting consultant Kaplan, Gehring, McCarroll Architectural Lighting
Main contractor Zhejiang Zhong Tian Construction Group Co., Ltd

Uses Hotel, office, retail
Number of buildings 1
Height 280 m (919 ft)
Above-ground storeys 56
Basements 3
Site area 30,478 m² (328,062 ft²)
Total gross area 240,169 m² (2,585,158 ft²)
Gross typical floor area 2,600 m² (27,986 ft²)
Total number of elevators 22
No of car parking spaces 203
Hotel brand JW Marriott
Principal structure materials Composite

Source: Skidmore, Owings & Merrill LLP (SOM)

2

3

4

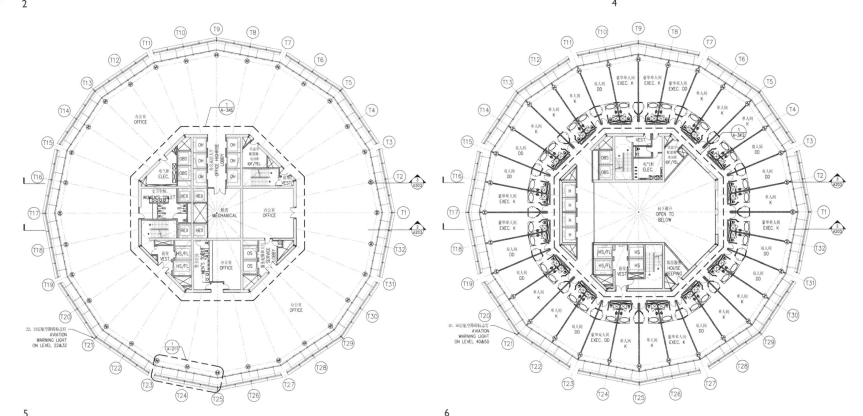

5

6

700 m

600 m

500 m

400 m

300 m

284 m | 931 ft

200 m

100 m

■ The new station, which is on the east side of the city, spans a clear town-planning axis that will terminate in a **double-tower** feature at its west end. The expanse of the station building together with the vertical emphasis of the mirror-image, 284-metre-high (931-foot) twin towers will form a crisp, gateway-style contrast. The towers themselves, built on windmill-shaped ground plans, will contain offices along with a hotel, apartments and a business club. Revolving recesses forming two-storey sky-lobbies give the towers their distinctive outlines.

1   Close-up of southwest perspective
2   Overview of southwest perspective
3   Lobby floor plan
4   Typical floor plan
5   Sky-lobby floor plan

Renderings & illustrations: ©gmp

Greenland Zhengzhou Central Plaza

Location Zhengzhou
Completion 2016
Client Zhongyuan Real Estate Business Department of Shanghai Greenland Group
Architect gmp (von Gerkan, Marg and Partners | Architects)
Local Design Institute Architectural Design & Research Institute of Tongji University (Group) Co., Ltd
Structural engineers schlaich bergermann und partner • Architectural Design & Research Institute of Tongji University (Group) Co., Ltd
MEP engineers Parsons Brinckerhoff • Architectural Design & Research Institute of Tongji University (Group) Co., Ltd

Uses Office, hotel, residential, commercial
Number of buildings 2
Height 283.9 m (931 ft)
Above-ground storeys 63
Basements 4
Site area 54,491 m² (586,536 ft²)
Gross above-ground building area 764,000 m² (8,223,627 ft²)
Principal structure materials Composite

Source: gmp (von Gerkan, Marg and Partners | Architects)

2

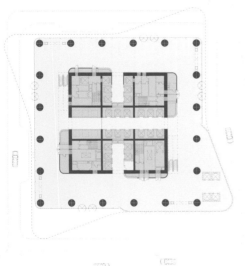

3

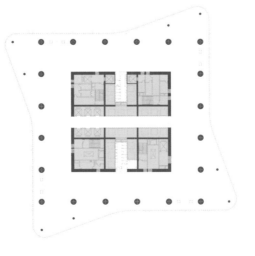

4

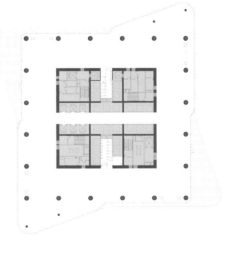

5

1

■ The 66-storey mixed-use tower is located in the Zhujiang development, planned as Guangzhou's new city centre near the Pearl River. While other mixed-use buildings typically step back, or slope, as they get taller, the challenge here was to define an iconic, monolithic form that accommodated all uses efficiently. Inspired by the segmentation and veining of **Chinese bamboo**, the tower is designed as a single volume that pinches in at the corners in relation to the changing programmatic functions stacked within. The field of staggered vertical strips on the façade stretch and compress like tendons in response to the varying floor-to-floor heights required for each distinct function.

1   Looking up at the tower's façade
2   Overall view
3   Typical hotel plan
4   Typical apartment plan
5   Typical condo plan
6   Typical office plan

Photography: ©Goettsch Partners

296 m | 972 ft

R&F Yingkai Square

Location Guangzhou
Completion 2015
Client Guangzhou R&F Properties Co., Ltd
Architect Goettsch Partners
Associate architect Guangzhou Residential Architectural Design Institute
Structural engineer Beijing R&F Properties Development Co.
MEP engineer Arup
Vertical transportation consultant Arup
Façade engineer Goettsch Partners (façade designer)
Landscape architect ACLA
Lighting consultant BPI
Other consultants Super Potato (hotel interior design) • Steve Leung Designers (residential interior design)
Main contractor Guangzhou R&F Properties Co., Ltd
Uses Hotel 28,300 m² (304,618 ft²) [53/F–66/F] • office 113,260 m² (1,219,120 ft²) [3F–52/F] • retail 2,000 m² (21,527 ft²) [1/F–2/F]
Number of buildings 1
Height 296.2 m (972 ft)

Above-ground storeys 66
Basements 6
Mechanical levels 9/F, 25/F, 39/F, 55/F
Refuge levels 9/F, 25/F, 39/F, 55/F
Sky-lobby levels 36/F, 36/F (mezzanine)
Site area 7,942 m² (85,487 ft²)
Gross above-ground building area 143,560 m² (1,545,267 ft²)
Gross basement area 30,710 m² (330,560 ft²)
Total gross area 174,270 m² (1,875,827 ft²)
Floor area ratio (FAR)/Plot ratio 18
Gross typical floor area 2,220 m² (23,896 ft²)
Basic planning module 1.25-m (4-ft) curtain wall module; 10-m (33-ft) bay
Total number of elevators 29
Speed of fastest elevators 6 m (20 ft)/s
Hotel brand Park Hyatt
Principal structure materials Concrete, composite superstructure

Source: Goettsch Partners

2

3

4

5

6

■ Their design inspired by the city flower of Nanchang, the **two towers** on Site A are the centrepiece of a new mixed-use, high-rise development that will support a balanced mix of office, retail and public spaces. Rising to a height of 300 metres (984 feet), they will be one of the tallest buildings in central China. Each tower consists of 110,000 square metres (1,184,030 square feet) of Class A office space, plus a two-storey, open-air observation deck that will offer sweeping views of the surrounding mountains. A pair of low-rise structures (each housing 5,000 square metres [53,819 square feet]) will accompany the skyscrapers and provide retail and conference functions for the towers.

SOM used parametric modelling software to design the exterior walls, whose form is based on studies of molten metal. The towers' organic, twisting profile will form a uniquely reflective and luminous surface. Grand in stature, yet sinuous in shape, these towers will appear unlike any others in the world. At the top of each tower, vertical axis wind turbines are oriented towards prevailing winds. This array of turbines will collect enough energy to power all of the high-efficiency elevators in the building.

1   Close-up view of façade exteriors
2   Street view
3   Typical office single tenant floor plan (zone 1)
4   Typical office single tenant floor plan (zone 2)
5   Typical office single tenant floor plan (zone 3)
6   Typical office multiple tenants (4–8) floor plan (zone 1)
7   Typical office multiple tenants (4–8) floor plan (zone 2)
8   Typical office multiple tenants (2–4) floor plan (zone 3)
9   Elevator diagram

Photography: ©G. Binder; renderings: ©SOM | Crystal GC; illustrations: courtesy SOM

Greenland Center NGC

Location Nanchang
Completion 2015 (estimated)
Client Greenland Group Nanchang
Architect Skidmore, Owings & Merrill LLP (SOM)
Architect of record East China Architectural Design & Research Institute (ECADI)
Structural engineer SOM
MEP engineer SOM
Landscape architect SWA Group
Lighting consultant KGM Lighting

Uses Office, retail, commercial
Number of buildings 2 towers + 2 smaller buildings
Height 300 m (984 ft)
Above-ground storeys 63
Basements 3
Site area 16,135 m² (173,675 ft²)
Gross above-ground building area 219,776 m² (2,365,649 ft²)
Total gross area 219,776 m² (2,365,649 ft²)
Principal structure materials Composite

Source: Skidmore, Owings & Merrill LLP (SOM)

2

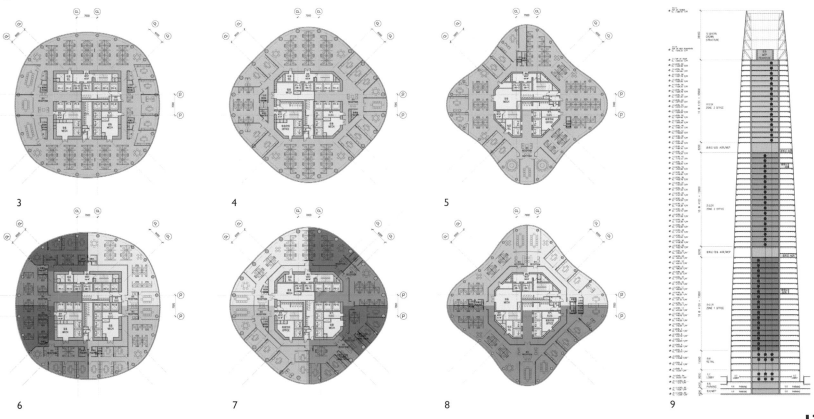

3

4

5

6

7

8

9

175

l

The Runhua Global Center's design is intended to be unique, a new city landmark. There are two towers with a total floor area of about 231,720 square metres (2,494,213 square feet), along with a four-storey podium, with three basement levels. Tower 1 is a 300-metre-high (984-foot) podium comprising 63 floors that include hotel facilities, Grade A office and retail areas; tower 2 is for apartments. The plane of tower 1 is a **'Y' type** with a more southern façade that enjoys sunshine. The depth of the plane is comparatively small with obvious advantages on sunshine, lighting and ventilation; furthermore, its plan is divergent, and with more view façades compared with other plan types. The 'Y' type plane of the tower is beneficial for building a comfortable urban space and to maximise the efficiency of the site's internal space. The symmetrical building form has two main façades with iconic features and building legibility.

1   Bird's-eye view
2   Rendering overview
3   Hotel floor plan
4   Office floor plan
5   Ground floor plan

Renderings & Illustrations: courtesy ECADI

Runhua Global Center

Location Changzhou

Completion 2016

Client Changzhou Runwanjia Real-Estate Co., Ltd

Architect East China Architectural Design & Research Institute (ECADI)

Structural & MEP engineers ECADI

Vertical transportation consultant ECADI

Façade engineer ECADI

Cost consultant Shanghai Xian Dai Architectural Design (Group) Co. Ltd

Main contractor China Construction Seventh Engineering Division Co. Ltd

Uses Commercial: 6,546 m² (70,460 ft²) [1/F, 3/F, 4/F] • hotel: 56,883 m² (612,283 ft²) [1/F, 3/F–29/F, 62/F, 63/F] • office: 80,098 m² (862,168 ft²) [1/F, 23/F–61/F]

Number of buildings 2

Height Tower 1: 300 m (984 ft) • tower 2: 146.5 m (480 ft)

Above-ground storeys Tower 1: 63 • Tower 2: 42

Basements 3

Mechanical levels 6/F, 22/F, 36/F, 50F

Refuge levels 6/F, 22/F, 36/F, 50F

Sky-lobby levels Hotel: 7/F • office: 23/F, 37F, 51F

Site area 31,957 m² (343,982 ft²)

Gross above-ground building area 137,442 m² (1,479,413 ft²) [tower 1]

Gross basement area 55,632 m² (598,818 ft²)

Total gross area 231,720 m² (2,494,213 ft²)

Floor area ratio (FAR)/Plot ratio 18.1

Gross typical floor area 176,088 m² (1,895,395 ft²)

Total number of elevators 33

Speed of fastest elevators 6 m (20 ft)/s

Elevator brands Schindler • Mitsubishi

Number of car/bike parking spaces 1100/580

Principal structure materials Steel, concrete

Source: East China Architectural Design & Research Institute (ECADI)

2

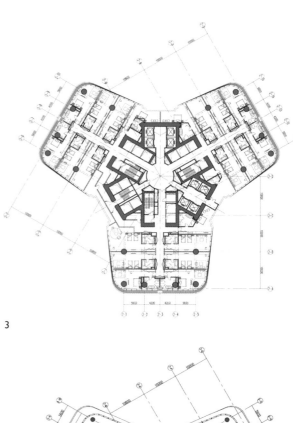

3

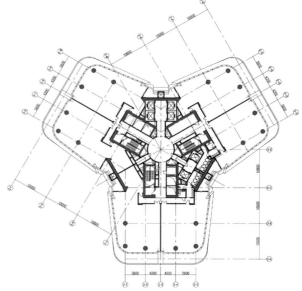

4

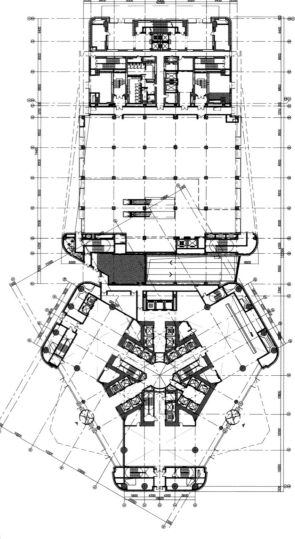

5

177

1

The Xiamen Shimao Straits Towers are inspired by the region's centuries-long history as a major international port of trade. The towers' shapes emulate the soft arches of a pair of Chinese junk **ship sails**. The site boasts panoramic views of the straits of Taiwan, and sits between the sea and a mountain range to the east. The two towers are bridged by a connective retail podium, which allows for residents, visitors and employees to transfer seamlessly between work, home and leisure. The project boasts leasable office space, retail space, residential apartments and a Hilton hotel, and provides residents and visitors alike with a dynamic variety of activities. Visually tied to the area's coastline, the design accentuates its local heritage while simultaneously representing the innovation that is driving Xiamen's modern growth. This landmark project utilises a specific vernacular and modern architectural language to symbolise the flow of the land into the sea, a subtle reminder of Xiamen's ancient past.

1 Connective retail podium bridges the two towers
2 Horizontal façade lines reference the ribs of Chinese Junk sails
3 Observation level floor plan
4 Typical hotel floor plan
5 Hotel sky-lobby floor plan
6 Floor plan (6/F)

Renderings: ©Gensler

Xiamen Shimao Straits Towers

Location Xiamen

Completion 2015

Client Shimao Group

Architect Gensler

Associate architect Shenzhen Aoyi Architecture & Engineering Design Company

Structural engineer DeSimone Consulting Engineers

MEP engineer Shanghai WSP Group

Façade engineer Guangzhou Siyida Curtain Wall Design Consulting Ltd.

Other consultants Arup (transportation) • Jingjinbao Environmental Acoustics Consulting (acoustics) • Shengmeihua Ltd (AV) • Bureau Veritas Building & Facilities Division (fire safety)

Uses Total: 39,014 m² (419,943 ft²) [retail] • office: 103,472 m² (1,113,763 ft²) • SOHO China office: 79,676 m² (857,625 ft²) • hotel: 44,995 m² (484,322 ft²); Tower A: parking [B1/F–3/F] • lobby [ground level] • retail [2/F–7/F] • office [8/F–27/F] • SOHO China Office [28/F–65/F]; Tower B: parking [B1/F–3/F] • lobby [ground level] • retail [2/F–7/F] • office [8/F–36/F] • hotel pool & gym [37/F] • hotel lobby [38/F] • hotel [40/F–53/F] • hotel restaurant & bar [54/F] • observation deck [55/F]; Retail podium: parking [B1/F–3/F] • lobby [ground level] • retail [2/F–7/F]; Plot A3 building 1: hotel ballroom • Plot A3 building 2: hotel conference hall

Number of buildings 5

Height 300 m (984 ft)

Above-ground storeys Tower A: 64 • tower B: 55

Basements 3

Mechanical levels Tower A: B1/F, B2/F, B3/F, 7/F, 27/F, 46/F • tower B: B1/F, B2/F, B3/F, 7/F, 22/F, 36/F

Refuge levels Tower A: B1/F, B2/F, B3/F, 7/F, 27/F, 46/F • tower B: B1/F, B2/F, B3/F, 7/F, 22/F, 36/F

Sky-lobby levels Tower B: 38/F, 56/F

Site area 22,354 m² (240,616 ft²)

Gross above-ground building area 273,847 m² (2,947,665 ft²)

Gross basement area 79,965 m² (860,736 ft²)

Total gross area 355,404 m² (3,825,537 ft²)

Floor area ratio (FAR)/Plot ratio 11.9

Number of car parking spaces 2,037

Hotel brand Hilton

Principal structure materials Steel, concrete

Source: Gensler

700 m
600 m
500 m
400 m

300 m | 984 ft

200 m
100 m

2

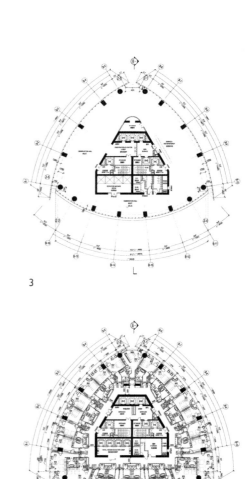

3

4

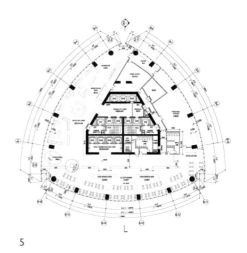

5

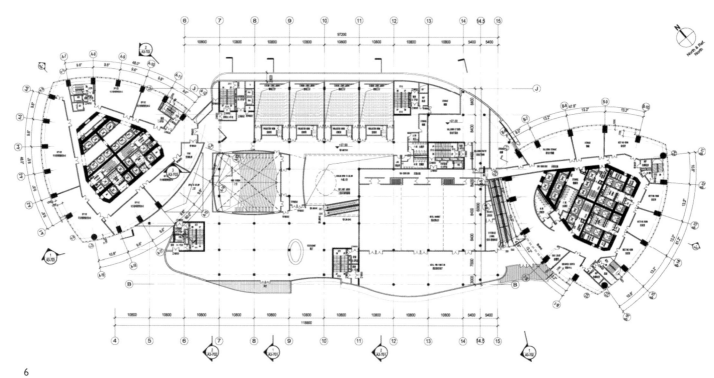

6

Gate to the East is located at Jinji Lake, Suzhou, in Jiangsu. The site's location is at the east end starting point of the central business district axial line of the Suzhou Industrial Zone – a very prestigious position – thus **a 'gate'** has been used as the project's architectural concept. There are two subways that cross the Suzhou area's central pedestrian belt, which bring a lot of foot traffic to the zone.

As a super-large urban complex, the build includes commercial facilities, observation points, offices, hotel-style apartments, a five-star hotel, along with other functions.

The total floor area of the project is more than 450,000 square metres (4,843,760 square feet), of which 340,000 square metres (3,659,729 square feet) is above-grade, and 110,000 square metres (1,184,030 square feet) is below-grade. The building also includes a podium of eight floors above-ground. There are two towers to the complex, the south and north towers.

1   View in context
2   Overall perspective
3   View of 'gate' at street level
4   Hotel floor plan (north tower)
5   Office floor plan (north tower)
6   Residence floor plan (south tower)

Credits: 1,2,4,5,6 courtesy ECADI;
3 ©Marty Carver

Gate to the East

Location Suzhou
Completion 2016
Client Suzhou Qianning Real Estate Co., Ltd
Architect RMJM Hong Kong
Associate architect East China Architectural Design & Research Institute (ECADI)
Structural & MEP engineers ECADI
Vertical transportation consultant Schindler Elevator Ltd
Façade engineers RMJM Hongkong Ltd
Project management consultant ECADI
Main contractor Shanghai Construction Group Co., Ltd
Uses Commercial, residential, office, hotel
Number of buildings 2, plus 1 podium
Height 301.8 m (990 ft)
Above-ground storeys South tower: 66 • north tower: 60
Basements 5

Mechanical levels 10/F, 27/F, 44/F, 58/F
Refuge levels 10/F, 27/F, 44/F, 58/F
Site area 24,319 m² (261,767 ft²)
Gross above-ground building area 336,681 m² (3,624,004 ft²)
Gross basement area 116,224 m² (1,251,025 ft²)
Total gross area 452,905 m² (4,875,029 ft²)
Floor area ratio (FAR)/Plot ratio 13.84
Gross typical floor area 2,000 m² (21,528 ft²)
Total number of elevators 61
Speed of fastest elevators 6 m (20 ft)/s
Elevator brand Schindler
Number of car/bike parking spaces 1901/400
Hotel brand Conrad
Principal structure materials Core & steel pipe concrete column
Other materials Glass curtain wall

Source: East China Architectural Design & Research Institute (ECADI)

2

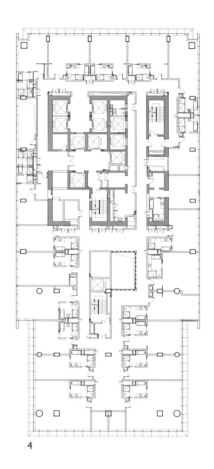

4

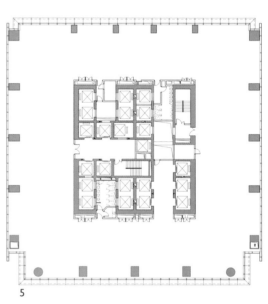

5

3

6

I

The Greenland Center JGC is located on the south of Puli Street, north of Gongqingtuan and east of the Shunhe Highway, Jinan City, Shandong Province. There are many historical and cultural relics surrounding the site, such as Baotu Spring and Wulongtan Park. The building is in the **centre of the city** and at the core of its commercial district. The site occupies a total area of 3.3257 hectares (8.2 acres) and includes a supertall high-rise tower of offices, commercial podiums, an underground garage and urban greenery. The total floor area of the project is around 200,000 square metres (2,152,782 square feet), of which about 146,000 square metres (1,571,530 square feet) is above-ground and 50,000 square metres (538,195 square feet) below grade.

The building is 303 metres (994 feet) high. There are 60 storeys, a five-storey high-rise podium and a three-level basement. In addition there are two podium groups: the east podium group comprises three-storeys on the ground with two levels underground, while the north podium group comprises four storeys above-grade, and one level underground.

1 Rendering of entrance plaza
2 Overview rendering
3 Office floor plan
4 Floor plan (5/F)
Renderings: courtesy ECADI

303 m | 994 ft

Greenland Center JGC

Location Jinan
Completion 2015
Client Shanghai Greenland Group Shandong Co., Ltd
Architect East China Architectural Design & Research Institute (ECADI)
Structural & MEP engineers ECADI
Vertical transportation consultant KONE
Façade engineers Merry Ocean Façade Technologies Co., Ltd
Cost consultant Shanghai Shen Yuan Engineering Investment Consulting Co., Ltd
Landscape consultant ASPECT Studios
Lighting consultant Shanghai Ying Tong Lighting Co., Ltd
Main contractor Shanghai Construction Group Co., Ltd
Uses Commercial, office
Number of buildings 1
Height 303 m (994 ft)
Above-ground storeys 60
Basements 3

Mechanical levels 15/F, 31/F, 31M/F, 45/F
Refuge levels 15/F, 31/F, 45/F
Sky-lobby levels 32/F (apartment) • 57/F (club lobby)
Site area 33,300 m² (358,438 ft²)
Gross above-ground building area 146,520 m² (1,577,128 ft²)
Gross basement area 51,019.4 m² (549,168 ft²)
Total gross area 197,539.4 m² (2,126,296 ft²)
Floor area ratio (FAR)/Plot ratio 4.4
Gross typical floor area 2,000 m² (21,528 ft²)
Total number of elevators 58
Speed of fastest elevators 6 m (20 ft)/s
Elevator brand KONE
Number of car/bike parking spaces 860/600
Principal structure materials Core + steel pipe concrete column
Other materials Glass curtain wall, stone curtain wall

Source: East China Architectural Design & Research Institute (ECADI)

2

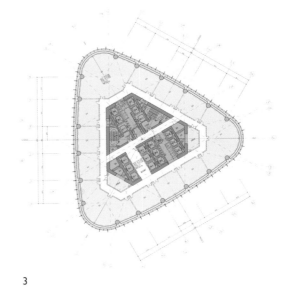

3

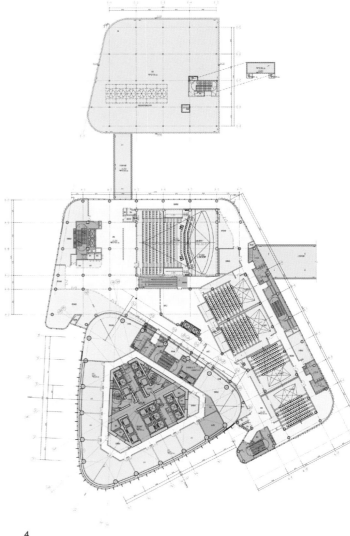

4

■ The East Pacific International (EPI) Centre occupies a highly prominent location on Shennan Road, Futia. It comprises five towers on top of a retail podium. The two towers to the eastern end provide over 100,000 square metres (1,076,391 square feet) of Grade A office space. The floors are designed around a central core, with 3-metre-clear (10-foot) floor space and full-height window to maximise daylight and views. Both main lobbies open into a grand plaza, which is landscaped for the enjoyment of office workers and public.

The central tower is a 100-metre-tall (328-foot) luxury urban hotel with more than 330 guest rooms. In addition to the amenities in the podium, including the ballroom, restaurants and swimming pool, there's also a banquet hall at the top floor and a roof garden.

The shopping mall occupies the lower three levels of podium. The large glass roof over the atrium brings abundant daylight into the retail space to generate open, spacious and relaxing ambience.

The twin towers at the western end feature as some of the tallest residential towers in China. The towers capture panoramic views of the city and the Shenzhen Bay. A multilevel sky-bridge connecting the two towers functions as the residential clubhouse. (This connecting structure presented a great challenge in the structural design.) The towers offer about 900 flats ranging between two and three bedrooms, along with duplex units with private gardens to meet the demands of different demographics.

Environmental issues are well considered in the design of the apartment towers. All units have **large windows** to allow maximum light gain and natural ventilation. Sky gardens are integrated into the building form to bring outdoor greenery into living spaces. A large landscaped garden with a large swimming pool for the use by the residents is designed at the podium roof.

1 Close-up view of the top of apartment towers
2 Perspective view from the northwest
3 South elevation
4 Section
5 Apartment entrance hall
6 Ground floor plan
7 Sky garden (45/F)
8 Typical apartment floor plan (low zone)

Renderings & illustrations: courtesy Wong & Ouyang (HK) Ltd

308 m | 1,010 ft
300 m | 984 ft

EPI Residences

Location Shenzhen

Completion 2013

Client Shenzhen East Pacific Real Estate Development Company, Ltd

Architect Wong & Ouyang (HK) Ltd

Associate architect A+E Design (local design institute)

Structural engineer Arup

MEP engineer Meinhardt

Landscape architect Earthasia HK

Lighting consultant Branston Partnership Inc., Lighting Design

Main contractor China Construction, 2nd Company, Shenzhen
• Jianhe Curtain Wall Co. Ltd (façade)

Uses Office, hotel, health club 45/F–49/F (serviced apartments)

Number of buildings 5 towers on a 2-storey podium

Height Offices: Block A – 150 m (492 ft), Block B – 100 m (328 ft) • hotel: 110 m (361 ft)
• serviced apartments: Tower A: 308 m (1,010 ft), Tower B: 270 m (885 ft)

Above-ground storeys 85

Basements 4 (1 retail, 3 car park)

Refuge levels 16/F, 30/F, 45/F, 60/F (SA)

Site area Office: 11,296.8 m² (121,598 ft²) • hotel & SA: 21,903.6 m² (235,768 ft²)

Gross above-ground building area 360,000 m² (3,875,008 ft²)

Gross basement area 30,000 m² (322,917 ft²)

Total gross area 390,000 m² (4,197,925 ft²)

Floor area ratio (FAR)/Plot ratio Office: 9.44 • hotel & serviced apartments: 13.3

Number of car parking spaces 1,400

Number of bike parking spaces 140

Residence brand The Langham, Futian Shenzhen

Residence service brand East Pacific Residences

Principal structure materials Reinforced concrete

Source: Wong & Ouyang (HK) Ltd

2

3

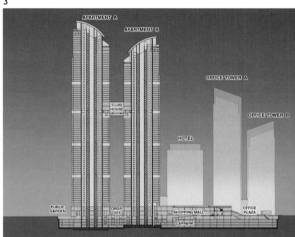

4

5

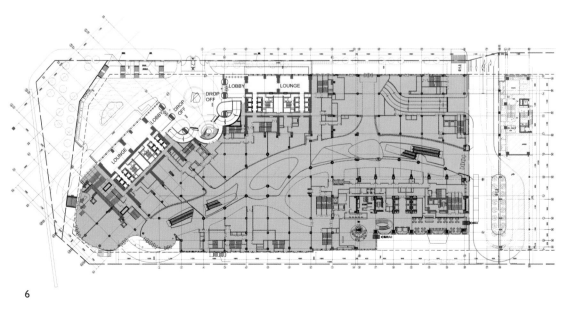

6

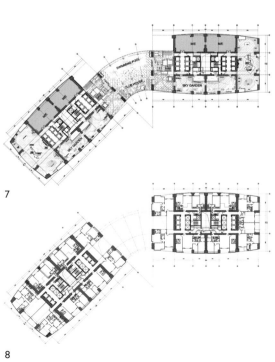

7

8

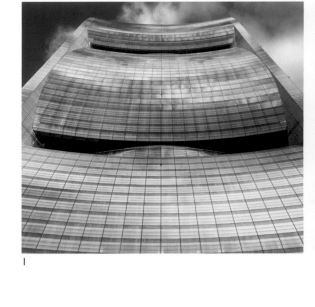

■ The 71-storey-tall Pearl River Tower's all-inclusive high-performance design philosophy combines unique active and passive sustainable measures to reduce its environmental impact, and allows the building to operate with approximately 30 percent less energy than a similar structure built to China's stringent energy codes.

The building's generally rectangular floor plate has been shifted slightly from Guangzhou's orthogonal grid into an **evocative curvilinear form** to maximise its utilisation of prevailing breezes and to better capture the sun's energy through the strategic location of photovoltaic (PV) technologies. PVs are integrated with the building envelope (asymmetrically located on the building's vaulted roof glass and incorporated into the sunshade devices on the east and west façades), serving the dual function of building skin and power generator.

East and west elevations are straight while the south façade is concave and the north façade convex. The south side of the building is dramatically sculpted to direct wind through four openings, two at each mechanical level, to accelerate the air and drive energy-producing vertical axis wind turbines. The power is then converted to electrical energy for the building. The building envelope's cavity is mechanically ventilated from the occupied space via low-level inlets under an inner monolithic glass panel.

The radiant ceiling cooling panel system is combined with direct outdoor air systems (DOAS) and an underfloor air delivery system; eliminating floor fan rooms and reducing air-shaft sizes resulted in a smaller building core. The double wall façade also allows greater flexibility to the layout of office space: the absence of fan coils, VAV boxes, filters, ductwork, insulation and other items typically requiring tenant-specific alterations throughout most of the floor plate

will result in reduced cost for tenant fit-out and future retrofits. Double-deck elevators have been installed to reduce the size of the building's core and create a more efficient floor plate. The mechanical design approach allowed architects to reduce the building's floor-to-floor height from 4.2 metres to 3.9 metres (13.8 feet to 12.8 feet; essentially saving five storeys of construction within the same square footage of exterior envelope).

Pearl River Tower will be one of the first supertall buildings certified as a LEED Platinum building by the USGBC – the highest level of sustainable design recognised by the internationally recognised organisation.

1 Looking up the curtain wall exterior
2 Overall view in context
3 Overall view at eye level
4 View of vertical axis wind turbine
5 Zone 1: typical office floor plan
6 Zone 2: typical office floor plan
7 Zone 3: typical office floor plan
8 Conference centre level floor plan

Photography: SOM | ©Tim Griffith; illustrations: ©SOM

310 m | 1,016 ft

Pearl River Tower

Location Guangzhou
Completion 2013
Client Guangzhou Pearl River Tower Properties Co., Ltd
Architect Skidmore, Owings & Merrill LLP (SOM)
Architect of record Guangzhou Design Institute
Structural engineer SOM
MEP engineer SOM
Vertical transportation consultant Fortune Shepler Consulting
Landscape architect SWA Group
Lighting consultant Pivotal Lighting Design
Other consultants Rolf Jensen & Associates (fire) • RWDI (wind) • Shen Milsom Wilke, Inc. (acoustics) • Meinhardt
Main contractor Shanghai Construction Group
Uses Office
Number of buildings 1

Height 309.6 m (1,016 ft)
Above-ground storeys 71
Basements 5
Site area 10,635 m² (114,474 ft²)
Gross above-ground building area 169,500 m² (1,824,483 ft²)
Gross basement area 44,600 m² (480,070 ft²)
Total gross area 214,100 m² (2,304,553 ft²)
Gross typical floor area 2,000 m² (21,528 ft²)
Total number of elevators 29
No of double-deck elevators 2 banks of 7
Speed of fastest elevators 9 m (29 ft)/s
Elevator brand Otis Elevator Company
No of car parking spaces 852
Principal structure materials Composite

Source: Skidmore, Owings & Merrill LLP (SOM)

2

3

4

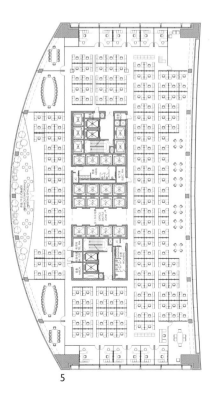

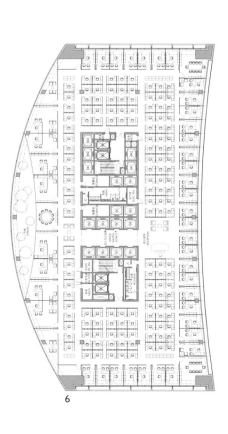

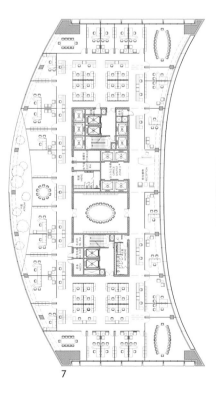

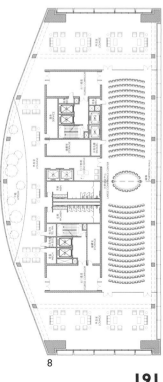

5

6

7

8

■ The Nanjing International Youth Cultural Centre is located on the river in Hexi New Town, Nanjing's new central business district. The project includes a conference centre, two towers and the plaza that terminates the CBD's main axis at the riverfront. The project is Nanjing's flagship development; its masterplan expresses the **continuity, fluidity and connectivity** between the urban environment of Hexi New Town, the agricultural farmland along the Yangtze River and the rural landscapes of Jiangxinzhou Island. An additional proposal by Zaha Hadid Architects includes a pedestrian bridge to link the plaza with the other side of the river. The Nanjing International Youth Cultural Centre occupies a site area of 5.2 hectares (12.85 acres) with a construction floor space of 473,010 square metres (5,091,437 square feet).

The taller of the two towers is 315 metres (1,033 feet) and is 68 floors high, and contains office floors and a five-star hotel. The shorter tower is 255 metres (837 feet) and is 61 floors high and houses a hotel for the conference centre on the plaza. The two towers share a five-level, mixed-use podium.

1 Looking up through the 'canyon' of the building façades
2 Southeast street view
3 Northeast bird's-eye view in context
4 Multifunctional hall
5 Conference hall
6 Ground floor plan

Renderings & illustrations: ©Zaha Hadid Architects

Nanjing International Youth Cultural Centre

Location Nanjing

Completion 2015

Client Hexi New Town Planning Bureau

Architect Zaha Hadid Architects

Architect of record China Architecture Design and Research Group

Structural engineer Buro Happold

MEP engineer Buro Happold

Vertical transportation consultant Dunbar and Boardman

Façade engineer Buro Happold

Landscape architect SWA

Lighting consultant Brandston Partnership Ltd

Other consultants Zhejiang University, China (acoustics) • China Art and Technology Institute (theatre)

Main contractor China State Construction Engineering Corporation Division 8 • China State Construction Engineering Corporation Division 3

Uses Hotel, retail, commercial, office

Source: Zaha Hadid Architects

Number of buildings 2 towers with 1 podium + 1 conference hall

Height T2: 315 m (1,033 ft) • T1: 255 m (837 ft) • conference hall: 45.6 m (150 ft)

Above-ground storeys Conference centre: 6 – 1/F: conference hall, concert hall, press room, exhibition hall, retail, VIP/VVIP lounge; 2/F: multifunctional hall, retail; 2M/F: conference hall, concert hall, plant room; 3/F: multifunctional halls; 4/F: plant room; 5/F: meetings rooms; 6/F: meeting rooms, restaurant, VIP lounge • podium: 5 – 1/F: four- & five-star hotel lobbies, office lobby, retail; 2/F: F&B, hotel amenities, retail; 3/F: F&B, hotel amenities; 4/F: F&B, hotel amenities; 5/F: hotel amenities, plant room • T1: 61 – 6/F–61/F: 1000-key four-star hotel • T2: 68 – 6/F–40/F: offices; 41/F–68/F: 300-key five-star hotel

Basements Conference centre: 2 – B1M/F: conference hall; B1: retail, kitchen, bicycle parking, car parking; B2: car parking • podium: 3 (T1/T2) – B1/F: hotel amenities, service facilities, car parking; B2/F & B3/F: car parking

Mechanical levels T1: 11/F, 26/F, 41/F, 52/F, 58/F • T2: 11/F, 25/F, 26/F, 41/F, 57/F, 61/F, 67/F

Refuge levels T1: 11/F, 26/F, 41/F • T2: 11/F, 25/F, 26/F, 36/F, 41/F, 57/F

Sky-lobby levels T2: 40/F

Site area 52,020.86 m² (559,948 ft²)

Gross above-ground building area Total: 358,291 m² (3,856,612 ft²) • conference hall: 113,491 m² (1,221,607 ft²) • podium – 32,800 m² (353,056 ft²) • T1: 92,000 m² (990,280 ft²) • T2: 120,000 m² (1,291,669 ft²)

2

3

4

5

Gross basement area Total: 114,719 m² (1,234,825 ft²) • conference hall: 79,919 m² (860,241 ft²) • podium (T1/T2): 34,800 m² (374,584 ft²)

Total gross area 473,010 m² (5,091,437 ft²)

Floor area ratio (FAR)/Plot ratio 9

Gross typical floor area Conference centre: varies • podium: 6,000 m² (64,583 ft²) • T1: 1,700 m² (18,299 ft²) • T2: 2,100 m² (22,604 ft²)

Basic planning module 8.4 m (28 ft) grid

Total number of elevators Conference centre: 46 • podium: 6 • T1: 12 • T2: 19

No of double-deck elevators 8

Speed of fastest elevators 6 m (20 ft)/s

Elevator brand KONE

Number of car parking spaces Conference centre: 914 • towers & podium: 183

Number of motorbike spaces 1,105

Number of bike parking spaces Conference centre: 796 • towers & podium: 53

Hotel brand Jumeirah Hotels

Principal structure materials Steel

Other materials Reinforced concrete, glass; glass fibre reinforced concrete (façade), glass fibre reinforced gypsum (interior)

6

193

The 74-storey China World Tower (Tower A) embodies quiet, purposeful elegance. As the tallest building in the city (at the time this book went to press), it has marked the broader China World Trade Center (CWTC) development as the centrepiece of Beijing's central business district.

The tower has a classic columnar proportion of a base, shaft/middle and crown integrated in the exterior surfacing and structural expression. The bold tapering profile will create a strong, **curved silhouette** that reaches for the sky. A confident, singular soaring form will contrast with the jumble of new buildings constituting the business district's skyline. Folded seamlessly into the urban fabric of streets and plazas,

330 m | 1,083 ft

the tower's base visually strengthens the lower tower levels, with transparency welcoming people to the spaces within. The ground floor contains clearly organised entries to the offices on the west and the hotel on the east. The tower's robust base visually and physically anchors the soaring spire.

The shaft's façades are layered with a series of vertical glass and metal fins to provide solar shading of the interiors. The faceted surface combined with glass/metal fins creates a textural yet transparent effect, with reflective surfaces becoming a 'waterfall' of light and detail.

Celebrating the public functions of the hotel at the top of the building, the upper levels take advantage of higher floor-to-ceiling heights and impressive views to create distinctive public rooms. The crown development demarcates the Shangri-La hotel and celebrates the public access and functions at the top of the tower.

Another building designed by SOM, Tower B (59 storeys and 288 metres [945 feet] high) will become the final touch to the CWTC when completed in 2016, next to Tower A.

1   Close-up of façade curtain wall, Tower A
2   Overall night view, Tower A
3   Vertical transportation diagram, Tower A
4   Tower A (right); Tower B (centre)
5   Office sky-lobby (32/F), Tower A
6   Hotel sky-lobby (64/F), Tower A

Credits: 1,4 ©SOM; 2 ©Gaohan; 3,5,6 courtesy China World Trade Center Co., Ltd

China World Tower

Location Beijing
Completion Tower A: 2010 • Tower B: 2016
Client China World Trade Center Co., Ltd
Design architect Skidmore, Owings & Merrill LLP (SOM)
Project architect Wong & Tung International Ltd
Architect of record Capital Engineering & Research Incorporation Ltd
Structural engineers Tower A: Ove Arup & Partners • Tower B: SOM
MEP engineers Tower A: WS Atkins/Parsons Brinckerhoff • Tower B: Parsons Brinckerhoff
Vertical transportation consultant Parsons Brinckerhoff
Façade engineers Tower A: Meinhardt • Tower B: KWP
Landscape architects Tower A: SWA Group • Tower B: Ohtori
Lighting consultants Tower A: BPI • Tower B: LPA
Wind consultants Tower A: RWDI/BMT Fluid Mechanics Ltd • Tower B: BMT Fluid Mechanics Ltd
Main contractor China State Construction Engineering Corporation (CSCEC)
Uses Tower A: office, hotel (278 rooms, upper levels) • Tower B: hotel (551 rooms, lower levels), office

Number of buildings 2
Height Tower A: 330 m (1,083 ft) • Tower B: 288 m (945 ft)
Above-ground storeys Tower A: 74 • Tower B: 59 (including rooftop mechanical)
Basements Tower A: 3 • Tower B: 4
Site area Tower A: 36,421 m² (392,000 ft²) • Tower B: 8,118.50 m² (87,387 ft²)
Total gross area Tower A: 295,000 m² (3,178,000 ft²) • Tower B: 148,000 m² (1,598,042 ft²)
Floor area ratio (FAR)/Plot ratio 1.5 (for the entire 3-phase CWTC complex)
Gross typical floor area Tower A: 2,750 m² (29,590 ft²) • Tower B: 1,900 m² (204,440ft²)
Total number of elevators Tower A: 60 • Tower B: 36
Speed of fastest elevators Tower A: 10 m (33 ft)/s, shuttle lifts; up to 8m (26 ft)/s, office • Tower B: 8 m (26 ft)/s, shuttle lifts; up to 7 m (23 ft)/s office
Elevator brands Tower A: Schindler • Tower B: Hitachi
No of car parking spaces 1,503 (shared)
Hotel brands Tower A: China World Summit Wing (Shangri-La Hotels & Resorts) • Tower B: Hotel Jen
Principal structure materials Towers A & B: composite

Source: China World Trade Center Co., Ltd; Skidmore, Owings & Merrill LLP (SOM)

2

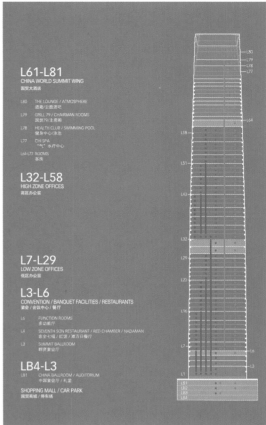

3

L61-L81
CHINA WORLD SUMMIT WING
国贸大酒店

L80   THE LOUNGE / ATMOSPHERE
       酒廊/云酷酒吧
L79   GRILL 79 / CHAIRMAN ROOMS
       国贸79/主席厅
L78   HEALTH CLUB / SWIMMING POOL
       健身中心/泳池
L77   CHI SPA
       "气"水疗中心
L64-L72 ROOMS
       客房

L32-L58
HIGH ZONE OFFICES
高区办公室

L7-L29
LOW ZONE OFFICES
低区办公室

L3-L6
CONVENTION / BANQUET FACILITIES / RESTAURANTS
宴会/会议中心/餐厅

L6   FUNCTION ROOMS
       多功能厅
L4   SEVENTH SON RESTAURANT / RED CHAMBER / NADAMAN
       家全七福/红馆/滩万行餐厅
L3   SUMMIT BALLROOM
       群贤聚宴会厅

LB4-L3
LB1   CHINA BALLROOM / AUDITORIUM
       中国宴会厅/礼堂

SHOPPING MALL / CAR PARK
国贸商城/停车场

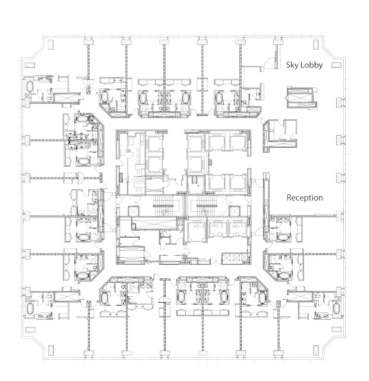

4

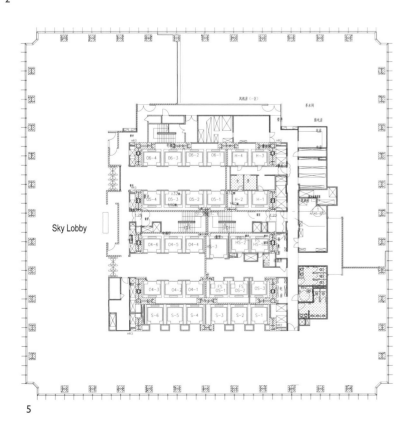

5

Sky Lobby

Sky Lobby

Reception

6

195

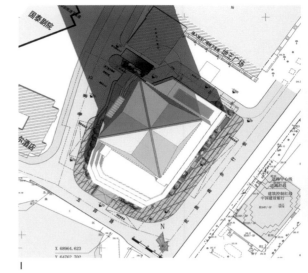

339 m | 1,112 ft

■ The Chongqing World Financial Center is an environmentally friendly, super high-rise building formed to provide Grade A office space and a first-class commercial shopping experience. The building is shaped in a distinctive abstract geometric form and its aesthetically pleasing contemporary design is balanced with the spirit of **oriental culture**, which pursues a noble and rich spiritual philosophy. The simple vertical lines and proportions aim to emphasise the top of the building, as well as to reduce the oppressive feeling from the building massing. The faceted building top is made with high reflectivity material that reflects sunlight from all directions, creating a lighting focal point to make the building stand out from Chongqing's foggy climate. The project's aim is to create a new landmark tailored to Chongqing's urban environment, and which helps to symbolise the rising start of Chongqing's new skyline.

1   Site plan
2   Rendering of building
3   Hotel floor plan
4   Office floor plan
5   View of tower in context

Renderings: courtesy C.Y. Lee & Partners Architects/Planners

Chongqing World Financial Center

Location Chongqing
Completion 2015
Client Chongqing Huaxun Real Estate Development Co., Ltd.
Architects C.Y. Lee & Partners Architects/Planners
    • Dayuan Architecture Design Consulting (Shanghai)
Structural engineer Arup
MEP engineer Arup
Vertical transportation consultant Arup
Façade engineer SuP Ingenieure GmbH
Cost consultant WT Partnership
Landscape architect DLC
Lighting consultant Brandston Partnership Inc
Main contractor China Construction Fourth Engineering Division Corp
Uses Parking (B1/F–B2/F) • shopping centre (B1/F–6/F) • international conference centre (7/F–8/F) • business facilities (9/F–70/F)

Number of buildings 1
Height 338.9 m (1,112 ft)
Above-ground storeys 72
Basements 6
Site area 5,800 m² (62,430 ft²)
Gross above-ground building area 163,700 m² (1,762,052 ft²)
Gross basement area 4,120 m² (44,347 ft²)
Total gross area 204,400 m² (2,200,143 ft²)
Floor area ratio (FAR)/Plot ratio 28.23
Gross typical floor area 2,103 m² (22,636 ft²)
Basic planning module 1.2 m² (12.9 ft²)
Brand of elevator Otis Elevator Company
Speed of fastest elevators 8 m (26 ft)/s
Number of car parking spaces 837
Principal structure materials Structural steel, aluminium extruded sections, aluminium plate, glass curtain

Source: C.Y. Lee & Partners Architects/Planners

2

3

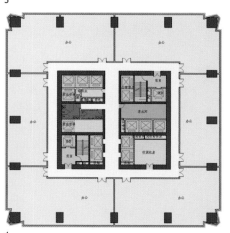

4

5

As the city's initial dock area on the Yangtze River, Chao Tian Men Plaza represents the great tradition of the shipping highway, which has fuelled Chongqing's development as one of China's largest modern cities. In designing the site, inspiration was drawn from historic images of great Chinese sailing vessels on the river, and the complex is intended to serve as a symbol of Chongqing's noble past as a trading centre. Gently arcing toward the water, the six towers of the complex form the 'apex' to the city's peninsula, like the **great masts of a ship**, with its sails pulling the city forward.

Bridging the four interior towers at the 60-storey level is the conservatory, which brings amenities and green spaces into the sky. The conservatory houses the hotel lobby, restaurants, pool, ballroom, spas, and clubhouse and gymnasium facilities for the residential apartments. It also links the towers to one another high above the skyline, affording uninterrupted views of both rivers and of central Chongqing. Chongqing's climate can fluctuate drastically, thus the glass enclosure ensures year-round enjoyment of the indoor gardens.

■ Located on a historically significant site at the confluence of the Yangtze and Jialing Rivers, the Raffles City Chongqing complex (also known as the Chongqing Chaotianmen Center) is composed of six slender towers that sit atop a five storey retail podium, featuring residential and office spaces, retail facilities, a serviced apartments residence, a hotel, restaurants and clubs. The project also integrates a public park and gardens and will be a major hub for land and water transport, housing a car park, metro station, bus interchange, ferry terminal and cruise centre. A major element of the design is a 402-metre-long (a quarter-mile), glass-enclosed conservatory, perched at the 60-storey level, accessible by four of the towers, providing a grand, common area for public activities.

At the ground level, the project includes an expansive park featuring gardens and landscape features, serving as one of the city's largest public amenities. The park gently slopes to the north, such that its entirety can be seen from the city, offering dramatic framed views to the water through the towers.

Beneath the park level, the podium offers five levels of retail gallerias, generously endowed with natural light and extensive views to both rivers. This ground level extends over the road, thereby providing pedestrian access to Chao Tian Men plaza and reconnecting the city to the water. Also included in the podium is a major public transport interface – housing terminals for subway, train and ferry services.

1 Aerial view at dusk
2 Bird's-eye view from the north
3 Cafe terrace
4 View along the central retail galleria
5 Section perspective through the conservatory
6 Axonometric drawing
7 Exploded axonometric diagram

Renderings & illustrations: courtesy Safdie Architects

Raffles City Chongqing

Location Chongqing
Completion 2019 (estimated)
Clients CapitaLand Ltd • CapitaMalls Asia Ltd • Singbridge Holdings Pte Ltd
Architect Safdie Architects
Executive architect P&T Group International Ltd
Structural engineer Arup
MEP engineer Parsons Brinckerhoff
Façade engineer ALT
Cost consultant Rider Levett Bucknall (quantity surveyor)
Landscape architect Williams, Asselin, Ackaoui & Associates Inc.
Other consultants CL3 Architects Ltd (interior design, hotel & convention) • The Buchan Group (interior design, retail) • Arup (LEED)
Uses Tower 1: residential (57,787 m² [622,014 ft²]), retail (228 m² [2,454 ft²]) • Tower 2: residential (57,026 m² [613,823 ft²]), retail (1,171 m² [12,604 ft²]) • Tower 3N: high-end residential (99,200 m² [1,067,780 ft²]) • Tower 3S: office (56,279 m² [605,782 ft²]), retail (160 m² [1,722 ft²]) • Tower 4N: office (64,733 m² [696,780 ft²]), hotel (41,062 m² [441,988 ft²]), retail (1,296 m² [13,950 ft²]) • Tower 4S: serviced apartments (28,964 m² [311,766 ft²]), office (28,661 m² [308,504 ft²]), hotel (2,067 m² [22,249 ft²]), retail (72 m² [775 ft²]) • Tower 5: residential (56,977 m² [613,295 ft²]) • Tower 6: residential (57,738 m² [621,487 ft²]) • conservatory: hotel (4,795 m² [51,613 ft²]), clubhouse/office (2,876 m² [30,957 ft²]), retail (2,428 m² [26,135 ft²]) • podium: retail (225,009 m² [2,421,977 ft²]), hotel (10,857 m²

Source: Safdie Architects

[116,864 ft²]), office (5,357 m² [57,662 ft²]), residential (6,909 m² [74,368 ft²]), project management offices (2,086 m² [22,453 ft²]), serviced apartments (1,034 m² [11,130 ft²])
Number of buildings 9 (8 towers, 1 podium)
Height 355 m (1,165 ft)
Above-ground storeys 79
Basements 3
Mechanical & refuge levels Total of 4 mechanical & refuge levels in each of the tall towers; 3 in each of the short towers
Sky-lobby levels 24/F, 42/F
Site area 92,000 m² (990,280 ft²)
Gross above-ground building area 917,000 m² (9,870,506 ft²)
Gross basement area 218,000 m² (2,346,532 ft²)
Total gross area 817,000 m² (8,800,000 ft²)
Floor area ratio (FAR)/Plot ratio 8.9
Gross typical floor area Varies
Basic planning module Varies
Total number of elevators 202
Speed of fastest elevators 6 m (20 ft)/s
Number of car parking spaces 3,900
Hotel brand InterContinental
Principal structure materials Reinforced concrete & steel

2

3

4

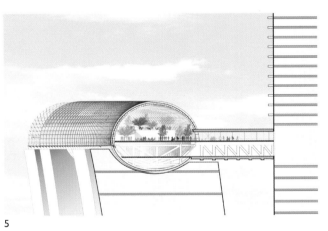

5

6

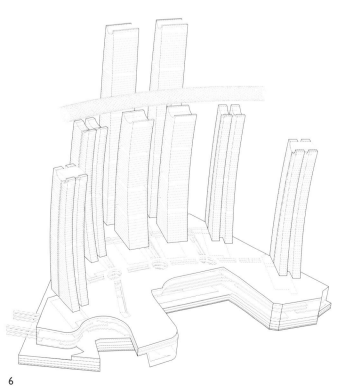

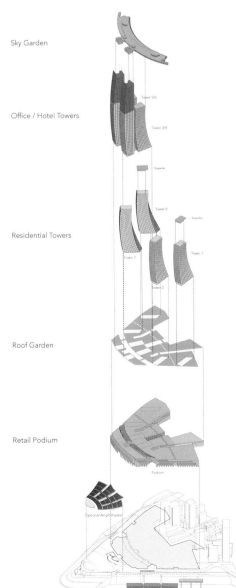

Sky Garden

Office / Hotel Towers

Residential Towers

Roof Garden

Retail Podium

7

■ Nanning Logan Century consists of a mixed-use tower that comprises office and hotel facilities, a retail complex with flagship stores, and a building housing high-end serviced apartments. The flower top of the office and hotel tower blooms in the sky, symbolising the blooming of Nanning's economy. At its apex, the **petal-shaped space** houses a grand sky lobby for a five-star hotel, on top of which is a public observation deck that's open to panoramic city views. The hotel's 250 guest rooms occupy the tapering portion of the tower (the high zone). The rest of the building bulk below is taken up by Grade A office space with 4.2-metre (14-foot) floor-to-floor heights.

To house these functions in a single tower its central core design was highly scrutinised to accommodate all elevator requirements for passengers and goods, fire services, as well as structural support. There are separate shuttle lifts for the public to reach the observation deck and hotel guests to go to the sky lobby; three lift zones for office users, plus independent entrances for hotel staff; the different ground levels allow for this clear and organised segregation of lobbies for different groups of users.

The various exterior façades are unified by the design of a curtain wall with aluminium vertical fins. These fins are not only decorative, but also cut down on solar heat gain by the projection factor of 300. The colour tone of the whole development ranges from white to grey with a hint of bluish grey for the visual glass. These building characteristics help to highlight modern design in Nanning, with this timeless piece of architecture.

1 View from street
2 Perspective at night
3 Bird's-eye view
4 Typical office floor plan

Renderings: courtesy Dennis Lau & Ng Chun Man Architects & Engineers (HK) Ltd

383 m | 1,256 ft

Nanning Logan Century

Location Nanning
Completion 2017
Client Logan Real Estate Co., Ltd
Architect Dennis Lau & Ng Chun Man Architects & Engineers (HK) Ltd
Structural engineer A+E Design
MEP engineer A+E Design
Façade engineer SUP Ingenieure Gmbtl
Cost consultant WT Partnership
Landscape architect AECOM
Uses Office, residential, retail, commercial
Number of buildings 3
Height Mixed-use: 383 m (1,256 ft) • serviced apartments 175.6 m (576 ft) • retail complex: 22.4 m (73 ft)
Above-ground storeys Mixed-use: 82 • serviced apartments: 50 • retail complex: 4
Basements 5
Mechanical levels 76/F (tower 1)
Refuge levels Tower 1: 5/F, 24/F, 43/F, 62/F • tower 2: 12/F, 20/F, 28/F, 36/F, 44/F

Sky-lobby levels 81/F
Site area 22,669 m² (74,373 ft²)
Gross above-ground building area Office: 145,851 m² (1,569,927 ft²) • commercial: 29,652 m² (319,171 ft²) • hotel: 47,579 m² (512,136 ft²) • car park & auxiliary: 3,964 m² (42,668 ft²) • serviced apartments: 75,577 m2 (813,504 ft²)
Gross basement area 86,723 m² (933,478 ft²)
Total gross area 389,346 m² (4,190,885 ft²)
Floor area ratio (FAR)/Plot ratio 5.54
Gross typical floor area Tower 1: 2,465 m² (8,087 ft²) • tower 2: 1,719 m² (5,640 ft²)
Total number of elevators Office: 21 • fire services & sightseeing: 2 • hotel: 9 • Tower 2: 8 • podium & basement 10
Number of car & motorbike parking spaces 1,633
Number of bike parking spaces 2,215
Hotel brand Sheraton
Principal structure materials Reinforced concrete & steel
Other materials Curtain wall, aluminium, glass

Source: Dennis Lau & Ng Chun Man Architects & Engineers (HK) Ltd

2

3

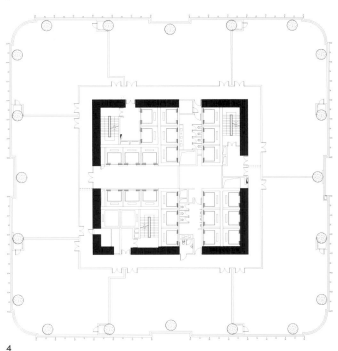

4

The Eton Place Dalian is located at the western edge of the central business district, offering breathtaking views to the city, harbour port, and Dalian Bay to the north and the beautiful mountains to the south. The site is at the juncture of two main streets, Zhong Shan Lu and Remin Lu, and is bound on the northern edge by ChangJiang Lu, a major thoroughfare running from the airport to central Dalian Station.

The vision for Eton Place Dalian is to create a contemporary focal point within Dalian's central business district. The project will set a new standard for high-end retail development for the city and will become the centre of commercial activity. It will provide a fresh, contemporary expression of the city's commitment to environmentally sensitive and healthy urban living in China. It will provide a vibrant, new, urban environment for shopping, business, tourism, entertainment, social and leisure activities, and become **a microcosm** of the 'New Urban Generation' connecting to the city at large with the natural environment.

The retail podium is the heart of the centre. Based on a planning module of 8.4 × 11 metres (27 × 36 feet) the building includes fashion boutiques, high-end luxury shops, a department store, a supermarket and an extensive food court.

Supertower 1 is a major landmark on the Dalian skyline and includes office space, a Five Star Suite Hotel (with approximately 200 rooms) and the Eton Hotel (with approximately 600 rooms). Amenities include two fitness centres with pools, restaurants, retail shops and landscaped sky gardens that ascend upwards through the building.

Supertower 2 contains approximately 700 units of serviced apartments, including one-, two- and three-bedroom units, as well as duplex units. This tower also includes restaurants, retail facilities and landscaped sky gardens.

1   View looking northeast
2   View looking south
3   View looking north
4   Hotel atrium, ST1
5   Typical office floor plan (low-rise), ST1
6   Typical five-star hotel floor plan, ST1
7   Ground floor plan, ST1
8   Typical hotel floor plan, ST1
9   Level 6 amenity floor plan, ST2
10   Typical serviced apartment floor plan, ST2
11   Ground floor plan, ST2
12   Typical SOHO floor plan, ST2

Credits: 1,2,4 ©Crystal CG; 3 ©G. Binder

383 m | 1,257 ft

Eton Place Dalian

Location Dalian
Completion 2017, supertowers 1&2 • 2015, mall • 2010, residential towers
Clients Eton Properties (overall project & towers) • Pavilion Real Estate (retail podium)
Architect NBBJ
Architect of record China Northeast Architecture Design Research Institute
Structural engineer Arup
MEP engineer Parsons Brinckerhoff
Vertical transportation consultant Parsons Brinckerhoff
Landscape architect Hassell
Lighting consultant BPI
Other consultants ALT Cladding (façade) • BMT Fluid Mechanics Ltd (wind)
Main contractor China Construction Second Engineering Bureau Ltd
Uses Retail, office, hotel, serviced apartments, SOHO, residential
Number of buildings 5 towers, 1 podium
Height Supertower 1: 383.1 m (1,257 ft) • supertower 2: 278 m (912 ft) • residential towers: 147 m (482 ft)
Above-ground storeys Supertower 1: 80 • supertower 2: 62 • residential towers: 43 • retail podium: 5

Basements 4
Mechanical & refuge levels Supertower 1: 7/F, 15/F, 29/F, 30/F, 45/F, 59/F, 74/F • supertower 2: 7/F, 15/F, 30/F, 45/F, 62/F
Sky-lobby levels Supertower 1: 76/F [hotel]
Site area 6.23 hectares (15 acres)
Gross above-ground building area 600,000 m² (6,458,346 ft²)
Gross basement area 93,586 m² (1,007,351 ft²)
Floor area ratio (FAR)/Plot ratio 10
Gross typical floor area Supertower 1: 2,000 m² (21,528 ft²) • supertower 2: 1,800 m² (19,375 ft²)
Basic planning module 1.5 m (4.9 ft) [ST1, ST2]
Total number of elevators Supertower 1: 29 • supertower 2: 15 • podium: 20
Speed of fastest elevators 8 m (26 ft)/s
Elevator brand KONE
Hotel brand Eton
Residence brand Eton
Residence service brand Eton
Principal structure materials Supertowers: hybrid structure (reinforced concrete & steel) • residential towers: concrete • podium: steel structure

Source: NBBJ

2

3

4

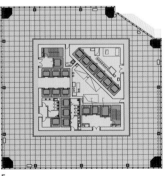

5

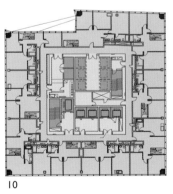

6

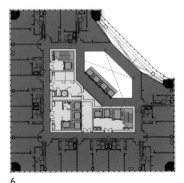

9

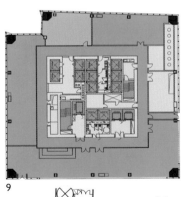

10

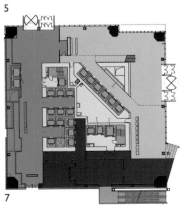

7

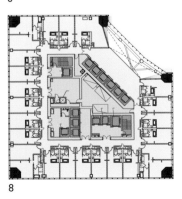

8

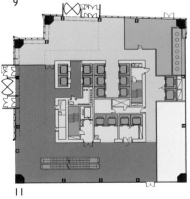

11

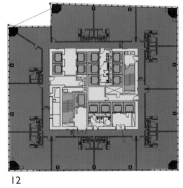

12

The China Resources Headquarters, a 392.5-metre-tall (1,288-foot) office tower, is located in the center of Houhai District in the ever-growing city of Shenzhen. The tall tower lies within the larger China Resources Business District Master Plan; bordered by Shenzhen Bay to the east, Shenzhen Sports Complex to the north and a linear greenbelt to the south. The headquarters tower is to become the **vertical icon** to mark the city's newest node.

Strategically positioned to overlook Shenzhen Bay, the China Resources Headquarters tower is linked to public transport through underground connections at B1. The experience is enriched by the addition of a park (2,000 square metres [21,527 square feet]) to the north where a small glass F&B pavilion floats, and a sunken plaza that functions as a hub space, connecting the office lobby at B1 mezzanine, a museum 3,000 square metres [32,292 square feet]), retail at B1, performance hall and auditorium.

The verticality of tower and its tapered sculptural form are further emphasised by 56 external columns. These 56 columns converge into 28 columns in the bottom and upper sections of the tower in the form of a diagrid. The diagrid not only strengthens the tower's structural integrity but it creates unique visual and functional conditions. At the lower section it creates a series of entry portals. At the upper section it creates an icon and helps to terminate the series of circular plans into a point. Such structural systems also offer column-free office interiors.

The tapering tower form works well, as the client plans to occupy the upmost part of the tower. Its corporate organisational structure allows for the design of smaller and more boutique office floorplates. The sky hall, located at the very top of the tower, is where various corporate functions are held and from where its occupants can have interior views of the spire and the work of the diagrid.

1 Internal view of crown from sky hall
2 Night overview from Shenzhen Bay
3 Typical office floor plan
4 Typical China Resources office floor plan
5 Sky hall floor plan

Renderings: courtesy Kohn Pedersen Fox Associates

China Resources Headquarters

Location Shenzhen
Completion 2017
Client China Resources
Architect Kohn Pedersen Fox Associates
Associate architect CCDI
Architect of record CCDI
Structural engineer Arup
MEP engineer Parsons Brinkerhoff
Vertical transportation consultant Parsons Brinkerhoff
Façade engineer Arup
Landscape architect Peter Walker Partnership
Lighting consultant BPI
Other consultants Lerch Bates (façade maintenance) • Faithful + Gould, Atkins group (sustainability) • MVA (traffic) • Arup (fire)
Main contractor China State Construction Engineering Company (CSCEC)
Uses Office (53 levels) • Skyhall (3 levels) • museum (ground level) • pavilion (ground level)
Number of buildings 3 (office tower, museum, retail pavilion)
Height 392.5 m (1,288 ft)

Above-ground storeys 67
Basements 5
Mechanical levels 4/F, 24/F, 48/F, 62/F
Refuge levels 13/F, 23/F, 36/F, 47/F, 62/F
Sky-lobby levels Sky lobby 1 (25/F) • sky lobby 1M (25M/F) • sky lobby 2 (49/F)
Site area 15.733 m² (169 ft²)
Gross above-ground building area Office tower: 193,168 m² (2,079,243 ft²) • museum 201 m² (2,163 ft²) • pavilion 203 m² (2,185 ft²)
Gross basement area basement area 59,413
Total gross area GFA 252,581
Floor area ratio (FAR)/Plot ratio 7.5–7.7
Gross typical floor area 3,300–3,600 m² (35,521–38,750 ft²)
Basic planning module 1.5 m (5 ft) [spacing]
Total number of elevators 53
Number of double-deck elevators 6
Speed of fastest elevators 9 m (29 ft)/s
Number of car parking spaces 754
Principal structure materials Steel tube in tube perimeter structure, concrete/steel core
Other materials Stainless steel cladding, insulated/laminated, Low-E glazing unit

Source: Kohn Pedersen Fox Associates

2

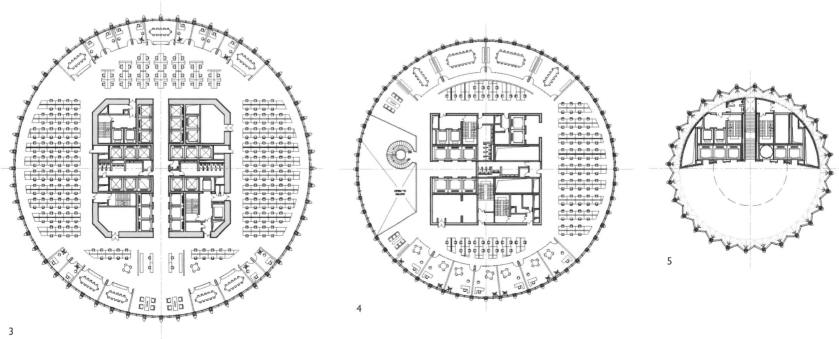

3

4

5

700 m

600 m

500 m

400 m 1,312 ft

300 m

200 m

100 m

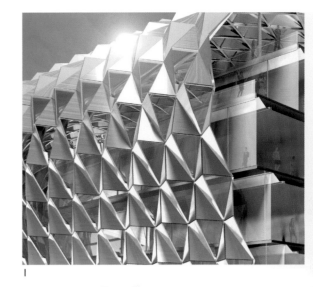

1

■ The ensemble of the Nanjing Olympic Suning Tower building (or NJ-T) at the city's CBD is a work of architecture of the highest aesthetic standard. Concavity and convexity explorations gave birth to two cutting-edge 'shells' of very different scales through which idea, design, form, structure, energy and technology will work in synergy. Both buildings – the vertical (tower) and the horizontal (retail) – emerge from the ground with striking sculptural impact, creating a provocative and iconic composition.

This **'earth vessel'** makes a statement for a new way of building. Its components are minimal, integrated with engineering and thus serve architectural, structural and mechanical purposes at once; its aesthetic and appearance derive from the coordinated whole of these systems and components. Transparency, ecology and user-comfort are the resulting benefits. The 'earth vessel' represents a new typology for a mixed-use tower, with a seductive form that combines the deep lease spans of the office space with the narrower lease spans required for hotels and residential uses. The long, narrow elliptical plan

of this design is ideal for the layout of residences and hotel rooms, with shallow lease spans and a large amount of developed façade length. To accommodate the greater depth required for office levels, the exterior tower façade bends outward at the lower floors, creating the large floor plates appropriate for office layouts.

Large-scale retail needs to be developed as an 'event', both as a memorable object in the city landscape and as a memorable interior spatial experience. The design concept proposes a softly rounded building form that follows the curves of the site and is wrapped in a luminous skin that flows down into an elliptical atrium. The retail becomes a sensuous, glowing landmark in the cityscape, with the skin cut away where it meets the street to reveal tall brightly lit show windows. The vessel's retail shell has a strong inward focus employing a large elliptical atria and arcades – to create an atmosphere that keeps the visitor focused on the retail experience (the intent is to create a grand interior gathering space that draws the visitor in and is so memorable that they will want to return again and again).

The geometry of the site, the views, the access and the relationship to the retail building determined in a large scale the location of tower.

Flowering trees are placed along the road and spread over the whole area and square surrounding the building complex. Wave patterns flow through the plaza, based on the idea of water, that is the essential base of living and a basic element of the nature all around Nanjing.

The ensemble is placed over a continuous landscaped plateau that keeps the access to pedestrian flows simple and legible. The plan's configuration allows for efficient vehicular and service access from virtually every corner of the site, the main access to the drop-off area occurs at Jiangdongzhonglu, secondary access and services are located along the streets in the south and west. The underground subway lines are along Jiangdongzhonglu and Hexidajie.

1 Close-up of façade
2 Rendering of overview
3 Interior view of atrium
4 Interior office lobby
5 Site plan

Renderings: courtesy JAHN

Nanjing Olympic Suning Tower

Location Nanjing	**Uses** Office, hotel, residential, retail, parking
Completion 2018	**Number of buildings** 2
Client Suning Real Estate Group Corp Ltd	**Height** 400 m (1,312 ft)
Architect JAHN	**Above-ground storeys** 88
Associate architects Shanghai Institute of Architecture Design & Research • Nanjing Architectural Design & Research Institute	**Basements** 4
Structural engineer Werner Sobek Stuttgart	**Site area** 317,000 m² (3,412,159 ft²)
MEP engineer WSP Flack + Kurtz	**Total gross area** 226,000 m² (2,432,644 ft²)
Vertical transportation consultant HH Angus & Associates Ltd	**Total number of elevators** 46
Façade engineer Werner Sobek	**Number of car parking spaces** 1,828
Landscape architect Rainer Schmidt Landschaftsarchitekten (RSLA)	**Principal structure materials** Steel & concrete composite
Lighting consultant AIK-Atelier de Yann Kersale	

Source: JAHN

2

3

4

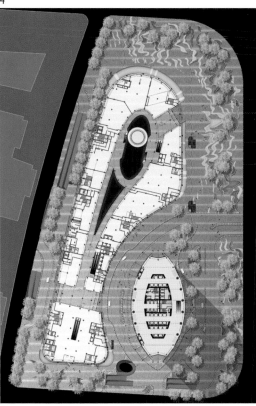

5

The majority of the tower is dedicated to multitenant office space. Special floors have been set aside as facilities for the Association of Southeast Asian Nations (ASEAN). The upper portion of the tower features a five-star atrium hotel. The topmost floors immediately above the hotel provide for an exclusive executive club, as well as a destination restaurant. Visitors can enjoy a 360-degree view of the surrounding area from a unique observation deck with two major levels – one enclosed and another open to the sky in a rooftop garden. A full complement of visitor and tourist facilities will be available at the sky deck, including a gift shop and cafe.

■ The goal for this project was to create a unique, powerful symbol for Nanning. As one of the tallest towers in the region, the project will command attention. The unique form of the Guangxi Financial Investment Center tower begins with a square base that widens to an octagon in the middle before gradually tapering back into a square plan at the top.

The lines of the podium building complement the tower form. Faceted, dynamic shapes continue the design language established in the tower to create a sculptural supporting component to the complex's shining star: the **iconic tower**.

A center skylight draws natural light deep into the hotel atrium. This natural light is enhanced by a narrow strip of windows recessed into the façade on the north and south sides of the tower, through the guestroom and hotel-amenity levels, where clearer glass is used to bring in more daylight.

The sweeping, curved lines of the tower create a unique presence on the skyline. The faceted glass façades reflect the sun and the surrounding city throughout the day in ever-changing patterns. At night, the facets of the tower are traced with LED lights to outline the powerful form, and the curving glass façades reflect the special night lighting that surrounds the base of the complex.

1 Observation deck and gardens of rooftop
2 View of tower's square base, widening to an octagon in middle and tapering back to square at top
3 Observation level floor plan
4 Office floor plan (high zone)
5 Level 4 floor plan
6 Level 7 floor plan

Renderings: ©John Portman & Associates

Guangxi Financial Investment Center

Location Nanning
Completion 2019
Client Guangxi Wei Zhuang Real Estate Co., Ltd
Architect John Portman & Associates
Associate architect Shanghai Institute of Architectural Design & Research (SIADR)
Structural engineer SIADR
MEP engineer SIADR
Vertical transportation consultant SIADR
Façade engineer SIADR
Project management consultant Shanghai Xiandai Engineering Consultants Co. Ltd
Cost consultant SIADR
Landscape architect SIADR
Lighting consultant SIADR
Traffic consultant Blue Design Institute
Uses Tower hotel: 34,908 m² (375,747 ft²) [63/F–78/F] • tower office: 160,943 m² (1,732,376 ft²) [4/F–60/F, 81/F–88/F] • tower observation: 3,822 m² (41,140 ft²) [89/F, 90/F] • tower podium & conference: 8,035 m² (86,488 ft²) [7/F, 8/F] • podium commercial: 23,182 m² (249,529 ft²) [1/F–5/F] • tower mechanical: 10,998 m² (118,381 ft²) [19/F, 20/F, 33/F, 34/F, 61/F, 62/F, 79/F, 80/F] • podium mechanical: 200 m² (2,153 ft²) • tower refuge: 6,900 m² (74,271 ft²) [11/F, 19/F, 33/F, 48/F, 62/F, 79/F] • tower lobbies: 3,565 m² (38,373 ft²) • basement parking: 79,165 m² (852,125 ft²)

Source: John Portman & Associates

Number of buildings 2
Height 409 m (1,342 ft) [tower] • 51 m (167 ft) [podium]
Above-ground storeys Tower: 90 • podium: 10
Basements 6
Mechanical levels 8: 19/F, 20/F, 33/F, 34/F, 61/F, 62/F, 79/F, 80/F
Refuge levels 6: 11/F, 19/F, 33/F, 48/F, 62/F, 79/F
Sky-lobby levels 4: 35/F, 36/F, 37/F, 38/F
Site area 17,356 m² (186,818 ft²) [usable area]
Gross above-ground building area 227,675 m² (2,450,673 ft²) [tower] • 34,036 m² (366,360 ft²) [podium] • 79,610 m² (856,915 ft²) [below-grade]
Gross basement area 30,000 m² (322,917 ft²)
Total gross area 310,000 m² (3,336,812 ft²)
Floor area ratio (FAR)/Plot ratio 4.95
Gross typical floor area Minimum: 2,025 m² (21,797 ft²) • maximum: 2,982 m² (32,098 ft²)
Basic planning module 1.5 m (4.9 ft)
Total number of elevators Total: 71 • tower: 57 • podium: 14
Number of double-deck elevators 22
Number of car/bike parking spaces 2,001/866
Principal structure materials Concrete, steel

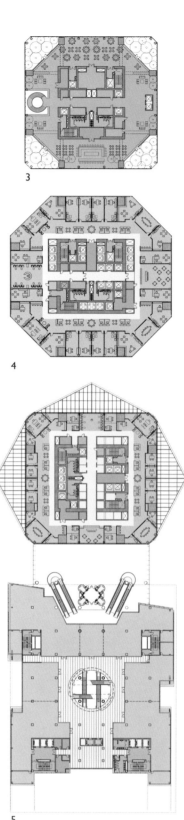

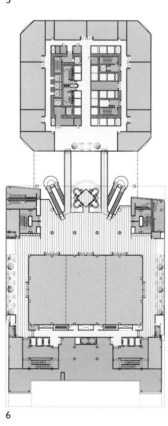

2

3

4

5

6

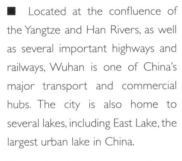

1

■ Located at the confluence of the Yangtze and Han Rivers, as well as several important highways and railways, Wuhan is one of China's major transport and commercial hubs. The city is also home to several lakes, including East Lake, the largest urban lake in China.

The design of the Corporate Center (Lots A1 to A3) aims to celebrate Wuhan's freshwater and commercial heritage, as well as its emergence as a political, economic and cultural centre. The development consists of the three towers and a podium building. Overall the project will contain a mix of office, residential and retail functions.

The sampans that once crowded the Yangtze River inspired the architecture of the three towers. The curving façades have a sail-like appearance and the three towers are arranged in a **line parallel** to the Yangtze, as if they are about to cruise upriver. To complete the composition, the tallest tower includes a soaring mast that reaches a height of more than 400 metres (1,300 feet).

The design of the towers' walls is a contemporary interpretation of traditional Chinese architecture. Decorative window screens that are found throughout the region have inspired the patterns on the glass. While the references are traditional, the performance is modern: the curtain walls will be made from energy-efficient double-glazing units that conform to the requirements of the LEED certification system.

At the base of the development is a dynamic four-level retail podium, which will house a convention centre, movie theatres, restaurants, a shopping mall and an outdoor rooftop garden with views of the Yangtze and surrounding city.

1   Retail podium
2   Aerial view in context
3   Typical office tower ground floor plan
4   Typical residential tower floor plan
5   Typical hotel floor plan

Renderings & illustrations: courtesy P&T Group

Wuhan Tiandi – Corporate Center

Location Wuhan

Completion 2016

Client Shui On Land

Architect Pelli Clarke Pelli Architects

Retail Designer Benoy

Associate architect P&T Group

Architect of record Wuhan Architectural Design Institute (WADI)

Structural engineer P&T Group

MEP engineer P&T Group

Vertical transportation consultant P&T Group

Façade engineer Arup

Cost consultant DLS

Landscape architect AECOM

Lighting consultant Brandston Partnership Inc. (BPI)

Other consultants Arup (green) • AECOM (traffic) • Graphia Brands (signage) • Wealth Island Consultants (hotel)

Main contractor China Construction Eight Engineering Division Corp. Ltd

Façade contractor Shanghai Mei Te Curtain System Co. Ltd

Uses A1 Tower: office (8/F–30/F), serviced apartments (33/F–56/F), hotel (59/F–74/F) • A2 Tower: office • A3 Tower: office • podium retail (1/F–6/F)

Number of buildings 4

Height A1 Tower: 436 m (1,430 ft) • A2 Tower: 156 m (512 ft) • A3 Tower: 190 m (623 ft) • retail podium: 35 m (115 ft)

Above-ground storeys A1: 73 • A2: 30 • A3: 37

Basements 3

Mechanical levels A1 Tower: 7/F, 16/F, 31/F–32/F, 47/F–48/F, 57/F–58/F, 75/F • A2 Tower: 17/F & 35/F • A3 Tower 21/F & 28/F • retail podium: varies

Refuge levels A1 Tower: 16/F, 31/F–32/F, 47/F–48/F, 57/F–58/F • A2 Tower: 17/F & 35/F • A3 Tower: 21/F & 28/F

Sky-lobby levels 60/F (hotel sky lobby, A1 Tower)

Site area 40,200 m² (432,709 ft²)

Gross above-ground building area Total: 402,564 m² (4,333,163 ft²); podium 149,025 m² (1,604,092 ft²) • A1 Tower 166,940 m² (1,796,927 ft²) • A2 Tower 35,890 m² (386,317 ft²) • A3 Tower 50,708 m² (545,816 ft²)

Gross basement area 115,938 m² (1,247,946 ft²)

Total gross area 518,502 m² (5,581,109 ft²), includes basement

Source: Pelli Clarke Pelli Architects

2

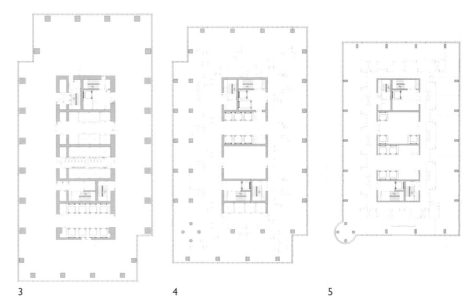

Floor area ratio (FAR)/Plot ratio 10

Gross typical floor area A1 Tower: varies 2,200–3,200 m² (23,680–34,445 ft²)
• A2 Tower: approx. 2,000 m² (21,528 ft²) • A3 Tower: approx. 2,000 m² (21,528 ft²)

Basic planning module 9 m (29.5 ft)

Total number of elevators A1 Tower: 18 passenger, 6 service • A2 Tower: 10 passenger, 2 service • A3 Tower: 12 passenger, 2 service

No of double-deck elevators Total: 14 (1 group of 8 [low-rise office] & 1 group of 6 [high-rise office]

Speed of fastest elevators 9 m (29.5 ft)/s for shuttle lifts in A1 Tower

Elevator brand KONE for A2 and A3 Towers, A1 Tower [TBA]

Number of car parking spaces 1,985

Number of motorbike & bike parking spaces 180

Hotel brand Four Seasons

Serviced apartment brand Four Seasons

Principal structure materials Reinforced concrete

Other materials Towers: glass curtain wall with anodised aluminium mullions and bullnose and granite accents • podium: coated aluminium panels, back-painted glass

3   4   5

1

438 m | 1,437 ft

■ Wuhan Tower is located on the starting point at the south end of the central axis of the central business district in the Wangjiadun zone, the geometric centre of Hankou in Wuhan. The centre acts as the gateway to downtown Wuhan and the hub connecting each of the city's functional zones: it is adjacent to Qingnia Road to the east, Jianshe Avenue to the south, Fazhan Avenue and Hanxi Road (the middle ring of urban traffic to the northwest). The building is 21 kilometres (13 miles) from Wuhan Tianhe International Airport, 1.8 kilometres (1.2 miles) from Hankou Railway Station, 17.8 kilometres (11 miles) from the Wuhan Economic Development Zone, and 24 kilometres (15 miles) from the Donghu high-tech zone.

The site's land shape contributes to the square floor plan of the tower, and the compact layout follows a typical floor plan: the upper part is devoted to hotel facilities, the middle to apartments, and the lower section to office space. The main tower is adjacent to Mengze Lake, and is designed to sit as far as possible from a super high-rise tower to its north. Its integrated and **straight profile** is of vital importance to the regional space, keeping it well proportioned with the city skyline and with the surrounding buildings.

1 Exterior façade
2 Rendering detail of top exterior
3 Overview of building
4 Typical hotel floor plan
5 Apartment lobby floor plan
6 Typical office floor plan
7 Rendering at street level

Renderings: courtesy ECADI

Wuhan Tower

Location Wuhan
Completion 2016
Client China Oceanwide
Architect East China Architectural Design & Research Institute (ECADI)
Structural & MEP engineer ECADI
Vertical transportation consultant Parsons Brinckerhoff
Façade engineer ECADI
Project management consultant ECADI
Cost consultant Widnell Sweett
Landscape architect SWA
Lighting consultant Grand Sight Design International Limited
Main contractor China Construction Third Engineering Bureau
Uses Parking B4/F–B1/F • commercial/retail: B1/F–4/F • office: 6/F–31/F • apartment: 32/F–63/F • hotel: 64/F–86/F • observatory: 87/F, 88/F
Number of buildings 1
Height 438 m (1,437 ft)
Above-ground storeys 88
Basements 5 (including one mezzanine)

Mechanical levels 6 (5/F, 18/F, 31/F, 47/F, 63/F, 86/F)
Refuge levels 6 (5/F, 18/F, 31/F, 47/F, 63/F, 86/F)
Sky-lobby levels Hotel: 65 • observation: 87
Site area 28,100 m² (302,466 ft²)
Gross above-ground building area 271,485 m² (2,922,240 ft²) [tower 1]
Gross basement area 82,315 m² (886,031 ft²)
Total gross area 353,800 m² (3,808,271 ft²)
Floor area ratio (FAR)/Plot ratio 9.05
Gross typical floor area 2,200–3,000 m² (23,680–32,292 ft²)
Basic planning module Basements/podiums: 8,500 mm x 8,500 mm (335 in x 335 in) • tower: 9,450 mm x 9,450 mm (372 in x 372 in)
Total number of elevators 68
Speed of fastest elevators 9 m (29 ft)/s
Elevator brand Mitsubishi
Number of car/bike parking spaces 1162/875
Hotel brand Grand Hyatt
Principal structure materials Reinforced concrete

Source: East China Architectural Design & Research Institute (ECADI)

2

3

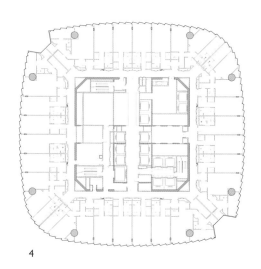

4

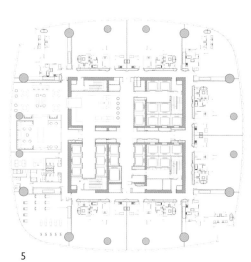

5

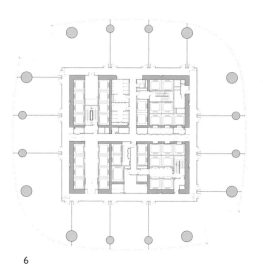

6

7

1

The tower is linked to a retail podium and incorporates highly efficient and flexible spaces. Its use of human-scale volumes, landscape and natural light provides pleasant and enjoyable working and living environments. The tower's curve gives a dimension difference between adjacent floors, while the standard floor-to-floor height of 4.2 metres (14 feet) allows daylight to penetrate deep into the floor plates. The perimeter column arrangement provides an unobstructed working environment on each level and views over Shenzhen. Lifts, E&M openings and service rooms lie within a rectangular central core, allowing for the flexibility of single or multi-tenancy opportunities.

A luxury hotel sits atop the last 26 storeys of the KK100 Tower. There's a unique 16-storey atrium sky lobby that leads into the six-star St. Regis Shenzhen. The hotel features standard rooms, panoramic rooms, suites and a presidential suite, as well as an executive lounge, lounge bar, restaurant, spa, swimming pool, business centre and fitness and recreational facilities. The rooms are arranged around the perimeter

■ At the time of completion in 2011, this 441.8-metre-high (1,449-foot) tower was the eighth-tallest building in the world. The project was a key feature of the Kingkey development masterplan design for 417,100 square metres (4,489,627 square feet) of mixed-use development. The megatower consists of 210,000 square metres (2,260,421 square feet) of accommodation, which includes one floor of basement retail connecting directly to a new metro station; 173,000 square metres (1,862,156 square feet) of Grade A office space (more than 70 floors); and a 35,000-square-metre (376,737-square-foot) hotel accommodating 290 rooms, complete with state-of-the-art conference and business facilities across 20 floors. A variety of fine-dining options are contained within the crowning sky garden feature on the top three floors.

of the tower to maximise the breathtaking views of the city, with the central atrium capturing natural light from the **glazed crown** at the top of the building.

The project's five 27-storey-high towers accommodate 1,620 residential apartments. With Shenzhen's growing population, clogged transport systems and an acute shortage of affordable land for development, the increased population density has become a major issue. This major mixed-use development promotes the idea of living and working in the same place, and reduces the need for commuting.

1   View of tower at base
2   Night view of tower from across the adjacent park
3   Typical hotel floor plan
4   Typical office floor plan
5   Tower main entrance
Following pages:
6   Interior of retail podium
7   Sky lobby atrium with panoramic viewing area

Photography: ©Carsten Schael

442 m | 1,449 ft

KK100

Location Shenzhen
Completion 2011
Client Shenzhen Kingkey Real Estate Development Co. Ltd
Architect TFP Farrells Limited
Associate architect Huasen Architectural & Engineering Designing Consultants Ltd Shenzhen
Structural engineers Arup • RBS Architectural Engineering Design Associates
MEP engineer Arup
Façade engineer Arup Façade
Lighting consultant Tino Kwan Lighting Consultants Ltd
Other consultants Arup [fire, wind, traffic] • E.W. COX Hong Kong Limited (BMU)
   • Kingsun Optoelectronic Col, Ltd (lighting design & installation)
Main contractor China Construction Fourth Engineering Design Associates
Uses Office: 173,000 m² (1,862,156 ft²) [4/F–72/F] • hotel: 35,000 m² (376,737 ft²)
   [75/F–100/F] • retail: 84,000 m² (904,168 ft²) [60,000 m² (645,835 ft²) above-ground;
   24,000 m² (258,334 ft²) below-ground)] • residential: 96,000 m² (1,033,335 ft²) [27 storeys]

Number of buildings Office/hotel: 1 • residential: 5 • retail: 1
Height 441.8 m (1,449 ft)
Above-ground storeys 100
Basements 4
Sky-lobby levels 39/F, 40/F, 95/F
Observation level 98/F
Site area 45,665 m² (491,534 ft²)
Total gross area 417,100 m² (4,489,627 ft²)
Total number of elevators Total: 66 • office: 51 [6 double-deck] • hotel: 15 [4 shuttle]
No of double-deck elevators 6
Speed of fastest elevators 8 m (26 ft)/s
Number of car parking spaces 2,000
Hotel brand St. Regis
Principal structure materials Composite

Source: TFP Farrells Limited

2

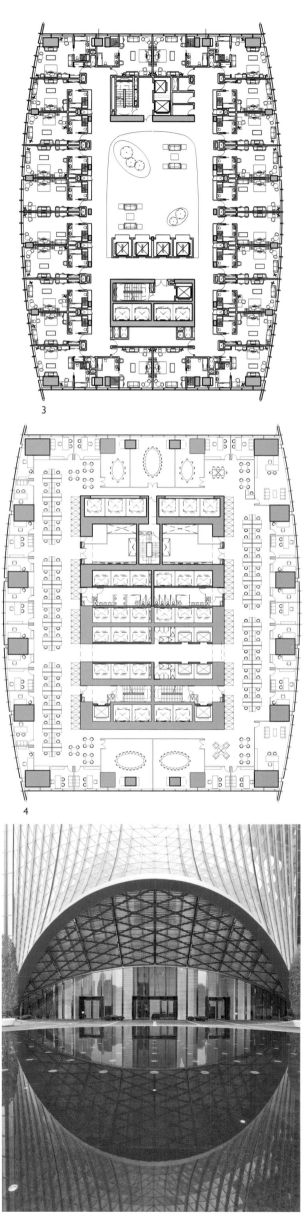

3

4

5

1

The China Resources mixed-use tower in Nanning is designed to provide an identifiable silhouette on the city's skyline, while offering architecturally sophisticated detail at the pedestrian scale. Composed of Class A office space and a luxury five-star hotel, the CR tower will establish a new level of quality as the city expands to the east. The compound massing for the project is a marriage of both programmatic efficiency and **sculptural expression**. The tower form tapers as it rises to further accentuate its verticality, culminating in an illuminated beacon of light visible from all directions.

The angled geometries of the façades and crown expression are inspired by crystalline forms, which represent both strength and timeless beauty. Designed to LEED Gold international standards, the building is encased in floor-to-ceiling performance glass that offers all users ample natural light and unobstructed views to the surrounding landscape. A series of sky decks provides outdoor amenity spaces for the hotel, offering unique experiences high in the sky and rarely found anywhere in the world. This design intends to blend environmental sensitivity with a unique architectural form that strives to position Nanning as a world-class destination.

1   Rendering of street view from southeast
2   Rendering of exterior overall view from northeast
3   Typical hotel plan
4   Office floor plan (high zone)
5   Office floor plan (mid zone)
6   Office floor plan (low zone)
7   Rendering of exterior aerial view from southeast
8   Ground floor plan

Renderings: ©Goettsch Partners

Nanning China Resources

Location Nanning
Completion 2019
Client China Resources Land Limited
Architect Goettsch Partners
Associate architect CCDI International (Shenzhen) Design Consultants Co. Ltd
Structural engineer RBS Architecture Engineer Associates
MEP engineer Parsons Brinckerhoff
Vertical transportation consultant Parson Brinckerhoff
Façade engineer Shanghai WSP Consulting Ltd
Landscape architect ADI Limited, Hong Kong
Other consultants MVA Systra Group (transport)
Uses Office, hotel, retail
Number of buildings 1
Height 445 m (1,460 ft) [to top of crown] • 410 m (1,345 ft) [to main roof]
Above-ground storeys 90
Basements 3
Mechanical levels 8: 6/F, 19/F, 31/F, 43/F, 56/F, 69/F, 72/F, 87/F

Refuge levels 7: 6/F, 19M/F, 31M/F, 43M/F, 56M/F, 69M/F, 72/F
Sky-lobby levels 45/F (office) • 71/F (hotel)
Site area 7,154 m² (77,005 ft²)
Gross above-ground building area 248,695 m² (2,676,931 ft²)
Gross basement area 30,934 m² (332,971 ft²)
Total gross area 279,629 m² (3,009,901 ft²)
Gross typical floor area Z1 avg. 3,723 m² (40,074 ft²) • Z2 avg. 3,071 m² (33,056 ft²) • Z3 avg. 2,960 m² (31,861 ft²) • Z4 avg. 2,768 m² (29,794 ft²) • Z5 avg. 2,726 m² (29,342 ft²) • hotel 1,983 m² (21,345 ft²)
Basic planning module 1.5
Total number of elevators 59
Speed of fastest elevators 10 m (33 ft)/s
Number of car parking spaces 213
Hotel brand Shangri-La
Principal structure materials Steel, concrete
Other materials Glass

Source: Goettsch Partners

2

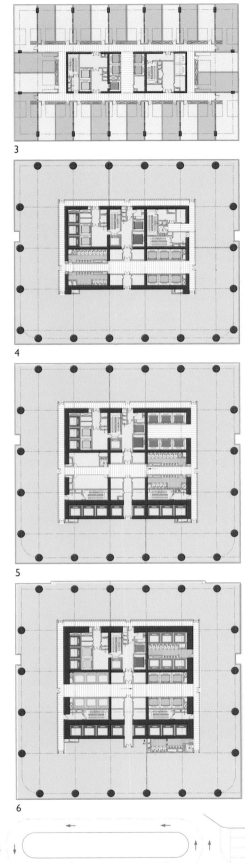

3

4

5

6

7

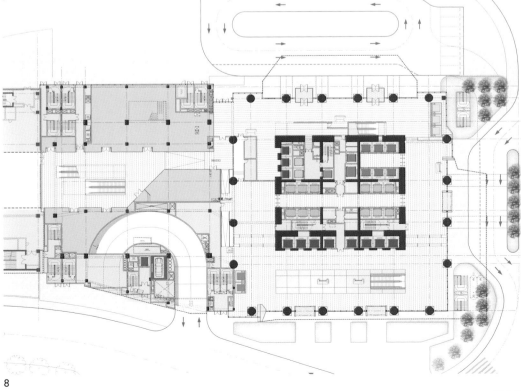

8

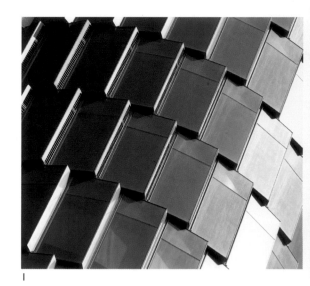

1

700 m

600 m

500 m

450 m | **1,476 ft**

400 m

300 m

200 m

100 m

■ The Greenland Center is a mixed-use complex comprising several buildings resting on two sites, parcels A1 and A2. Parcel A1 contains a podium connecting two towers. The 450-metre-high (1,476-foot) Zifeng Tower consists of offices and hotels, and the 100-metre-tall (328-foot) tower contains office space. Parcel A2 contains a 63-metre-high (207-foot) tower of offices with its own podium.

The shape and placement of the buildings are designed to echo the geometry of the existing roads and maximise exterior views of the city. The buildings' composition maintains the east-to-west view corridors along East Beijing Road and provides a visual link to the nearby historic drum and bell towers.

Landscaping is a significant part of the project. The buildings are set back from the street with several large landscaped public open spaces. South of parcel A1 there's a sunken garden that will connect to the future subway. There is also a roof garden at the top of the podium in parcel A1 to reduce the heat island effect and offer views of the drum and bell towers. The 450-metre-high tower incorporates sky gardens that wind up the façade like a **coiling dragon**.

1   Close-up of façade curtain wall
2   Overall view
3   Typical floor plan (high-rise)
4   Typical floor plan (low-rise)
5   Podium floor plan
6   Base of office tower with podium

Credits: 1,2,6 ©ECADI | ©Liu Qihua;
4,5,6 courtesy SOM

Zifeng Tower at Greenland Center

Location Nanjing	**Number of buildings** Parcel A1: 2 towers + 1 podium • parcel A2: 1 tower + 1 podium
Completion 2010	**Height** 450 m (1,476 ft)
Client Greenland Group	**Above-ground storeys** 66
Architect Skidmore, Owings & Merrill LLP (SOM)	**Basements** 4
Associate architect TK	**Site area** 28,294 m² (305,000 ft²)
Architect of record East China Architectural Design & Research Institute (ECADI)	**Total gross area** 308,000 m² (3,320,000 ft²)
Structural engineer SOM	**Total number of elevators** 54
MEP engineers SOM	**Speed of fastest elevators** 7 m (23 ft)/s
Landscape architect SWA Group	**Elevator brand** KONE • Schindler
Lighting consultant PHA Lighting Design	**No of car parking spaces** 1,200
Other consultants Rolf Jensen & Associates (fire)	**Hotel brand** InterContinental
Main contractor Shanghai Construction Group	**Principal structure materials** Composite
Uses Office, hotel, retail	

Source: Skidmore, Owings & Merrill LLP (SOM)

2

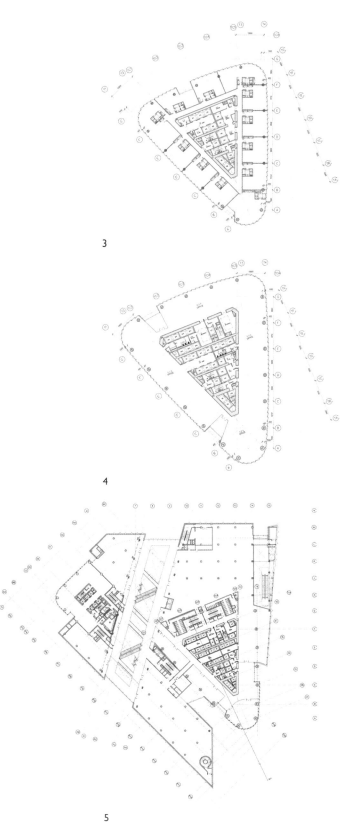

3

4

5

6

■ Tianjin R&F Guangdong Tower is a 289,860-square-metre (3,120,027-square-foot) mixed-use development in the city of Tianjin. Occupying a central parcel in the city's newly planned business district, the tower will be one of China's tallest buildings at 468 metres (1,535 feet). The complex features 125,670 square metres (1,352,700 square feet) of Grade A office space, a 335-key Grand Hyatt hotel, 149 condominiums, and 8,550 square metres (92,031 square feet) of retail. The tower is designed to establish a signature visual profile in the city skyline and provide a destination for the people of Tianjin and beyond.

The building's design responds to the programmatic needs of each function, as well as to the decreasing size of the core. The tower unwraps around its vertical axis as it ascends, similar in nature to a shell or **ancient scroll**. In this manner, the form relates to the historical context of the site's location in the Tanggu district, a port of sea trade. The unwinding form also creates unique opportunities to introduce two-storey atria into the program in each vertical zone. These landscaped interior spaces provide ideal circulation for multifloor tenants, daylighting for deeper lease spans, and inviting social meeting spaces within the building's upper floors. The landscaped interiors are an instrumental part of the overall environmental sensitivity to the new downtown's iconic centrepiece.

Clearly defining the building's circulation pattern is critical to achieving a successful mixed-use project. The site's vehicular circulation is divided by function for efficient access to the tower from the main roads. Pedestrian circulation is further segregated throughout the site, with a landscaped plaza on the building's north side that creates a welcoming arrival space for the complex. Internally, each of the primary building programs is separated at the ground floor, providing clear and intuitive wayfinding for the occupants. A network of 55 elevators provides access from the ground floor to each of the primary building functions, delivering guests to their destinations within the tower quickly and efficiently.

The primary palette of high-performance glass and metal is employed for the exterior design of the building. Floor-to-ceiling glass maximises views and ambient light, as well as landscaped roofs and interior atria for both their visual and energy benefits. The design promotes material and façade approaches that are integral to the performance of the building systems, not decorative. Above all, the architectural 'skin' seeks to positively impact the pedestrian scale through transparency and texture, while minimising the project's environmental footprint.

1 Rendering of building base view from the southwest
2 Rendering of exterior overall view from the southeast
3 Typical hotel elevator plan
4 Ground floor plan

Renderings: ©Goettsch Partners

R&F Guangdong Building

Location Tianjin
Completion 2018
Client Guangzhou R&F Properties Co., Ltd
Architect Goettsch Partners
Associate architect East China Architectural Design & Research Institute
Structural engineer Arup
MEP engineer J. Roger Preston Limited
Vertical transportation consultant J. Roger Preston Limited
Façade engineer Goettsch Partners (façade designer)
Landscape architect SWA Group
Lighting consultant BPI
Other consultants MVA (traffic) • RWDI (wind engineer)
Uses Office 125,670 m² (1,352,700 ft²) [7/F–48/F] • hotel 55,900 m² (601,702 ft²) [54/F–74/F] • hotel amenity podium 22,000 m² (236,806 ft²) [1/F–6/F] • residential/condominiums 22,700 m² (244,341 ft²) [79/F–91/F] • retail 8,550 m² (92,031 ft²) [1/F–2/F]
 Number of buildings 1
 Height 468 m (1,535 ft)
 Above-ground storeys 91

Basements 5
Mechanical levels 12/F, 28/F, 39/F, 49/F, 53/F, 64/F, 75/F, 78/F
Refuge levels 12/F, 28/F, 39/F, 49/F, 53/F, 64/F, 75/F
Sky-lobby levels 29/F (office), 51/F (hotel)
Site area 12,110 m² (130,350 ft²)
Gross above-ground building area 247,695 m² (2,666,167 ft²)
Gross basement area 42,165 m² (453,860 ft²)
Total gross area 289,860 m² (3,120,027 ft²)
Floor area ratio (FAR)/Plot ratio 21
Gross typical floor area Office 2,600–3,600 m² (27,986–38,750 ft²) • hotel 2,000 m² (21,528 ft²) • apartment 1,750 m² (18,837 ft²)
Basic planning module North and south façades: 1.25-m (4-ft) curtain wall module; 10-m (33-ft) bay • east and west façades: 1.2-m (3.9-ft) curtain wall module; 12-m bay (39-ft)
Total number of elevators 55
Speed of fastest elevators 8 m (26 ft)/s
Number of car parking spaces 852
Hotel brand Grand Hyatt
Principal structure materials Concrete, composite

Source: Goettsch Partners

468 m | 1,535 ft

2

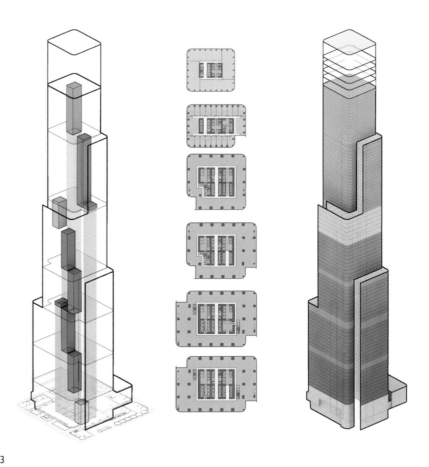

3

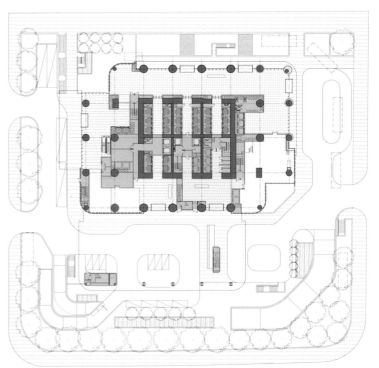

4

■ The ICC tower sets new standards for both scale and sustainability in building design. It accommodates offices, a 360-degree observation deck on the 100th floor and one of China's highest hotels. The tower is the centrepiece of the Union Square reclamation project, which includes a new urban centre with residential, office, retail, hotel and recreation spaces, as well as a new transport hub, Kowloon Station, connecting Hong Kong to Chep Lap Kok airport by rail. The ICC tower, currently the tallest building in Hong Kong, accents this new development and provides a new model of **green urban design**.

The tower's subtly tapered re-entrant corners and the gently sloped curves at its base are designed to optimise its structural performance. These curves splay out at the base of the tower, rooting the tower in its surroundings, while creating sheltering canopies on three sides and a dramatic atrium on the north side. The atrium gestures towards the rest of the development and serves as a public connection space for retail and train station functions. The air-conditioning system has central intelligent control and energy consumption monitors, and collects data and analyses it for day-and-night and seasonal variations to provide a baseline for energy-saving adjustments. The elevators use a passenger smart card system to maximise the efficiency of vertical transport by assigning lifts to groups of people with similar destinations, minimising waiting times for lifts and wasteful starting/stopping of the cabs. The tower is also designed to save water by harvesting condensed water from the air-conditioning units for use in either cooling towers or toilet flushing. This scheme succeeds in wedding the high-rise building model with a highly efficient structural and operational agenda.

The Ritz-Carlton, Hong Kong opened in 2011 and boasts a 360-degree view of the entire city and surrounding islands. Situated at floors 102 to 118, the hotel offers 312 contemporary guest rooms. There's also a glass-enclosed infinity pool with an LED screen ceiling and an outdoor terrace on the 118th floor. The hotel also boasts one of the largest ballrooms in the city at 930 square metres (10,010 square feet) and is decorated with a sea of crystal chandeliers. An additional four meeting rooms complements the hotel, comprising 1,300 square metres (13,993 square feet) of meeting space.

The 116th floor contains the Ritz-Carlton Spa (by ESPA), and is one of the world's highest hotel spas. It comprises 860 square metres (9,257 square feet) of treatment rooms and relaxation areas; every treatment room offers floor-to-ceiling windows with panoramic views.

1 Close-up of façade
2 View from harbour
3 Circulation diagram
4 Overview in context
5 Typical office floor plan
6 Typical hotel floor plan
7 Observation deck floor plan

Credits: 1,2,4 ©Tim Griffith; illustrations: courtesy Kohn Pedersen Fox Associates

484 m | 1,568 ft

International Commerce Centre

Location Hong Kong
Completion 2010
Client Sun Hung Kai Properties
Architect Kohn Pedersen Fox Associates
Associate architect Wong & Ouyang (HK) Ltd
Structural engineers Arup • Leslie E. Robertson Associates
MEP engineer J. Roger Preston Group
Vertical transportation consultant Lerch Bates & Associates, Inc.
Façade engineer Permasteelisa Group
Project management consultant Harbour Vantage Management Limited
Cost consultant WT Partnership
Landscape architect Belt Collins & Associates
Other consultants ALT Cladding & Design, Inc. (façade) • LTW Design Works (interior design) • Arup (fire) • WTP (quantity surveyors) • RWDI (wind) • Meinhardt
Main contractor Sanfield Building Contractors Limited

Uses Office, hotel, retail, public observatory & airport rail link
Number of buildings 1
Height 484 m (1,568 ft)
Above-ground storeys 108
Basements 4
Site area 274,064 m² (2,950,000 ft²)
Gross above-ground building area 260,000 m² (2,798,617 ft²)
Total number of elevators 83
Speed of fastest elevators 9 m (29 ft)/s
Elevator brand Schindler
Number of car parking spaces 1,700
Hotel brand Ritz-Carlton
Principal structure materials Composite

Source: Kohn Pedersen Fox Associates

2

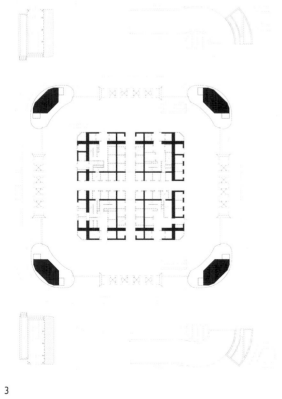

3

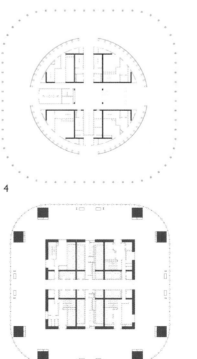

4

5

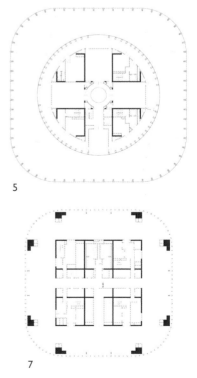

6

7

700 m

600 m

530 m | **1,739 ft**

500 m

400 m

300 m

200 m

100 m

■ The Guangzhou CTF Finance Centre, a mixed-use East Tower and podium, is located across from Guangzhou West Tower in the city's burgeoning Tianhe District. The centre is linked to public transport through underground connections at the B1 and B2 levels, and to adjacent buildings via second level pedestrian bridges.

The tower houses an office, residential and hotel program. A stepped podium with spiralling roof terraces houses hotel functions, as well as a retail, restaurant and cinema program.

The design of the Guangzhou CTF Finance Centre is derived from its multiple uses – the building steps to accommodate the changing floorplates of the various program types – but also from the form of the adjacent West Tower and TV Tower – the city's other two landmark supertall structures. The building's **chiselled setbacks** are sculpted to acknowledge the various heights of the nearby towers, and to provide a crescendo on the city's ever-expanding skyline. The overall effect of the tower is of a crystalline form ascending to the sky. This formal vocabulary extends to the podium, which extends upwards from the tower, with stepping terraces that frame a large atrium skylight.

The tower's façade is designed to emphasise its gentle curved form and verticality. Long stripes of white terracotta extend from the tower's base to its chiselled setbacks and top. By day, the tower's terracotta and metal façade stands out among its all-glass neighbours. At night the glistening terracotta sparkles on the skyline. The building's podium, sheathed in a metal screen of warm bronze, provides an active and vibrant presence along the large central green axis of the Tianhe District.

The building will employ a number of energy efficient tools in order to reduce its environmental footprint (in addition to its strong multilevel connections to public transport); these include the use of high-efficiency chillers, façade materials with high thermal properties, solar panels on the podium roof and heat recovery from the water-cooled chiller condensers.

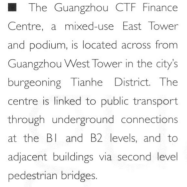

1

1   Close-up of façade
2   Rendering overview
3   Hotel floor plan (top floor)
4   Typical hotel floor plan
5   Hotel sky-lobby floor plan
6   Serviced apartment hotel sky-lobby floor plan
7   Office sky-lobby floor plan
8   Office floor plan
9   Ground floor plan

Renderings: courtesy Kohn Pedersen Fox Associates

Guangzhou CTF Finance Centre

Location Guangzhou
Completion 2016 (tower), 2017 (retail & hotel)
Client CTF Group
Design architect Kohn Pedersen Fox Associates
Local design institute Guangzhou Design Institute
Executive architect Leigh & Orange (CHINA) LTD
Executive interior designers L+T Architects Hong Kong (retail & office)
   • EKIT II Design Hong Kong (hotel)
Structural engineer Ove Arup & Partners HK Ltd
MEP engineer Parsons Brinkerhoff
Façade engineer ALT Limited
Project management New World Development Company Ltd
Cost consultant Rider Levett Bucknall
Landscape architect P Landscape Co., Ltd
Lighting consultants Lighting Planners Associates Inc. (exterior)
   • Isometrix Lighting Design (interior)

Other consultants Yabu Pushelberg (interior design, hotel) • Perception Design (HK) Ltd (interior design, serviced apartments) • Callison (interior design, retail) • RWDI (wind)
Uses Office: 208,000 m² (2,238,893 ft²) • residential: 75,000 m² (807,293 ft²) • hotel: 46,000 m² (495,140 ft²) • retail, restaurant & cinema: 47,000 m² (505,904 ft²) [podium]
Number of buildings 1
Height 530 m (1,739 ft)
Above-ground storeys 111
Basements 5
Gross above-ground building area 398,000 m² (4,284,036 ft²)
Total gross area 508,000 m² (5,468,066 ft²)
Total number of elevators 86
Speed of fastest elevators 20 m (66 ft)/s
Elevator brand Hitachi, Ltd
Number of car parking spaces 1,705
Principal structure materials Composite

Source: Kohn Pedersen Fox Associates

2

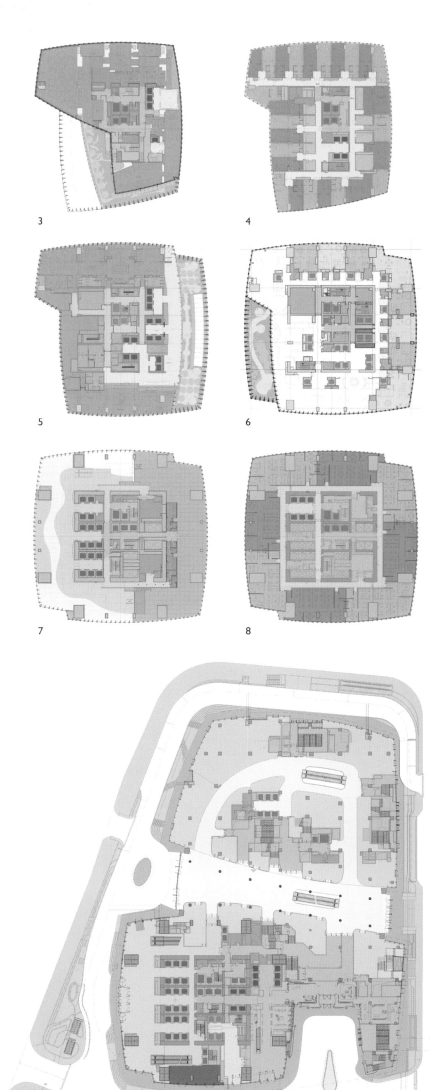

3

4

5

6

7

8

9

■ Atkins is behind the design for the two supertall towers of the World Financial Center. One 568-metre-high (1,863-foot) tower, dubbed the 'Pearl of the North', holds an executive club within its unique rooftop sphere. The 308-metre-high (1,010-foot) second tower features the only five-star hotel in the city entirely above 200 metres (656 feet), starting from its projecting sky-lobby and restaurants. Together with **the Pearl** – a symbol of wisdom, luxury and purity – these striking shapes are the jewels in the crown of this new development, soon to become the icon of Shenyang's ongoing transformation.

The site south of the iconic TV tower forms part of the 58.5-hectare (145-acre) development on the prestigious 'Golden Corridor' Youth Street in the central business district. The towers overlook the famous Youth Park and the Nanyun River to the east. The complex also contains five luxury residential towers each about

200 metres (656 feet) high, above a culturally themed lifestyle shopping mall, which will retain the original branded bookshop on the site.

There are several key design principles in the concept of the Pearl of the North. Its design evolves from the fabled history of Shenyang being the ancestral home of the last Qing Dynasty emperors and the first industrial city in China. The gentle parting of the curtain walls framing the lobby canopies recalls the nomadic tent entrances of the last Qing Dynasty emperor's ancestors. The slender V-grooves on the elevations suggest molten steel flowing down, thus slimming the profile of an already slender mass and visually connecting the sphere at the top with the canopies below.

Situated in a severely cold climate

falling below -30°C (86°F) frequently in winter, energy conservation is a cornerstone in the design. The supertall tower will meet LEED Gold Certificate standard and the 3-star rating in the Chinese system by employing various strategies, such as adopting a triple-glazing curtain wall system. Structurally each tower comprises a braced steel frame with a steel reinforced concrete core. The aim is to achieve the lowest steel tonnage record in similar types of towers.

1   Entrance perspective
2   Aerial view perspective
3   Ground level floor plan (T1)
4   Floor plan of level 10 (T1)
5   Floor plan of level 112 (T1)

Renderings: courtesy Atkins Consultants (Shenzhen) Co., Ltd

World Financial Center

Location Shenyang

Completion 2018

Client Baoneng Holding (China) Co., Ltd

Architect Atkins Consultants (Shenzhen) Co., Ltd

Associate architect The Institute of Architectural Design & Research, Shenzhen University

Structural engineers RBS Architectural Engineering Design Consultant Co.Ltd • The Institute of Architectural Design & Research, Shenzhen University

MEP engineers Parsons Brinckerhoff • The Institute of Architectural Design & Research, Shenzhen University

Vertical transportation consultant Parsons Brinckerhoff

Façade engineer Inhabit Group

Lighting consultant Brandston Partnership Inc.

Landscape architect Botao Landscape (Australia) [of Peddle Thorp Architects]

Main contractor China Construction Third Engineering Bureau Co., Ltd

Uses T1: Financial trading 10,685.4 m² 115,017 ft²) [9/F–11/F] • office 249,765.53 m² (2,688,454 ft²) [12/F–107/F] • club 9,232.85 m² (99,382 ft²) [108/F–112/F] • T2: office 84,173 m² (906,031 ft²) [3/F–5/F, 8/F–42/F] • hotel, exhibition & facilities 59,362 m² (638967 ft²) [1/F, 5/F–7/F, 44/F–63/F]

Number of buildings 2

Source: Atkins Consultants (Shenzhen) Co., Ltd

Height T1: 568 m (1,863 ft) • T2: 308 m (1,010 ft)

Above-ground storeys T1: 114 • T2: 63

Basements 5

Mechanical levels T1: 7/F–8/F, 24/F–25/F, 41/F–42/F, 58/F–59F, 75/F–76/F, 92/F–93/F, 106/F–107/F, 114/F • T2: 7/F, 25/F, 43/F, 47/F

Refuge levels T1: 7/F, 24/F, 41/F, 58/F, 75/F, 92/F, 106/F • T2: 7/F, 25/F, 43/F, 47/F

Sky-lobby levels T1: 26/F–27/F, 50/F–51/F, 77/F–78/F • T2: 44/F–46/F

Site area 58,424.10 m² (628,872 ft²)

Gross above-ground building area T1: 321,484 m² (3,460,425 ft²) • T2: 143,535 m² (1,544,998 ft²)

Gross basement area 2,845.56 m² (30,629 ft²) [just below T1, not including area of basement under the podium]

Total gross area 462,778 m² (4,981,301 ft²) [total above-ground building area of T1 & T2]

Floor area ratio (FAR)/Plot ratio 13.5

Gross typical floor area T1: 3,500 m² (37,674 ft²) • T2: 2,040 m² (21,958 ft²)

Total number of elevators T1: 80 • T2: 32

Number of double-deck elevators T1: 17 • T2: NIL

Speed of fastest elevators T1: 10 m (33 ft)/s • T2: 7 m (23 ft)/s

Number of car parking spaces 3,500

Hotel brand Ritz-Carlton

Principal structure materials Steel reinforced concrete

2

3

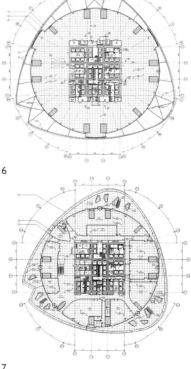

4

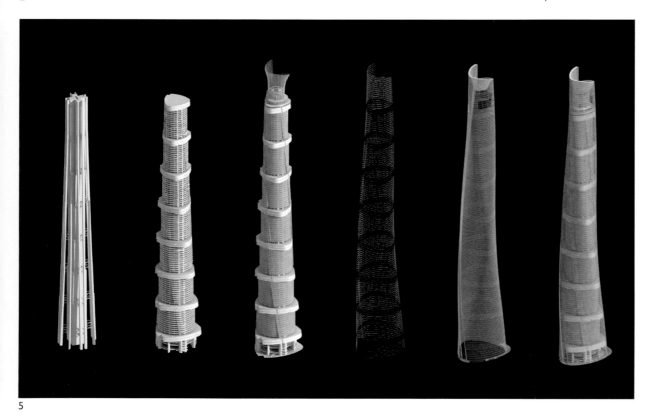

5

6

7

700 m | 2296 ft

636 m | 2,087 ft

600 m | 1968 ft

500 m | 1640 ft

400 m | 1312 ft

300 m | 984 ft

200 m | 656 ft

100 m | 328 ft

■ The 125-level tower will comprise offices, luxury apartments and condominiums, a five-star hotel, and a private club with spectacular views at the tower's penthouse level. The tower features a uniquely streamlined form that combines three key shaping concepts—a tapered body, softly rounded corners and a domed top—to reduce wind resistance and vortex action that builds up around supertall towers. The building's extremely efficient **aerodynamic performance** will allow it to minimise the amount of structural material needed for construction.

The tower's three corners taper upward, culminating in an arched tip above the dome at the top. The corners will be smooth curved glass, contrasting with the more textured curtain wall cladding of the body of the tower. Apertures in the curtain wall at regular intervals will assist in venting wind pressure against the tower; the apertures will also house window-washing systems and air intake and exhaust systems on mechanical floors.

The project will also feature several sustainable elements, such as energy recovery using an enthalpy wheel integrated into the ventilation system; this will capture energy from the building's exhaust systems and use it to pre-heat or pre-cool air entering the building. There'll be a greywater recovery system, which takes waste-water from the hotel laundry, sinks and showers and reuses it in the building's evaporative

cooling system. The high-efficiency lighting system will use low-energy-consuming ballasts and lamps to reduce required power consumption, and it will incorporate daylight-responsive controls, which automatically turn off electric lights when sufficient daylight is available. Finally, the building will be fitted with water-conserving low-flow plumbing fixtures, which reduce the total amount of potable water required as well as the associated pumping energy.

1 Exterior wall vent detail
2 Overall tower in context
3 Tower section looking east
4 Floor plan with elevators
5 Sky atrium

Renderings & illustrations: ©Adrian Smith + Gordon Gill Architecture

Greenland Center WGC

Location Wuhan
Completion 2017
Client Greenland Group
Architect Adrian Smith + Gordon Gill Architecture
Architect of record East China Architectural Design & Research Institute (ECADI)
Structural engineer Thornton Tomasetti
MEP engineer PostivEnergy Practice
Vertical transportation consultant Forcade
Façade engineer Lerch Bates
Landscape architect SWA Group
Lighting consultant Fisher Marantz Stone
Civil/traffic/parking consultant Prism Engineering

Main contractor Greenland Group
Uses Offices: 200,000 m² (2,152,782 ft²) • luxury apartments & condominiums: 50,000 m² (538,195 ft²) • five-star hotel: 45,000 m² (484,375 ft²) • private club: 5,000 m² (53,819 ft²)
Number of buildings 1
Height 636 m (2,087 ft)
Above-ground storeys 125
Basements 6
Site area 14,494 m² (156,012 ft²)
Total gross area 300,000m² (3,229,173 ft²)
Hotel brand Ritz-Carlton
Principal structure materials Composite

Source: Adrian Smith + Gordon Gill Architecture

2

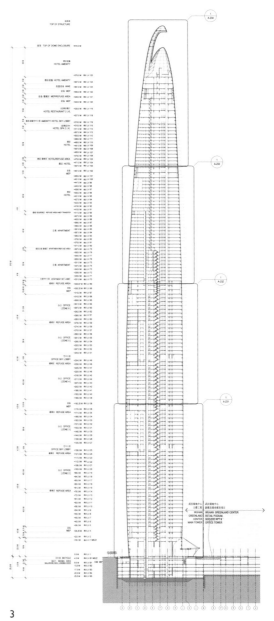

3

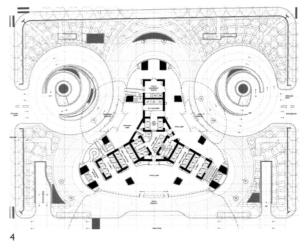

4

5

I

■ Located in the centre of Shenzhen, the Ping An Financial Centre (PAFC) is a 'transit-integrated tall building' occupying a major node in the increasingly connected megacity of Hong Kong/Shenzhen/Guangzhou.

PAFC will be 660 metres (2,165 ft) tall, comprising around 460,000 square metres (4,951,399 square feet) of floor area across 115 levels, with a daytime population of 17,000. And yet, despite its size, it will also have significant sustainability credentials.

As a design, 'Ping An' is the combination of the Chinese characters for 'peaceful' and 'safety', evoking the entrepreneurial spirit of Shenzhen. Architecturally, the exposed columns provided the opportunity to articulate structural elements on the façade. Linen-finish stainless steel was selected for

the column finish to enhance the ductility of the overall form. Eight stainless-steel columns trace the edges of the tower and converge into the spire in one continuous gesture. Each column is clasped by a stone buttress, stylised like the talons of some great bird gripping the earth before taking flight. Vertical strands of stainless steel are drawn tightly along the full height of the tower to express the underlying tension.

Its stretched, **needle-like shape** is streamlined and notched with continuously tapering corners, for both aerodynamic performance and visual effect, as well as for returning the maximum possible number of square, functional floor plates on a compact site. Overall, the shape of the tower achieves a 32 percent reduction in overturning moment and a 35 percent reduction in wind load compared to China code. With an extremely dense program, well-chosen materials and mechanical engineering strategies are predicted to sustain an 18.25 percent energy savings beyond ASHRAE standards,

and a 46 percent annual savings in energy costs over a conventionally constructed commercial office building of the same scale. High performance is factored into the building, from the structural health-monitoring system to its synchronised movement of its independent elevator cars, and the optimisation of cleaner, cooler air at the pinnacle for use through sophisticated use of Building Information Modelling (BIM).

I   Overview in context
2   Rendering of overall façade
3   Observation deck floor plan (113/F)
4   Typical floor plan (high zone)
5   Typical floor plan (mid zone)
6   Typical floor plan (low zone)
7   View of retail floors (left)
     & podium atrium (right)

Renderings & illustrations: courtesy Kohn Pedersen Fox Associates

Ping An Financial Centre

Location Shenzhen
Completion 2016
Client Ping An Life Insurance Company of China
Architect Kohn Pedersen Fox Associates
Architect of record CCDI
Structural engineer Thornton Tomasetti
MEP engineer J. Roger Preston Group
Cost consultant Rider Levett Bucknall
Other consultants ALT Cladding (façade) • MVA Transportation, Planning & Management Consultants (traffic) • LPA (lighting) • Arup (sustainability & fire) • RWDI (wind)
Main contractor China Construction First Group Construction & Development Co., Ltd

Uses Office, retail
Number of buildings I
Height 660 m (2,165 ft)
Above-ground storeys 115
Basements 5
Site area 18,931 m² (203,772 ft²)
Total gross area 459,525 m² (4,153,987 ft²)
Total number of elevators 80
Speed of fastest elevators 10 m (33 ft)/s
Number of car parking spaces 1,174
Principal structure materials Composite

2

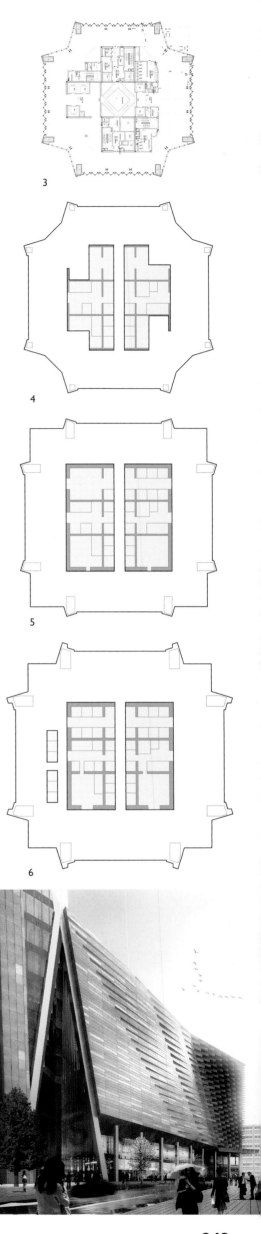

3

4

5

6

7